G000060383

Māori and the Environment: Kaitiaki

Māori and the Environment: Kaitiaki

Edited by
Rachael Selby,
Pātaka Moore
and Malcolm Mulholland

First published in 2010 by Huia Publishers,
39 Pipitea Street, P O Box 17-335
Wellington, Aotearoa New Zealand
www.huia.co.nz

ISBN 978-1-86969-402-9

Copyright © the authors 2010
Cover design and cover image: Te Tahi Tākao – Te Wānanga-o-Raukawa

All rights reserved. No part of this publication may be reproduced, stored in a retrieval system,
or transmitted in any form or by any means, electronic, mechanical, including photocopying,
recording or otherwise, without prior permission of the publisher.

National Library of New Zealand Cataloguing-in-Publication Data

Māori and the environment : kaitiaki /
compiled and edited by Rachael Selby, Pataka J.G. Moore and Malcolm Mulholland.
ISBN 978-1-86969-402-9
1. Environmental protection—New Zealand.
[1. Taiao. reo. 2. Tūkinotanga ā-taiao. reo]
I. Selby, Rachael. II. Moore, Pataka J. G. III. Mulholland, Malcolm, 1976-
333.7208999442—dc 22

Published with the support of Te Wānanga-o-Raukawa

TE WĀNANGA-O-RAUKAWA
e kore au e ngaro, he kākano i ruia mai i Rangiātea

Contents

Foreword

For a thousand years prior to the first wave of immigration, Māori lived in harmony with the environment. As tangata tiaki, we appreciated the need to protect the mauri or the physical life force of everything in the natural environment. The responsibility to live respectfully with the environment was observed as kaitiakitanga – a value promoted by our tipuna to maintain the delicate balance between tangata whenua and the natural environment.

Kaitiakitanga in Ngāti Kahungunu terms seeks balance in sustaining our natural resources as the basis for our wellbeing – rather than as limitless commodities to use at our will. Each iwi, each hapū, each whānau will have their own unique kawa which guides them in the vital role of guardians of our natural resources, protectors of the flora and fauna for the benefit of future generations.

And yet in 19th and 20th century New Zealand, during a period of colonial settlement, the land, sea and forest suffered from exploitation in the mistaken belief that the land and sea were indestructible and would provide for our wellbeing mai rā ano.

The great forests of Tāne were felled and little thought given to the centuries they had taken to grow to maturity. The prevailing ideology was that of the economic benefits accrued to the traders who shipped the timber overseas or sold it locally. The economic development of New Zealand was inextricably linked with the destruction of the forests.

Throughout the 19th century, clearing the land for pasture received hardly a second thought. The precedence awarded to farming land was to be expected in the land of milk and honey. There was little consideration, if any, of the impact of many practices now recognised as destructive.

While dairy farming has brought great wealth to New Zealand it has polluted our creeks, streams and rivers, the providers of tuna, shellfish and koura.

Similarly, the prosperity associated with horticulture in many areas of New Zealand, has to be offset by the runoff of chemicals from land to waterways that have compromised the health of the streams, lakes and rivers, the providers of flounder, whitebait and other fish.

And if communities have benefited from inexpensive sewage disposal into lakes and rivers and the ocean, it must be noted that the environment has also been put at risk by these practices. Indeed the cost of pollution is demonstrated in the warnings posted at beaches not to take traditional foods: such as shellfish, oysters, pāua and mussels. Regrettably, our natural paradise is threatened by the effects of activity designed more around profit than people. Swimming and fishing in many of our waterways is a dangerous activity and remains so until we commit to a long term programme of restoration.

But all is not lost. There is now evidence of a change in land use in Aotearoa: from the conversion of valleys, rolling hills and mountains into grazing land to greater diversity of use. There is an appreciation of the pockets of natural forest remaining. Some are protected with covenants and through the Conservation estate. There is also recognition that our lakes, rivers, wetlands and coastal areas cannot sustain another century like the last and that we need to restore them with urgency. Many of these issues are the subject of treaty claims, are issues for all New Zealanders and many are addressed in this book with passion and vigour by kaitiaki Māori.

This compendium is timely as it provides an historical overview of issues and concerns about the environment and in particular it provides well researched and presented case studies from Māori scholars, researchers and academics about areas in which they have or are developing impressive expertise.

The book documents changes in environmental practices, policies and priorities for Māori and other New Zealanders. It is a time for a re-evaluation of our environmental goals and this book provides a basis from which to begin that. It implores all New Zealanders to urgently address issues of sustainability.

Timeliness is also relevant when we think of two key areas in the current policy agenda. The first is the WAI 262 claim; which asserts exclusive and comprehensive rights to flora and fauna, cultural knowledge and property as taonga protected by Article Two of the Treaty of Waitangi. The claim dates back to 1988, when kaumātua from Ngāti Kuri, Te Rarawa, Ngāti Wai, Ngāti Porou, Te Whānau a Rua and Ngāti Kahungunu (Ngāti Koata joined later) met to discuss the protection of mātauranga Māori. A fundamental premise of the claim is the opportunity for Māori to fulfil their role as kaitiaki when plants and animals were being lost and ecosystems dismantled.

The Wai 262 Treaty claim report is expected at the end of 2009, and will be a key resource in relation to taonga species and the traditional knowledge associated with them.

This book also comes hot on the heels of the announcement by the Prime Minister John Key that Government would repeal the controversial Foreshore and Seabed Act. The progress achieved is a key milestone of the Māori Party coalition agreement with National has been phenomenal and this book reflects some of the complex issues emerging from implementation of the Act.

The book consists of 19 chapters written by twenty five Māori researchers and writers. More than half have completed doctoral studies in universities in New Zealand and overseas, a further six are enrolled in doctoral programmes. The rest have completed Masters research and post-graduate qualifications in wānanga and universities. Some are now working in academic institutions; others are working for their people. All are kaitiaki and work for hapū and iwi in various ways: either as advocates, in governance roles, as committee members, chairing marae committees and rūnanga and supporting environmental restoration projects. They move effectively between the worlds in which we live.

This pool of intellectual force is to be celebrated by us all. Through the influence of these writers, we now have a base of literature by Māori to contemplate and it will be of particular interest to other indigenous communities whose self-determination was compromised during 19th and 20th century colonisation. They too will recognise the issues and appreciate many of the challenges Māori confront today defending the environment.

The litany of painful experiences for hapū and iwi in working with local and regional bodies to safeguard and defend the environment stands out in this book. Their inspiration remains in the fight for the wellbeing of the next generations, ka whawhai tonu mātou.

Discharge of pollutants to water continues and yet the cry for more environmentally acceptable practices has developed into a roar from the kaitiaki writing in this book. Resource management practices and policies are constantly under review and comprise a common thematic debate throughout the book. Current issues such as climate change, the use of 1080 poison, the Foreshore and Seabed Act and wetlands restoration are close to the hearts of kaitiaki throughout New Zealand. Some of the writers share their experiences as Māori of working with models for consultation and partnership with various Councils and local government.

This book demonstrates the tenacity of tangata whenua as kaitiaki. It reminds us of the resilience of the indigenous project; that the people will not be put off, nor will they give up what have become lifelong struggles. Many have picked up the rākau and mantel from kaitiaki who have died during the struggle and left their children and mokopuna to continue the fight. Kaitiakitanga cannot be postponed or taken lightly. It is a daily obligation to our nation.

These writers are environmental historians, detailing the whakapapa of environmental attitudes, values, practices, policies and changes. They introduce new tools for consideration, new analysis about the benefits of co-operation and collaboration. They challenge current practices and suggest new and old ways of working together. They represent a diversity of views which are not surprisingly, also very similar.

This book makes a powerful contribution to our history and records our desire and readiness to make a greater contribution to the future. It is a promise to hold fast to the kaupapa and a promise to realise our dreams for a better future. I commend this book to you all.

Dr Pita Sharples
Minister of Māori Affairs

Acknowledgements

This book is a collection of papers by Māori writers from whānau, hapū and iwi throughout Aotearoa New Zealand, many of whom are kaitiaki within their own rohe (tribal area), and throughout Aotearoa. Many have extended their interest in kaitiakitanga to other places in the world, particularly with indigenous communities and in forums such as the United Nations and World Indigenous consortiums. They have all given generously of their time, shared their knowledge, refined original manuscripts, refocused their chapters and responded to many requests from the editors. We acknowledge and thank all the writers for their contributions. Tēnā koutou katoa.

Thanks to Anne Austin for her expertise, skills and attention to detail, while editing and proof reading all chapters to achieve consistency of the manuscript.

Our thanks are extended to Te Wānanga-o-Raukawa for their generous financial grant to support the publication of this book.

Finally, to Huia Publishers for their achievements in supporting Māori writers, we are pleased to have worked with them on this venture.

Nō reira, tēnā koutou katoa.

Rachael Selby
Pātaka Moore
Malcolm Mulholland

Introduction

Kaitiakitanga is an inherent obligation we have to our tūpuna and to our mokopuna; an obligation to safeguard and care for the environment for future generations. It is a link between the past and the future, the old and the new, between the taonga of the natural environment and tangata whenua. The natural environment is located between Ranginui and Papatūānuku, between Earth and Sky, and is shared by their descendants, tangata whenua and all other people. In order to live in harmony with the environment and each other, and to ensure our long term survival, we must respect and protect the environment. As tangata whenua and as kaitiaki we have responsibility for the environment and for those that share the environment. Kaitiakitanga is not an obligation which we choose to adopt or to ignore; it is an inherited commitment that links mana atua, mana tangata and mana whenua, the spiritual realm with the human world and both of those with the earth and all that is on it

All the contributors to this book are kaitiaki and exercise kaitiakitanga in many ways. All are recognisable for speaking out and speaking up for kaitiakitanga. Regrettably our voices are sometimes heard and seen as angry voices, as pleading voices and voices in opposition to the injustices which are visited upon Papatūānuku and Tangaroa. For over a thousand years Māori lived in harmony with the environment exercising kaitiakitanga, recognising our needs and those of the realms around us.

When new migrants came to Aotearoa in the 19th century they arrived in awe of the beauty they observed and in awe of the possibilities the land and environment afforded them. These opportunities were for many, economic. Forest was cleared from the hills and valleys, from the mountains and ranges, to make way for pasture and for sheep and cattle which represented and delivered wealth and opportunity in a new land. Communities and towns grew beside waterways: sources of food, sustenance and spiritual nourishment for Māori. Those same waterways were seen by new migrants as the natural places to flush human, animal and industrial waste. The resultant pollution was a setback to marae and Māori communities whose protesting voices were ignored by councillors who made decisions largely based on the economic and cultural wellbeing of the new majority population known as Pākehā. These decision-makers frequently made choices based on short term gains ignorant of long term costs. They lacked forethought and insight. Even today hindsight is not used to its full advantage and poor decisions continue to be made impacting on our ability to exercise kaitiakitanga and continuing to have grossly negative impacts on the environment.

This clash of cultures remains, with Māori communities smarting from the impact of one hundred and seventy years in a democratic system which is resolute in practicing a 'majority rules' version of democracy. Māori kaupapa and values have been smothered as the development of New Zealand and the decisions made about the value of the environment by local and regional councils have done more damage to the environment in that one hundred and seventy years than was done in the previous one thousand years prior to occupation by the descendants of British and European colonists.

Our role as kaitiaki has been ignored and many of our efforts to protect the gifts of our ancestors have been futile as is reported over and again in the chapters presented in this book. The chapters explain how kaitiaki respond to specific situations: to exploitation, to threats to the environment, to local and regional council [mis]management, to legislation enacted by government which threatens kaitiakitanga, to business and foreign interests. They also explain how specific hapū and iwi have responded in local areas to local issues. The authors in this book provide case studies which trace the events of the past, the impacts on the present and the challenges for the future which will require our mokopuna and descendants to undo the damage of the past.

These scholars address the impact of environmental damage on our people, our spirituality, our whānau, our mental and emotional wellbeing. They look to the future by providing solutions to problems created in the past. Many decisions require vision and long term commitment, finance and imagination. Many of the key decision-makers in our communities are elected representatives whose terms of office depend on playing populist politics. This discourages them from making long term decisions for fear of being thrown out of office at the next ballot box by others without long term obligations to future generations.

The first section, kaitiakitanga, represents historical issues, future subject matter and concerns for today for Māori and non-Māori. Some of the problems are global, some are local but are not unique. The first two chapters are about hapū kaitiakitanga. Margaret Mutu, like many kaitiaki, uses her expertise to work at undoing the damage done as a result of poor decisions made in the past which have impacted on tangata whenua in the north of New Zealand. She explains what kaitiakitanga means to Ngāti Kahu and how the hapū has implemented kaitiakitanga. She explains the statutory framework within which this responsibility is brought to bear. Legal frameworks can assist or impede the efforts of kaitiaki and regardless of the legal frameworks Māori responsibilities as tangata whenua remain. Margaret Mutu provides distressing examples of illegal activity overlooked by officials; of illegal discharges, of destruction of traditional food sources, of extensive environmental damage and objectors having to mount serious challenges and protests before those with apparent authority under Pākehā legal frameworks are prepared to exercise their legal powers.

Hapū have multiple responsibilities: to whānau, to neighbouring hapū, to their own iwi and neighbouring iwi, to manuhiri whether they are transient or whether they have settled here, to the gifts of our ancestors and the children of the future. Rachael Selby and Pātaka Moore cast a similar shadow. The stories are the same, only the location is the lower west coast of the North Island. This chapter explains the impact of fifty years of environmental damage by councils, neighbouring horticultural growers and pig farmers, twenty five years of sewage discharge into Lake Horowhenua and the Hōkio Stream and the potential impacts of mis-managed rubbish disposal and the battles which have ensued between local officials and a small hapū based on the southern banks of the Hōkio Steam. Like Ngāti Kahu and many other marae, Ngāti Pareraukawa has numerous ongoing projects to minimise the degradation of waterways, to challenge Councils making decisions which will have far reaching negative impacts hundreds of years into the future. Ngāti Pareraukawa has a plan to instil a Māori world view in the children so that they will naturally continue the role of kaitiaki. Passion is not enough, rather technical knowledge, environmental law and philosophy complement a Māori world view. Knowledge and skills to examine and analyse technical reports are necessary. The ability to battle and fight and protest are necessary. This is a Ngāti Pareraukawa legacy. The relationships with local, regional and national government are explored in several chapters.

One of the last Labour government's legacies was the passing of the Foreshore and Seabed legislation in 2004. Wellington and New Zealand witnessed a march on parliament in that year which resulted in the birth of the Māori Party. Māori were galvanised in response to the poor decisions of the government. Tracey Whare has worked globally on environmental issues for the United Nations in Geneva and on the Declaration of the Rights of Indigenous peoples. In her chapter she examines background to the Foreshore and Seabed Act, the responses, what it means, the implications for Māori and others, the key players, the instruments and mechanisms in the legislation, and the Ngāti Porou case. Ngāti Porou had begun negotiations with the Crown before the enactment of the Foreshore and Seabed Act and their experiences serve as a case study of ongoing developments with the Crown which is currently reviewing the legislation.

Veronica Tāwhai questions the role as kaitiaki of Māori who live outside their traditional iwi and hapū. This is equally relevant for those who live, for example, in Auckland, and who want to contribute to a rural marae environment many hours drive away, as it is for those who have been located for a lifetime away from home and want to participate within the region in which they reside. How to express their interests is uncertain. The involvement of Māori within 21st century Māori organisations follows no simple formula. Veronica Tāwhai argues that Māori living away from their traditional whenua may maintain an interest both in the environmental integrity of their regions, and the local environment in which they live. The method by which Māori individuals might express their interests as kaitiaki Māori is blurred. Some of the people who have contributed to this book manage these relationships by maintaining a career in the city and spending time travelling to home marae to maintain a significant role. Others are isolated and do not participate. Many have various relationships with tangata whenua and their expertise is appreciated while still others have expertise which is needed but they have not found a way to inject it.

Rangi Mataamua and Pou Temara examine the impact of Tūhoe becoming a global people, now resident in all corners of the earth. Tūhoe have become an urban-dwelling people. They are modern 21ˢᵗ century Tūhoe who in many cases have never gazed upon Maungapōhatu, or journeyed to Waikaremoana, or have never walked along the Whakatāne River. They lament the change in lifestyle of Tūhoe in one generation and the lost connection with the environment. This is not unique to Tūhoe and the claim of Rangi Mataamua and Pou Temara, that if many of them "ever found themselves lost in the forest with no food, [they] would either starve to death or die from exposure" may sound dramatic, pessimistic, perhaps even a hint of amusement may surface. These two men ask how Tūhoe exercise kaitiakitanga today and how this will occur in the future. Their challenge applies to many of us. We may well ask how we will be recognised as Māori in another thousand years, what we will be renowned for, how we will be practising as kaitiaki.

Change is as certain as night and day. All the scholars in this book examine the impact of change: changes in legislation such as the Resource Management Act and the Foreshore and Seabed Act, in rural and urban living, in values and beliefs about where to discharge pollutants and sewage, change in attitudes and beliefs about landfills, and about poisons like 1080, and the impact of change in diet and the move from being a tuna and fish eating people to meat eaters.

Change in this new millennium is now linked to climate and climate change. There are sceptics and there are adherents. Lisa Kanawa has systemically explored the issues as they relate to Māori. She provides climate change projections for all regions of New Zealand and promotes the idea that Māori will adapt to climate change as we have to other changes in the past thousand years. She predicts that climate change will be embraced as an opportunity for Māori.

The second set of six chapters focuses on Wai Māori. These chapters explore both kaitiakitanga and rangatiratanga within a dynamic and changing environment. They explore the significance of water, the consequences of polluting our waters and the impact on the mauri and the wairua of water and water bodies. Malcolm Mulholland's chapter, The death of the Manawatū River, draws our attention to a significant river in the lower North Island and one which has endured a century of discharge and pollution along its journey from the mountain to the sea. The chapter highlights the failure of communities, local bodies and now regional bodies to protect this taonga. It is a significant example of a river which needs kaitiaki to crusade to save it. Because it is a river which journeys through the whenua of many hapū and iwi, councils have exploited this by playing hapū and iwi off against each other when consulting. The Manawatū was, fifty years ago and one hundred years ago, admired for the quality of eels, for the abundance of fish, for excess and surplus. Today it is the discharge point of so many pollutants that it is, as Malcolm Mulholland claims, dying. When we are asked by our mokopuna what we have done as kaitiaki for the Manawatū River, we want to show how we fought with all our might to halt the decline and won. Currently we need much more effective engagement with the bodies granting consents to win.

Gail Tipa and Craig Pauling take us from the North Island to Ngāi Tahu and the South Island to explore the health and management of waterways. Craig Pauling details the state of the Takiwa tool used by Ngāi Tahu "allowing tāngata whenua to systematically record, collect, collate and report on the cultural health of significant sites, natural resources and the environment within their respective takiwā." This will promote opportunities for significant involvement as kaitiaki in environmental management. As is recorded in this book, many waterways are in poor health being points of inappropriate discharge and contaminants. They are no longer safe for food gathering. It is noteworthy that Craig Pauling acknowledges the extensive knowledge held by Māori which is undervalued and underutilised in a management context because it is perceived to be scientifically indefensible.

Gail Tipa goes further, outlining a Cultural Opportunity Assessment that has been developed for Māori to "assess their opportunities to engage in a range of cultural experiences in a catchment under differing stream flows". Water has become so valuable in the world not only for drinking and for human health but for economic reasons. Climate change and variable rainfall have become part of the New Zealand landscape. The manipulation of rivers and streams, the changes to flow, the impact on communities and the value of water are themes throughout this book.

The management of water bodies, namely rivers and lakes is addressed in the next two chapters by April Bennett and Te Rina Warren. The Waikato

River and Rotorua Lakes have been the subject of recent treaty claims with Waikato-Tainui and Te Arawa settlements providing the opportunity to restore and protect these water bodies. The Rangitīkei river, as outlined by Te Rina Warren, was diverted in its upper reaches north east of Waiouru, to supply water for a hydro power station. Along its 240 kilometre journey it has been polluted by various communities and suffered from poor management. Ngā Pae o Rangitīkei was set up by the marae, hapū and iwi within the catchment of the river and is a model for management of a natural resource.

Wetland ecosystems have been lost throughout the country with changing land use, competing values and priorities. Margaret Forster uses experiences of the Ngāi Te Ipu, Ngāti Hinepua and Ngāti Hine hapū in the Wairoa-Mahia region to examine the "social and cultural impacts of drainage, ecological degradation and loss of wetland biodiversity". The relationship between Māori and Pākehā values is a tension explored throughout the chapters either explicitly or implicitly.

The third section of this book continues the themes of the first two sections and adds a further dimension. The chapters collectively address issues of heritage and protection. Merata Kāwharu further explains kaitiakitanga, the environment and the marae. Her chapter outlines the values and principles of the marae enabling us to conceptualise and understand the concept of environment. She weaves the Māori Heritage Council's National Māori Heritage Statement Tapuwae in and relates this to 'marae locales' using the Ngāti Whātua community at Ōrākei to apply the concepts developed in Tapuwae.

The shared understanding of environmental relationships by indigenous peoples is explored by Mason Durie in his chapter which addresses what constitutes outstanding universal values. This chapter draws on Pacific views which are then able to inform a wider understanding of heritage, universality and determine what are deemed to be precious sites.

Shaun Ogilvie, Aroha Miller and James Ataria grapple with the highly controversial practice of dropping 1080 poison from aircraft. While there is a need to protect many species from pests such as rodents and possums there is considerable opposition. This chapter explores the advantages and disadvantages and the results of a research project reassessing 1080 use which received submissions from Māori. Many concerns have been addressed and this chapter highlights the importance of effective communication with Māori communities. Their scientific testing finds there is only minute uptake of 1080 by native plants. Cherryl Smith's chapter also deals with poison sprayed from the air but in another time and context. She researches the implications for Māori Vietnam war veterans of Agent Orange, a powerful herbicide defoliant used to clear forests in Vietnam. Because Māori were over-represented in this war they are over-represented in bearing the impact and consequences of Agent Orange on themselves and their descendants. The oral testimonies and recordings of the veterans indicate that this assault on the environment and the people, while expedient, continues to have long term impacts on many Māori whānau.

The exploitation of environmental resources is addressed jointly by Jessica Hutchings and Angeline Greensill in what they outline as a paternalistic colonial mindset which assumes superiority in knowing what is best. The exploitation extends to indigenous peoples as greater profits encourage corporations to further extend their activities without being accountable. While sustainable management has occurred for thousands of years the new millennium has seen the balance tipped and the environment at greater risk than any time in the past. Jessica Hutchings and Angeline Greensill deal with two neo-liberal policies that specifically relate to biodiversity and Māori. One is the proposed framework for bio-prospecting in Aotearoa/New Zealand. The other is a defeated bi-lateral (free-trade) agreement on the regulation of natural medicines referred to as the proposed Australian and New Zealand Therapeutics Authority (ANZTPA). Both frameworks impact on the rangatiratanga of Māori.

For generations Māori relied on tuna as a major food source. As a result of the poor management of many lakes, rivers and streams, the availability and the quality of tuna has declined steadily over the past five decades. Marie Nixon-Benton has documented the benefits of a diet rich in the unsaturated fatty acid omega-3 derived primarily from the long-finned eel or tuna. She also found that a diet rich in tuna assisted in the prevention of Type II diabetes mellitus and hence promoted health and wellbeing.

Huhana Smith's chapter draws together themes which have been explored in all three sections. She uses a case study to explain the restoration of an ecosystem by Ngāti Tūkorehe (based on the west coast of the North Island). The context in which she locates this case study is within the structures and policies for protecting Māori cultural heritage within natural and cultural landscapes.

These contributions by kaitiaki from the north to the south, the west to the east, demonstrate the relationship that Māori have with the environment. As such this book serves not only as a reminder of those obligations but as a record of what those obligations entail for future generations. Not only do the concerns raised within the book need to be registered for ourselves as Māori, but they also need to be listened to by local, regional and central government which continue to make decisions about the environment based on a least expensive option rather than on the most sustainable. Should New Zealand embrace the kaupapa of kaitiakitanga then both Māori and non-Māori will have greater opportunities to leave future generations with sound environmental principles. Māori should take a lead role as active kaitiaki to promote these principles in the wider community for the benefit of all.

Rachael Selby, Malcolm Mulholland and Pātaka Moore

KAITIAKITANGA

Ngāti Kahu kaitiakitanga

Margaret Mutu [1]

Over the past two decades, Ngāti Kahu has watched with increasing alarm as Pākehā have sought to generate ever-increasing profits from exploiting Ngāti Kahu's lands and seas. Our role as kaitiaki throughout our territories, while theoretically respected and protected under the Resource Management Act 1991, has been severely challenged and threatened on many occasions as the Department of Conservation, along with district and regional councils, ignore and ride roughshod over our legal rights allowing the desecration of our wāhi tapu and despoliation of our lands. They rely on Māori being too poor to force government agencies and developers to adhere to the Act. Yet Ngāti Kahu have on several occasions taken legal action against the Department of Conservation and the Far North District Council, relying on the generosity of both Pākehā and Māori lawyers to carry out the work on either a voluntary or a *pro bono* basis or using legal aid.

In this chapter, before recounting a selection of our experiences over the past two decades in trying to carry out our kaitiaki responsibilities, I will first explain what being kaitiaki means to Ngāti Kahu and the statutory framework within Pākehā law which is supposed to uphold and protect our kaitiakitanga.

Introduction

Ngāti Kahu are the descendants of Kahutianui, daughter of Tūmoana and ancestor of Te Rarawa, and Te Parata who reached Aotearoa on board the Māmaru. We hold mana whenua over the area of Te Hiku o te Ika (the Far

North) which stretches from the Rangaunu harbour in the north, south to
Te Whatu (Berghan's Point), inland along the Maungataniwha range and
from the western end of the range back to Rangaunu, taking in Takahue,
Pāmapuria and Kaitāia. Today, there are twelve Ngāti Kahu hapū in fifteen
marae communities in Ngāti Kahu's territories. Our marae are located on
the remnants of our lands still under our control, which is less than 6% of
our land territories.[2] Ngāti Kahu's population, based on whakapapa rather
than census data, is approximately 15,000 and more than 80% of Ngāti
Kahu live outside our territories, mainly in cities such as Auckland.

Our role as kaitiaki has been passed down through the generations
and is carefully rearticulated in hui, in wānanga, and every time another
development taking place within our territories threatens the integrity
of our mother earth, Papatūānuku. By the 1980s our kaumātua were
becoming so concerned that some of them started recording and writing
down what our role is. They also played a key role in formulating the
sections of the Resource Management Act which acknowledge and protect
our role as kaitiaki, and the provisions to uphold and implement these
that are in the New Zealand Coastal Policy Statement. Today, Ngāti Kahu
relies heavily on their work, and particularly that of Māori Marsden[3] and
McCully Matiu,[4] when presenting cases in the Pākehā court system.

McCully Matiu provided the following explanation which was
supported by hapū and iwi throughout the country and quoted in the
Report and Recommendations of the Board of Inquiry into the New
Zealand Coastal Policy Statement in 1994:[5]

> *Kaitiakitanga is the role played by kaitiaki. Traditionally, kaitiaki
> are the many spiritual assistants of the gods, including the spirits of
> deceased ancestors, who were the spiritual minders of the elements
> of the natural world. All the elements of the natural world, the sky
> father and earth mother and their offspring; the seas, sky, forests and
> birds, food crops, winds, rain and storms, volcanic activity, as well as
> people and wars are descended from a common ancestor, the supreme
> god. These elements, which are the world's natural resources, are
> often referred to as taonga, that is, items which are greatly treasured
> and respected. In Māori cultural terms, all natural, and physical
> elements of the world are related to each other, and each is controlled
> and directed by the numerous spiritual assistants of the gods.*

These spiritual assistants often manifest themselves in physical forms such as fish, animals, trees or reptiles. Each is imbued with mana, a form of power and authority derived directly from the gods. Man being descended from the gods is likewise imbued with mana although that mana can be removed if it is violated or abused. There are many forms and aspects of mana, of which one is the power to sustain life.

Māoridom is very careful to preserve the many forms of mana it holds, and in particular is very careful to ensure that the mana of kaitiaki is preserved. In this respect Māori become one and the same as kaitiaki (who are, after all, their relations), becoming the minders for their relations, that is, the other physical elements of the world.

As minders, kaitiaki must ensure that the mauri or life force of their taonga is healthy and strong. A taonga whose life force has been depleted, as is the case for example with the Manukau Harbour, presents a major task for the kaitiaki. In order to uphold their mana, the tangata whenua as kaitiaki must do all in their power to restore the mauri of the taonga to its original strength.

In specific terms, each whānau or hapu (extended family or sub-tribe) is kaitiaki for the area over which they hold mana whenua, that is, their ancestral lands and seas. Should they fail to carry out their kaitiakitanga duties adequately, not only will mana be removed, but harm will come to the members of the whānau or hapu.

Thus a whānau or a hapu who still hold mana in a particular area take their kaitiaki responsibilities very seriously. The penalties for not doing so can be particularly harsh. Apart from depriving the whānau or hapu of the life sustaining capacities of the land and sea, failure to carry out kaitiakitanga roles adequately also frequently involves the untimely death of members of the whānau or hapu.

An interpretation of kaitiakitanga based on this explanation must of necessity incorporate the spiritual as well as physical responsibilities of tangata whenua, and relate to the mana not only of the tangata whenua, but also of the gods, the land and the sea. The manner in which we implement our kaitiaki responsibilities is determined by our tikanga, our rules and system of laws. Introduced Pākehā law cannot change our responsibilities. It can instead either assist and support us as kaitiaki, or make it very difficult for us to carry out our responsibilities. So, for example, only mana whenua – that is, those who belong to the land – can be kaitiaki and hence exercise kaitiakitanga. For Ngāti Kahu, that is the whānau and hapū of Ngāti Kahu who are each responsible for the particular area over which they hold mana whenua. The definition of kaitiaki in the Resource Management Act 1991 had to be amended in 1997 to stop Pākehā asserting they could be kaitiaki and redefining the word to suit their purposes.[6] We have often had to explain that non-Māori are not kaitiaki because they are not mana whenua. Along with that we also have to explain that they still have a responsibility to look after, respect and use the land properly and appropriately.

There is also the fact that legal ownership of land as defined through the English-derived legal system is irrelevant in respect of the kaitiakitanga responsibilities of mana whenua. Yet Pākehā, including lawyers and judges, will try to argue that the legal title overrules kaitiaki considerations, when in terms of tikanga it cannot do so. The erroneous notion of the supremacy of Pākehā law derives from the delusions of White Supremacy which the English brought with them when they arrived in this country in the 1800s (Ballara 1986; Jay, 2005; Lee, 2007, pp. 29–32). This racism was outlawed in New Zealand with the introduction of the Race Relations Act in 1971 at the behest of the United Nations and their 1965 International Convention for the Elimination of all forms of Racial Discrimination. New Zealand ratified the Convention in 1972 after the Office of the Race Relations Conciliator was established. However, the website of the Human Rights Commission notes "The introduction of the Act was not without controversy. Many people considered that race relations in New Zealand were good and the legislation was unnecessary..." (http://www.hrc.co.nz/index.php?p=13819). As a result racism, and particularly that against Māori, is still widely practised in New Zealand and is deeply entrenched in local and central government. The attitude is perpetuated through Pākehā mass media (Stavenhagen 2006, paragraphs 66 and 104) . This leads to government agencies and developers evading the clear statutory provisions which protect the role of Māori as kaitiaki.

Statutory provisions

On the face of it, the statutory provisions of Pākehā law that do exist in respect of our role as kaitiaki should, if implemented correctly, support and assist us.[7]

The relevant statutory considerations which can assist Ngāti Kahu in our kaitaiki role are

- the Conservation Act 1987 and S.4 in particular, which requires that the Department of Conservation to 'give effect to the principles of the Treaty of Waitangi'.
- the Local Government Act 2002. Section 4 states '...to improve opportunities for Māori to contribute to local government decision-making processes...'
- the Resource Management Act 1991 (RMA). Section 6(e) concerns the recognition and provision of matters of national importance including the relationship of Māori and their culture and traditions with their ancestral lands, water, sites, wāhi tapu, and other taonga. Section 7(a) concerns the requirement to have particular regard to kaitiakitanga. Section 8 concerns the requirement to take into account the principles of the Treaty of Waitangi. There is considerable overlap in practice between these subsections and all other subsections of Part II. There is also a significant and growing body of case law considering sections 6(e), 7(a) and 8 of the Act (Mutu 2007:17). The Fourth Schedule of the Act sets out the matters that should be considered when preparing an assessment of the effects that a proposal will have on the environment and many of these relate specifically to Māori and our role as kaitiaki.
- the New Zealand Coastal Policy Statement 1994 (NZCPS) guides local authorities in their day-to-day management of the coastal environment. It contains numerous sections that set out specifically how the provisions of the RMA are to be interpreted and implemented in respect of the Māori role in managing the coast.[8] Section 62(2) of the Act requires that regional policy statements not be inconsistent with the NZCPS.
- the Regional Policy Statement for Northland.
- and the Proposed Far North District Plan.

Photo 1: *The mouth of the Rangaunu harbour. The barging terminal was proposed for the northern shores in the centre of this photo.*

Photo 2: *Waikākari showing the damage to the sand dunes caused by off-road vehicles.*

Trying to prevent desecration of our wāhi tapu and despoliation of our lands

The whānau and hapū of Ngāti Kahu have more than 40 generations of knowledge and expertise relating to our lands, seas and natural resources. Despite innumerable efforts on our part to inform both central and local government about our resources and to explain how they are best managed, we are constantly appalled at their seemingly wilful and deliberate lack of knowledge and, at times, amazing stupidity as they attempt to manage but only succeed in mismanaging Ngāti Kahu's natural resources. During the 1990s, for example, unsustainable exploitation of Ngāti Kahu's fisheries by commercial fishermen resulted in Ngāti Kahu issuing public notices declaring all commercial fishing vessels banned from fishing in our waters.[9] While this move drew considerable support from local communities, including Pākehā, and some fishing companies went elsewhere to fish, others ignored the ban. Over the years it has become clear to us that racism on the part of many Pākehā prevents them from accepting our advice and directions.[10] As a result we have sustained many environmental disasters and witnessed the desecration of many of our wāhi tapu.

(a) Rangaunu harbour

At the northern extent of our territories is the Rangaunu harbour which we share with our neighbouring iwi, Ngāi Takoto. For years, the Far North District Council and the Northland Regional Council allowed timber mill waste to pollute the harbour, threatening and at times closing the oyster farms some of our whānau owned in the harbour. And then they tried to push through consents to construct a barging terminal in the harbour to transport the logs from the timber mills. Patukoraha hapū and Ngāi Takoto iwi, the kaitiaki for the harbour, fought the councils on both issues over many years. They managed to stop the barging terminal proposal before it was formally notified. The councils finally started to impose conditions on the waste water discharge consents of the timber mill and the harbour is now slowly improving.

(b) Waikākari

Just outside Rangaunu on the Karikari peninsula is the beautiful Waikākari with its white sand beach and sand dunes which are all wāhi tapu. The dunes have an extensive golden pingao covering.[11] The Department of

Conservation claims management responsibility for the beach and dunes. This beach ranks among the best surf beaches in the country. In photo 2 you can see the tracks made by off-road vehicles through the sand dunes. Te Whānau Moana hapū of Karikari has repeatedly directed the Department to stop the vehicles desecrating our old burial grounds and destroying the fragile and rare pingao but they refuse to listen. So Te Whānau Moana erected barriers, although the off-road vehicles usually demolish them, and evicts vehicles from the dunes.

(c) Karikari

The next beach along the peninsula is the seven-kilometre-long white sand Karikari. Like Waikākari, the beach has extensive sand dunes that are all wāhi tapu and have extensive pingao coverage. Te Whānau Moana still live on the northern half of this beach and use and monitor it on a daily basis. We have had particularly bitter experiences in recent years.

In the 1970s and 80s Te Whānau Moana fought a long and bitter battle to stop a developer building a huge tourist complex on the southern end of the beach. Our kuia and kaumātua did so to protect the extensive wāhi tapu along the beach and inland in several places and relied heavily on Pākehā lawyers who were prepared to do the legal work for little or no pay. The Environmental Defence Society also assisted by starting the legal action.[12] The permits granted by the Mangonui County Council (the predecessor of the Far North District Councl) were eventually overturned by the Court of Appeal.[13] After the developer died in the early 1990s, his widow put the land on the market for a giveaway price of one million dollars. Te Whānau Moana begged the Minister in Charge of Treaty of Waitangi Negotiations, Douglas Graham, to purchase it so that it could be included in the land bank being developed to settle Ngāti Kahu's land claims. The Minister refused and the government chose instead to allow it to be sold to an American merchant banker to build a large, exclusive tourist resort.

Neither the American nor the Far North District Council consulted with Te Whānau Moana of Karikari beach or Ngāti Kahu about the proposed development and the council issued resource consents for it in 1999 without publicly notifying it. When we found out about the consents from the Environmental Defence Society, Ngāti Kahu took the matter to the courts, suing both the American's company, Carrington Farms, and the Far North District Council[14] over the matter. A young Māori lawyer working in a large Auckland legal firm agreed to take the case *pro bono* and fought for over 18 months to get the matter to court.

In the meantime the American proceeded with the development disregarding the legal action before the courts. Deciding to turn our swamp from which we collect tuna (eels) into a lake, he blocked off a swamp outlet behind the sand dunes by digging up the dunes. He had no resource consent for the work. Workers abandoned the job when they started digging up kōiwi; the site manager refused to stop work, falsely claiming they were cow bones. Desperate pleas to both the Far North District Council and the Department of Conservation went unheeded. The blockage held but the swamp was under huge strain as a result of the removal of extensive vegetation coverage on a large area of land that was part of the development. This action had stripped the land of its water-holding capacity, and the swamp had to try to cope with massive increases in the volumes of water draining into it. As huge volumes of top soil were also being washed into the swamp, it had to find an alternative outlet. So after a few months it forced its way through to the sea about two kilometres north of the blockage, taking out over five hundred metres of dunes, including many hectares of pingao.

For weeks, the beautiful white sands of Karikari were black and the sea a dirty brown. Dead pingao was strewn along the beach. The huge pipi bed in the path of the break out was swept away and took several years to re-establish itself several kilometres down the beach. The magnificent white sand dunes by the Waimango stream seen in photo 4 have now almost gone. The American lied to the Council saying that that was how the beach had always been. And the Council, in its ignorance, believed him over the protests of Te Whānau Moana.

When a hearing date was finally confirmed, the American asked to settle out of court. He entered into an agreement with us which the High Court sealed.[15] Both he and the Far North District Council apologised to Ngāti Kahu. The American promised never to touch the dunes or several other wāhi tapu, to cut back the size of the development substantially and to get permission from Te Whānau Moana before undertaking any more development.[16] Within months of signing the agreement he breached it, having mounted an extensive campaign to divide Te Whānau Moana. The Far North District Council refused to uphold the agreement. The American

Photo 3: Karikari.

Photo 4: The pingao on the dunes on Karikari. In the middle distance are the very high dunes which have now reduced significantly in height.

then tried to close off the beach and issue trespass notices to Te Whānau Moana kaumātua. Te Whānau Moana ignored them and kept the beach open for the public. The American continues to advertise Karikari beach as his private beach on the world-wide web and there is an on-going feud between Te Whānau Moana of Karikari beach and the American and his company.

Other developers who have also managed to acquire lands on Karikari beach have followed the lead of Carrington Farms, having been assured that the Far North District Council will turn a blind eye to their illegal activities.[17] But when one of them abused and swore at a Te Whānau Moana representative for advising them that they could not build on a burial cave, Ngāti Kahu called in the Historic Places Trust. Ignoring very specific instructions, the developer continued digging up the burial cave and did not stop until he had dug up two full skeletons and several taonga. The Trust issued an order that all work stop but ignored the pleas of Te Whānau Moana that the developer be prosecuted. As a result it is Te Whānau Moana, rather than the Pākehā authorities, who have the legal responsibility and the resources to do so, who has to monitor the developer to make sure the work ban is complied with.

(d) Waikura and Mērita

On the eastern side of Karikari peninsula is the picturesque Ōmahuri (Maitai Bay) and Mērita (see photo 5). In 1968 the Crown confiscated the two beaches and the surrounding land from two Te Whānau Moana whānau. The Commissioner of Lands had visited the area and decided that the Crown should own and run the camping grounds the whānau had run for the public for many years. Not satisfied with confiscating just the camping grounds, they also confiscated the two surrounding farms. The two whānau fought bitterly to have their lands returned and in the 1980s one of them was returned. But the financial return to the Crown from the other camping ground at Waikura was significant and, despite having no real reason for doing so, they refused to return it.

The Department of Lands and Surveys and then the Department of Conservation managed the camping ground. Both crammed more people into the site than it could sustain. They dumped rubbish from the camping ground illegally on the boundary to the adjacent Māori land. They dumped

Photo 5: The two beaches, Ōmahuri and Mērita with Maitai pā between them. The pasture area was confiscated by the Crown in 1968. The beach to the left and the adjacent beach were returned in the 1980s. The DOC camping ground is to the left of Maitai.

Photo 6: The northern end of Mērita. One of the illegal toilet blocks was located where the car is in the foreground.

untreated sewage from the camping ground septic tanks in open pits on the Māori land, disregarding the vehement protests of the owners living there. They circulated maps to campers showing neighbouring Māori land as available for public recreation and the trespassers from the camping ground regularly abused tangata whenua on their own lands. They allowed visitors to desecrate the numerous wāhi tapu, including burial grounds and a large, very ancient pā site. They constructed toilet blocks on wāhi tapu, one just a few metres above the high water mark, and did not maintain the septic tanks properly. As a result, in the peak summer period, raw sewage flowed down the open drains and out to sea as the septic tanks overflowed.

All these activities were illegal and the Department of Conservation was also in clear violation of section 4 of the Conservation Act which required it to "give effect to the principles of the Treaty of Waitangi". Over the years Te Whānau Moana appealed repeatedly to both Departments, to various Ministers, to the New Zealand Conservation Authority,[18] to our MPs, to the health authorities and even to the media.

Finally, the Northland Regional Council intervened to help Te Whānau Moana. They ordered that the illegal rubbish and sewage dumps be closed and instructed the Department of Conservation to apply for permits to take and discharge water. It took several years for the Department to respond but they eventually did, applying for water permits in 1990 under the Water and Soil Conservation Act to avoid the much more stringent requirements of the imminent Resource Management Act 1991. Northland Regional Council issued the permits but did not include all the necessary conditions needed to manage the camp properly. So Te Whānau Moana took the Council and the Department of Conservation to the Planning Tribunal. The Tribunal decision[19] made it clear that the Department's behaviour was unacceptable and set a large number of conditions on the water permit, including significantly reducing the number of camping sites. Although the Department did not appeal the decision, it chose to ignore most of the conditions.

Te Whānau Moana spent many years trying to cajole the Department into complying. They did close the rubbish dump and stop dumping sewage on our land. They also removed the most offensive toilet block and reduced the number of camp sites. But our patience eventually ran out and in 2004 the whānau repossessed the camping ground, forcing the Department to

Photo 7: Perehipe. *Kōiwi were washed out of the dunes at the centre and to the right of this photo. Illegal storm water pipes drained from the houses above.*

Photo 8: Tokerau. *This part of the beach was a black-brown colour for several months as a result of illegal discharges.*

the negotiating table with Ngāti Kahu's Treaty of Waitangi claims negotiators. Since then there have been many changes in the management of the camping ground. The wāhi tapu are now protected, all the offensive toilet blocks have been removed, the septic tanks replaced, we haven't seen raw sewage in the drains for several years, and we rarely have to deal with trespassers. And although the Crown has yet to formally return the land, the whānau is back living on the land permanently.

(e) Perehipe

Several kilometres south of Maitai is the Pākehā settlement that they have called Whatuwhiwhi.[20] A generation ago there were very few Pākehā at Whatuwhiwhi, or on the Karikari peninsula. There are now more than 2500[21] and the pace of housing development, particularly along the coastline, has risen exponentially. Once again, the pleas of Te Whānau Moana to slow down the rate of development, to ensure the protection of wāhi tapu and to monitor building activity have been ignored. In 2003 illegally piped storm water washed out wāhi tapu on the dunes on Perehipe beach adjacent to the eastern reaches of the settlement. Kōiwi were scattered over the beach. This time Te Whānau Moana called on archaeologists, and the Far North District Council was ordered to fence off the wāhi tapu and remove the illegal drainage pipes. Te Whānau Moana kaumātua have been trying to persuade the council to comply for several years now without success.

(f) Tokerau

Immediately to the south of the Whatuwhiwhi settlement is Tokerau, a ten-kilometre white sand beach, again with sand dune system which extends the full length of the beach. Extensive housing development along the northern end of the beach has robbed it of its magnificent natural character and outstanding landscape values. Illegal water discharges have been piped directly onto the beach. Several years ago heavy rains dislodged the peat soils inland from the dune system after the area had been denuded of its vegetation. The illegal drainage pipes discharged a black-brown sludge directly onto the beach discolouring large sections of it. Shellfish harvested from the beach in the following months were deformed and health authorities closed the beach twice. When Te Whānau Moana tried to have the damage remedied, the Northland Regional Council refused to

Photo 9: Taipā. The kokota beds used to stretch from the bridge to the estuary mouth to the right of the photo.

Photo 10: Waipapa (Cable Bay). The Far North District Council issued a consent for a footbridge across the road through the pohutukawa trees at the northern end of the beach just before the rocks. The condominiums are located up the hill to the left.

act against the developers. As a result no-one was prosecuted and the illegal drain pipes continue to discharge onto the beach to this day.

(g) Taipā

Several kilometres south of Tokerau, in the territories of Ngāti Tara and Matakairiri hapū, is Taipā. The river estuary there is renowned for its huge kokota beds and whānau have collected the shellfish from there for centuries. In the 1980s whānau noticed that the estuary was becoming polluted by runoff from adjacent farms and the kokota beds were suffering. Repeated requests to both the Far North District Council and the Northland Regional Council to stop, or at least reduce and control the runoff went unheeded. As a result the kokota beds which used to extend from the bridge in photo 9 to the mouth of the estuary have been reduced to just the area around the mouth.

(h) Waipapa and Koekoeā

Just south of Taipā in the territories of Matarahurahu hapū is Waipapa, the beach the Pākehā called Cable Bay, and Koekoeā which they called Coopers beach. Building activity along this part of the coast and right down to Mangonui has been increasing markedly over the past decades. The Far North District Council's predecessor, the Mangonui County Council, constructed sewerage systems designed only to cope with the population of the area as it was several decades ago. The Far North District Council recklessly approved increasing development with seemingly little consideration for the carrying capacity of the sewerage systems at Waipapa and Koekoeā. As a result the systems regularly overloaded, particularly during heavy rain, and discharged raw sewage onto the beaches. It took several years for the Council to upgrade the systems.

When the Council approved a huge upmarket condominium development on a wāhi tapu at Waipapa in 2006 without publicly notifying it, Matarahurahu protested. However, when it also approved a foot bridge from the development across State Highway 10 onto the beach, the whole community, Pākehā and Māori, joined Matarahurahu in protest. The Pākehā community were incensed that the Council had refused permission for a foot bridge for school children across the highway at Taipā outside the Area School, but would allow one for a small group of very wealthy condominium owners. Particularly bitter arguments and confrontations followed and there was extensive media coverage of the protest action. For a long time the Council remained cowed by the developer's threats of legal action if his profits were threatened. But increasing public anger finally forced the Council to back down. Recent media reports seem to indicate that the developer is now experiencing financial difficulty and is unable to complete the project because of the negative media coverage.[22] Far more important to Matarahurahu, however, is that the wāhi tapu has sustained extensive damage from the earthworks and building activity.

(i) Mangōnui

The Pākehā settlement at Mangōnui has been an on-going problem for both Matarahurahu and Ngāti Ruaiti hapū for many decades. The harbour at Mangōnui has sustained extensive environmental damage as a result of unwise development, and especially as a result of erecting buildings too close to the sea. Sewage discharge has impacted severely and negatively on the harbour. Extending State Highway 10 across the southern reaches of the harbour was particularly damaging and destroyed extensive fishing and shellfish areas belonging to Matarahurahu.

In 1994 Mangōnui residents decided they wanted to reclaim part of the harbour adjacent to the shopping area to provide extra public parking and recreation areas. The shops and a hotel had all been built at the foot of a cliff and were too close to the sea. There had already been several reclamations carried out on the harbour and they had all had negative impacts. Now they wanted to reclaim several thousand square metres more. The reclamation would destroy all the marine life in its path and, like all the others, impact severely and negatively on the rest of the harbour.

From the outset Matarahurahu made its opposition known. They knew the harbour far better than any of the Mangōnui residents and patiently tried to explain why the reclamation could not happen. Over many decades Matarahurahu had witnessed significant changes in the harbour. Tidal flows had changed, not only at the points of reclamation but also much further inland. Matarahurahu rejected the notion that western scientists working for the Mangōnui residents were more expert in this matter than they were. They had seen and experienced the changes themselves where the scientists have not and were, essentially, guessing.[23]

Matarahurahu had also observed a marked reduction in the harbour's capability as a nursery for and provider of customary sea foods for Matarahurahu and other hapū, in particular several fish and shell fish species. Maturahurahu knew this as regular harvesters of seafood from the area concerned. They had observed these changes over a period of many decades and, once again, rejected western scientists' assertions to the contrary as guesswork.[24]

Matarahurahu had also experienced the killing off of the sea life above the reclamation at Paewhenua, an island in the inner reaches of the harbour. That reclamation had been carried out to accommodate State Highway 10 and even the Mangōnui residents recognized how bad the effects of that reclamation had been.[25]

Matarahurahu informed the Mangōnui residents that apart from being the owners of the Mangōnui harbour, they also have overall responsibility as kaitiaki for its well-being and that of the surrounding lands and waterways and that they would not allow any more damage to their harbour.[26]

Yet the Mangōnui residents completely ignored Matarahurahu and carried on with their application. In 2003, when the application was in its final stages and the Far North District Council had invested a lot of time and effort into planning the reclamation, the Mangōnui residents and the Far North District Council were instructed by the Northland Regional Council to talk to Matarahurahu. The meeting was arranged to coincide with one of the monthly hui of Te Rūnanga-ā-Iwi o Ngāti Kahu and was held at Kenana marae. The meeting clearly articulated Matarahurahu's opposition and the Rūnanga chairperson warned the council not to proceed without Matarahurahu's permission.[27] The marae chair instructed them to put their car park and walkway on piles. The council ignored both directives and Northland Regional Council issued a resource consent for the reclamation.

Kenana marae immediately sought and received legal aid to lodge an appeal in the Environment Court. After many months of legal battling, the matter was finally settled out of court after the Doubtless Bay Citizens and Ratepayers Association and the Far North District Council agreed to build the structure on piles. Matarahurahu agreed to allow minimal reclamation to support the structure but imposed extensive restrictions on the nature of the reclamation and the materials to be used in it.[28]

Construction went ahead but in 2007 one of the Mangōnui residents became the mayor of the Far North District Council. He immediately halted the construction work, which was almost complete. Kenana marae reminded the council of the Environment Court agreement but the Mangōnui residents seemed, once again, not to listen. At the time of writing Kenana marae had asked the chairperson of Te Rūnanga-ā-Iwi o Ngāti Kahu to intervene on their behalf to enforce the agreement.

Photo 11. Mangōnui harbour extra parking and recreation area. Matarahurahu hapū insisted that rather than sitting on a reclamation and causing further damage to the harbour, the structure had to be on piles with minimal reclamation.

Conclusion

Ngāti Kahu's experience of trying to carry out our responsibilities as kaitiaki of our natural resources is that it has become increasingly difficult over the recent decades as Pākehā development has encroached at an alarmingly increasing rate into our territories. Protection afforded us by Pākehā statutes has only assisted us when we have taken cases to the courts. But the cost of doing so is prohibitive and unless lawyers work for us voluntarily, or on a *pro bono* basis, or we can access legal aid for our cases, we have little chance of being able to pursue our legal rights. That does not absolve us of our responsibilities, it simply makes it much harder for us to carry them out. It also makes us more determined to carry them out in accordance with our own tikanga.

We do not accept that ignorance and so-called 'cultural misunderstanding' – a euphemism for racism – are legitimate excuses for desecrating our wāhi tapu and despoiling our lands and seas. And we will never accept the White Supremacy (racism) which nurtures these attitudes and will continue to seek the support of the United Nations to stop it being practised in New Zealand as was so strongly recommended by their Special Rapporteur, Professor Rodolfo Stavenhagen, after he visited New Zealand in 2005.[29]

END NOTES

[1]Professor Margaret Mutu is the chair of Ngāti Kahu's iwi parliament, Te Rūnanga-ā-Iwi o Ngāti Kahu, and chair of Karikari marae of Te Whānau Moana hapū of Ngāti Kahu.

[2]Approximately 12,000 acres out of more than 250,000 acres of dry land are still in Ngāti Kahu control.

[3]Māori Marsden's writings have been gathered and published as *The Woven Universe – Selected Writings of Rev. Māori Marsden.* (Royal 2003).

[4]McCully Matiu's teachings are recorded in the book *Te Whānau Moana – Ngā Kaupapa me Ngā Tikanga – Customs and Protocols.* (Matiu & Mutu 2003).

[5]*Report and Recommendations of the Board of Inquiry into the New Zealand Coastal Policy Statement* (Department of Conservation, Wellington, 1994) pp. 16–17.

[6]The *Resource Management Act* 1991 defines kaitiakitanga as "…the exercise of guardianship; and in relation to a resource, includes the ethic of stewardship based on the nature of the resource itself." (section 2). The 1997 amendment reads "Kaitiakitanga means the exercise of guardianship by the tangata whenua of an area in accordance with tikanga Māori in relation to natural and physical resources; and includes the ethic of stewardship."

[7]The fact that Pākehā law does not assist Māori in our role as kaitiaki because the provisions that do assist us are ignored has been analysed by Hirini Matunga (2000). He explains why and how the current legislation is deficient and therefore can be used by government departments and councils to evade their Treaty of Waitangi responsibilities if they choose to do so.

[8]See Mutu (2002, pp. 85–92) for a list of these sections in the NZCPS and a discussion of their application to the Carrington Farms development on Karikari peninsula which was opposed by Te Whānau Moana hapū of Ngāti Kahu.

[9]*Northland Age,* Kaitāia, April 1998.

[10]One strategy Ngāti Kahu has used to try get past this racism is to employ an Englishman, who has been trained by our kaumātua, is married into Ngāti Tara hapū of Ngāti Kahu, and has a degree in resource management, as our resource management officer in Te Rūnanga-ā-Iwi o Ngāti Kahu. He reports having some success with the Northland Regional Council and some resource management consultant firms, and with a very few

Department of Conservation officials. However, he still finds that the Far North District Council and some resource management consultant firms ignore the objections of mana whenua and refuse to consult. (Mutu, 2008, p. 5).

[11]Pingao, *desmoschoenus spiralis,* is a coastal sedge grass that became threatened by marram grass and is now relatively rare around the country.

[12]The Environmental Defence Society is an incorporated society specialising in legal action on environmental issues. It is made up of lawyers, planners and resource management specialists.

[13]New Zealand Law Reports, 1989. *The Environmental Defence Society Inc. and Taitokerau District Māori Council v Mangonui County Council* [1989]. NZLR 257.

[14]The Environmental Defence Society and Te Runanga-a-Iwi o Ngati Kahu v the Far North District Council (FNDC) and Carrington Farms Ltd, High Court, Whangarei.

[15]High Court of New Zealand, 5 March 2001. 'Settlement Agreement between the Environmental Defence Society Inc., Te Rūnanga-ā-Iwi o Ngāti Kahu and the Far North District Council and Carrington Farms.'

[16]For a full description of the background to this agreement see Mutu (2002).

[17]The Far North District Council has also refused to register or even note the location of the many burial grounds about which Te Whānau Moana has notified them, denying that they exist.

[18]Details of the early attempts by Te Whānau Moana and Te Rorohuri hapū to stop the Department of Conservation desecrating and despoiling Waikura and Mērita are provided in correspondence of the Karikari Trust to the Minister of Conservation and the New Zealand Conservation Authority of 23 November 1993.

[19]Decision No. A93/93 of the Planning Tribunal in *The Beneficial Owners of Karikari II Residue Block vs The Northland Regional Council* and *The Minister of Conservation.*

[20]Its proper name is Pārakerake. Whatuwhiwhi is located further along the coast.

[21]Ministry of Education Census Population Data for Karikari Peninsula 2007. The Māori population on census night was 1300. (J. Norman, personal communication, 17 December 2007.)

[22]*Northland Age,* 26 February 2008, p.1.

[23]Letter Rūnanga-ā-Iwi o Ngāti Kahu to Far North District Council 13 March 2003.

[24]Ibid.

[25]Ibid.

[26]Ibid.

[27]Minutes of Te Rūnanga-ā-Iwi o Ngāti Kahu hui, 18 January 2003.

[28]Environment Court New Zealand, Consent Order in the matter of Kenana Te Ranginui Marae Trust v Northland Regional Council, Far North District Council and Doubtless Bay Citizens and Ratepayers Association Incorporated.

[29]Stavenhagen, R., 2006. *Report of the Special Rapporteur on the situation of human rights and fundamental freedoms of indigenous people. Mission to New Zealand.* E/CN.4/2006/78/Add.3. 13 March 2006. Geneva, United Nations Human Rights Commission.

Nōku te whenua o ōku tūpuna: Ngāti Pareraukawa kaitiakitanga

Rachael Selby and Pātaka Moore

Ko Tainui te waka
Ko Tararua te maunga
Ko Hōkio te awa
Ko Ngātokowaru te marae
Ko Ngātokowaru te whare tupuna
Ko Ngāti Pareraukawa te hapū
Ko Ngāti Raukawa te iwi
Ko Te Whatanui te tangata

Ngātokowaru marae is located three kilometres inland from Te Moana o Raukawa (known as the Tasman Sea) on the west coast of the North Island of New Zealand. It is situated on the southern bank of the Hōkio Stream, the single outlet of Lake Horowhenua. The Hōkio Stream meanders four kilometres from the lake to the sea. The marae, situated on a ridge facing the Tararua ranges and the rising sun in the east, overlooks the lake and much of the town of Levin, in the distance. When the marae was established in the 19th century the vista was bush-clad to the lake's edge, the hinterland and mountains. Today the outlook is across grazing farmland with intensive agriculture, horticulture and viticulture, a polluted lake, State Highway One, the main trunk railway between Wellington and Auckland, and the bright lights of Levin. In the background the Tararua ranges no longer support the diverse birdlife and the range of flora and fauna the mountain ranges supported for thousands of years.

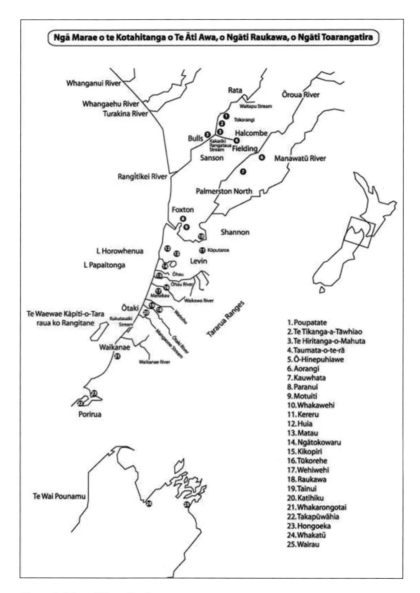

Figure 1. Map of Ngāti Raukawa marae.

Following the 1817 migrations of Ātiawa from Taranaki, Ngāti Raukawa from Maungatautari, and Ngāti Toarangatira from Kāwhia in the Waikato, mana whenua over land and environment was well established between Manawatu and Wellington by these three iwi (Royal 1994: 24). Ngāti Raukawa settled the region from the Rangitīkei River to the Kukutauaki Stream north of Waikanae (a stream that, incidentally, struggles to flow in the 21st century). This area is commonly described in the whakatauki: Mai i Waitapu ki Rangataua, mai i miria te kakara ki Kukutauaki. This whakatauki is an axiom describing geographic landmarks which identify iwi and hapū boundaries of Ngāti Raukawa whenua from the Rangitikei to the Kukutauaki Stream north of Waikanae. They are points of environmental significance. From the early 1800s until today, Ngāti Raukawa has maintained mana whenua within these boundaries where twenty marae have been established and are the homes of more than twenty-four hapū.

The descendents of Te Whatanui and his sister, known today as Ngāti Pareraukawa, settled at Raumatangi, Hōkio (Royal 1994: 25) and seasonally relocated to the banks of the Manawatū River to fish, maintain relationships with neighbouring hapū, and tend the crops and land on which they had settled. The urupā was established on a knoll at Raumatangi and remains the primary final resting place of Ngāti Pareraukawa. It is often referred to as ngā oneone mahana o Raumatangi, the warm sands of Raumatangi, a place welcoming of those who have journeyed there. Today it is maintained by the families whose tūpuna, mātua and tamariki lie there at rest. It is also recognised as a place that holds an important record of the history of the hapū.

For over a century, until 1950, Ngāti Pareraukawa lived and flourished on the land that supported the families and successive generations born at Hōkio and on the lands farmed on the southern banks of the Manawatū River. As their tūpuna had survived for nearly one thousand years after the arrival of the Tainui waka to Aotearoa, so Ngāti Pareraukawa lived off the land, wetlands, and water bodies surrounding them. New migrants from Britain, Europe and Australia arrived during the 19th century. They cleared the land for farming and built relationships with new neighbours that provided new opportunities. During both World Wars members of the hapū supported the new government and the colonists by sending young men to foreign wars in Europe and others joined the Māori Battalion to serve in battlefields far away. Later, whānau members served in Korea and other foreign places, believing there were benefits in serving alongside other New Zealanders building a new society together.

The Hōkio Stream provided food, sustenance and cleansing qualities, a transport route and a reference point to travel from and return to. Several homes and a homestead were built at Hōkio and blocks of land were allocated to sons and daughters who wished to farm. The whare tupuna, Ngātokowaru, which had opened on Christmas Day 1900, served the hapū until the 1950s when a series of events resulted in the near abandonment of the marae, the homes and surrounding lands. The events that ensued compromised the ability of Ngāti Pareraukawa to exercise kaitiakitanga over our landscape, manaakitanga to our visitors, and rangatiratanga over our futures.

Actions taken by Crown agents and new settlers without consideration for the tangata whenua or the long-term impacts of their actions further alienated our people from the land, rivers and lake. Many actions, taken in the name of progress, have subsequently been regretted by our local communities. Since colonisation, Pākehā interests have almost always been given priority at the expense of Māori interests. For example, today the common practice of using waterways as sites for effluent discharge is frowned on, unacceptable to most people. However, in the recent past, communities sited rubbish dumps, abattoirs, cowsheds and piggeries beside waterways in the belief that waterways had the power to deal with the discharge without a negative impact. Such practices and decisions were never acceptable to Māori and never will be. When Māori communities objected to such activities there was a range of responses. It was implied that either Māori did not understand that there would be 'no negative impacts', or we were 'hindering progress', 'being obstructive', 'unrealistic', 'difficult', 'ignorant or ill informed'. Māori values and beliefs that demanded effluent be kept separate from food sources were considered unreasonable. The very concept of giving effect to Māori values and beliefs was somehow 'backward' and 'primitive'. Our experience tells us that our values were ignored and never respected.

The hapū, Ngāti Pareraukawa has, like many hapū throughout the country, a history of being regarded by Pākehā as objectors, protestors and submitters. We have spent many days sitting in less than comfortable surroundings waiting to be heard, waiting to speak to a submission, waiting for formalities to be concluded, waiting for others to finish their submissions, waiting for our time, waiting for our turn.

This chapter outlines some of the ways in which we have waited with patience for our time, waiting for those with decision-making powers to hear our views, to listen while we explain the impact of their decisions on our people. We have a reputation with local and regional Councils for being objectors, for always protesting. Our young people support their elders at many hearings, protests, in parliament, and in front of local government commissions. We are preparing our children to take over the reins of those who have spent a lifetime trying to protect the environment, protect our waterways, protect our lands. Now we are challenged by elders to continue the fight so that their efforts were not in vain.

Photo 1. Ngāti Pareraukawa join the protest against discharge into the Manawatū river.

Hōkio Stream

Māori settled beside lakes and streams for good reason. These water bodies were 'pull' factors attracting whānau to them: they provided water for cleaning, cleansing and drinking, for cooking, food storage and recreation. The stream was a transport route from coast to lake and on to the forest with all its gifts of birds, berries and plants necessary for food, medicinal use and daily life. The forest also provided the timber for homes and other buildings preferred by the new migrants arriving in New Zealand in large numbers from the 1850s to the 1880s. In 1840 there were 2000 settlers in New Zealand. By 1881 the non-Māori population had risen to 500,000. (King 2003: 169). Māori had lost control of what had become a British colony.

The Hōkio Stream, abundant in fish life, had the capacity to provide sustainably for thousands of people all year round. It teemed with many species of kokopū and kōaro (native trout), kākahi (fresh water mussel), koura (crawlies and freshwater crayfish), inanga (whitebait), pātiki (flounder), and other species migrating seasonally between the salt and fresh water. The Hōkio Stream was and remains well known for the quality and quantity of healthy tuna (eel) (Adkin 1948: 19) and fed the people all year round. Interviews with Māori elders abound with accounts of large eel migrations throughout the early and mid-20th century when thousands of eels migrated in the autumn with the cool rains. Neighbouring whānau and hapū themselves visited Hōkio to share in the abundance that was guaranteed every autumn. Eel weirs were renewed and eel boxes were constructed annually after Christmas and placed in the stream to weather and be ready to store tuna for the coming winter. It was the staple food for Māori in the area. The boxes provided the capability to store food for the winter and spring. The diet of tangata whenua was fish and birdlife even after the settlers arrived with their animals such as pigs, sheep and cattle.

It is difficult to envisage how important the Hōkio Stream and Lake Horowhenua were in the lives of people living a subsistence existence and managing their environment. To pollute critically important places like lakes and streams in the name of progress is unfathomable to Māori. When in 1953, the Levin Borough Council introduced a sewage system and piped the sewage into the Lake the negative impacts were felt more by Ngāti Pareraukawa than any resident living in the township of Levin.

In many ways Ngāti Pareraukawa, the marae and the surrounding homes, were invisible to the Borough Council and to the new settlers of Levin. As the whānau waded into the stream to set up the hīnaki in the autumn in anticipation of the eel run, toilet paper and faeces floated around them. One kaumātua, born in 1927, who was interviewed for an oral history project recalls kicking the faeces aside to get to the hīnaki. His visual account of how it hung together in the water remains with many who listened to his recorded oral history account (Winiata 2003).

The tangata whenua living quietly on the western side of the lake were now the recipients of Levin's former septic tank contents. Living off the stream was no longer possible. Allowing children to swim in the stream was dangerous and compromised tikanga and values. Using the water for bathing children, the sick and the elderly was unthinkable. It was necessary to 'modernise' and install tanks to collect rainwater. This single act of discharging sewage into the lake, without any concern for the people living on the stream, compromised the fundamental values and practices of the people who had lived there for over a century. Over the next 20 years the hapū all but abandoned the marae while still pleading with the Council to remove the sewage from the lake and stream.

Within a decade of sewage discharge, the marae was virtually reduced to a place where the lives of the dead were celebrated before they were carried across to the warm sands of Raumatangi for interment. Some of the kaumātua believed the marae could no longer be used and there was talk of rebuilding south of the current site, away from the polluted stream. There was even a suggestion of relocating to the town to be closer to modern facilities. Yet there was always acknowledgement that the reason the tūpuna had settled beside the stream was because of its value. The pull of the stream was stronger than the desire to modernise and this belief has remained in the hearts of the people – hence the desire to return to the original site of the marae and to restore kaitiakitanga.

In the past decade the area between the marae and the stream has been cleared of noxious weed and foreign tree species such as willow. The stream has been cleaned and the descendants of those who left in the 1950s have returned to reunite with the land and the Hōkio Stream. The impact of thirty years of sewage discharge remains. The physical disconnection with the stream is one detrimental impact. The knowledge and skills that early

Photo 2. Hōkio Stream before restoration work by Ngāti Pareraukawa.

Photo 3. The Hōkio Stream following restoration work.

twentieth century residents accumulated daily has not been transferred to three generations of Ngāti Pareraukawa. The elderly recall the clear clean stream, eel runs, fishing, swimming, and food gathering: those under the age of fifty think of a muddy stream, a place to be avoided, a dirty unclean space. The children are now being returned to the stream to learn the skills of their great grandparents and tūpuna.

Sewage in and out of the lake

The discharge of sewage into New Zealand waterways and coastal areas is a theme that runs parallel with urban development. Accounts of progress and development in New Zealand include the debates that have raged in the mid- and late-20th century about discharge of sewage. These accounts seldom record the impact on the Māori communities who relied on water bodies for food, water, storage of food, and for cultural and cleansing activities. The story of Levin is a story of sewage. Moving from septic tanks to sewage became urgent in the 1950s when the government invested in "a psychopaedic hospital, a horticultural research centre, a boy's training centre and a maternity hospital" (Dreaver 2006: 242). The Borough Council came under intense pressure to develop a sewage scheme to support the growth of Levin. Townspeople regarded it as a modern and desirable asset without any concern for the environmental impact on the lake, stream and coastline and without any thought for the people living and relying on the lake and stream. Laurie Roberts, a long-serving mayor in the 1970s, came to Levin as a "drainage contractor for the sewerage scheme in 1951" (Dreaver 2006: 267). The development of sewage was seen as progress and attractive, without any consideration of the environmental costs.

Half a century of protest about sewage discharge by hapū such as Pareraukawa is virtually unrecorded and our attempts to build positive relationships with Councils have been severely compromised because of our ongoing battle to have the lake and stream at our back door restored to their former status.

It is no coincidence that the residents of the marae settlement at Ngātokowaru abandoned the marae and moved away in the early 1950s. The Winiata homestead was later dismantled and the marae was no longer a place of permanent residents from the 1950s.

In the early 1970s the grandchildren of the original owners met and amidst the drive to protect and preserve Māori values, beliefs and tikanga, the decision to build a new carved and decorated meeting house was made. This was in many ways a statement: our ancestral land was important and regardless of development around us, we would return to our ancestral home, exercise kaitiakitanga and prepare the environment, land and buildings for future generations. This decision brought dozens of whānau back to the marae, including many who were willing to pick up the environmental issues again. The Values Party was at its height and with their support and that of a local Hōkio Residents group, submissions were made to the Manawatu Catchment Board to have the effluent discharge removed from the lake which was in a "high degree of eutrophication, over enriched by sediments as well as by the nitrate and phosphate discharged from sewerage ponds" (Dreaver 2006: 272).

The new Meeting House was opened in March 1978, and by 1979 the Manawatū Catchment Board convened to hear objections to the discharge into the lake. A small sub-group representing Ngāti Pareraukawa proposed that the Council investigate discharge of sewage to land rather than the lake and presented a paper to this effect. They had researched similar schemes in North America and Europe and proposed that the Levin Borough Council investigate this option. It was soundly rejected by the Council and the Marae Committee and its supporters waited for the outcome of the hearing. The decision was eventually made. The Council was to remove the effluent discharge from the lake but was granted a water right to discharge directly into the Hōkio Stream. For Ngāti Pareraukawa this was unacceptable. The pollution would be moved from one point of the ecosystem to another. Our stance was and continues to be that pollution of water bodies is unacceptable to Māori regardless of the fact that it was acceptable to non-Māori.

Subsequently, the Council decided that the terms and conditions for the stream discharge could not be met and applied for a further consent to discharge into the lake while they engaged consultants to investigate discharge to land (the same proposal that had been submitted by our sub-group). Eventually a new proposal was accepted and the Council laid pipes to carry the discharge to 'The Pot' an area of sand hills south of the marae where the effluent has been discharged to land since 1987. It is ironic that the Council received awards for their creative solution and applaud themselves for their innovation. Although it is a marked improvement on discharge to water it reinforces that Hōkio is the Council's preferred waste-disposal location, a preference, which is an ongoing irritant to Ngāti Pareraukawa.

Our hapū remains as one of the guardians of the area. When there is 'emergency discharge' into the lake it is frequently our hapū that challenges the Council or notifies others with more clout, who can protest. As recently as August 2008 the Green Party Co-leader, Russell Norman, challenged the Horowhenua District Council mayor to a debate on the Council's waste management practices when there was overflow from the effluent ponds into the lake. When this was denied by the Mayor, the Green Party chartered a plane with a photographer to record with footage and to photograph the evidence that was then broadcast on national television news and news sites, and published in the local newspaper. Anecdotal evidence suggests the Council then challenged the local newspaper about the negative press.

There are still residents who perceive the lake as available for emergency discharge of waste. Despite our response that they should forget that the lake is there and increase their waste disposal storage capacity, this has not been done in an environmentally sustainable way. Another challenge for the Council is to increase the land-disposal area proportionately to the increase in population. This increase has not occurred since 'The Pot" was established.

As more Levin residents have become aware of the extreme negative impacts of poor decisions by former Councils on the health of the lake and stream, perhaps there is now a greater awareness that human beings have done more damage to the environment in the last 50 years than was done in the previous thousand years of our occupancy on this land. Only recently has kaitiakitanga been recognised as a practical way of challenging detrimental environmental decisions while posing sound environmentally based alternatives.

The Arawhata Stream

This stream feeds Lake Horowhenua from the south, drawing on surface and ground waters from an intensive agricultural and horticultural catchment. The soils on the plains surrounding Levin are renowned for their fertility and have since the early 1900s produced fruit and vegetables for the Wellington market. The Arawhata Stream was once a vigorously clear flowing stream regarded by Māori as the 'soul of the lake'. It cleansed the lake because it had the ability to pour clean fresh water directly into the lake helping flush the lake out through the Hōkio Stream. For thousands of years the Arawhata Stream provided the lake with the necessary volume of water to maintain the functioning of the lake as a vibrant ecosystem.

In the mid-20th century a drainage system was developed throughout the district drawing water from the land westward to Lake Horowhenua. This enabled the land surrounding Levin to be used intensively for horticulture and agriculture. At the same time (1947) that the stream was dredged and straightened, the lake was lowered by approximately two metres, ostensibly to improve drainage in the catchment area. In effect the stream dynamics and ecology of the lake and streams were radically altered in order to increase the amount of productive pastoral land available for farmers. Fertilisers were used intensively at this time to increase farm production without concerns for negative impacts on the ecosystems which received the excess. The lowering of the stream had many other impacts on Ngāti Pareraukawa as a large number of customary eel weirs were removed and replaced with only a few dysfunctional concrete and metal structures.

In the mid-20th century much energy was devoted to increasing productive land. The coastal plain on which Levin was built was an ideal environment in which to establish intensive farming, including dairy farming, dry stock farming, horticulture, and market gardening. Many of the decision makers were farmers who stood for the county and borough councils. While history records that farmers have served this country well, it has neglected to note that these benefits have been at the expense of the environment and local peoples. Māori were seldom represented on any such bodies and the form of democracy practised was that the majority ruled; since Māori were a minority of the population their voice was silent.

The fertiliser applied in the Arawhata Stream catchment is funnelled into the Arawhata Stream. This nutrient enrichment is a form of pollution that creates algal blooms and weed growth in the stream and the lake. The impact in the Hōkio Stream and on the coast is also evident. The land use within the Arawhata stream catchment reduces the ability of the stream to cleanse the lake. The lowering of the lake and the farming activities have resulted in five decades of pollution. The lake bed has significant sediment build-up, which in effect suffocates the lake and contributes to a deteriorating ecosystem. The discharge of sewage into the lake for over 30 years also contributed negatively to the current state of Lake Horowhenua.

A number of decisions made to benefit land owners and farming production in the wider council region have had serious negative environmental impacts on stream and lake ecosystem functionality. The impact on Ngāti Pareraukawa based on the southern banks of the Hōkio Stream is that the pollution that results from both the drainage systems and the farming practices negates the stream's ability to provide sustainably for the hapū. The fish and the tuna are no longer available because the health of the stream has been compromised. The benefits received by the Levin community, the farmers and those who service the farming community are not necessarily accrued by hapū whose values are compromised. Despite years of monitoring that reveals alarming nutrient levels no action has been taken to curb unsustainable land practices such as fertiliser leaching and agricultural chemical runoff, other than to continue monitoring.

The Piggery

In 1953 one of the descendants of the original owners of the marae made the decision to sell the block of land immediately west of the marae to a local pig farmer. It was said he farmed twelve sows from which to breed. An average litter of eight piglets per sow would result in around a hundred pigs on site. Each day, the pigman's truck rattled up the marae driveway to gain access to his property and to bring drums of food scraps from Levin's local hotels for the pigs. There was little impact on the marae as the pig population was low, the marae was seldom used, and the homestead had been dismantled in the mid-1950s. Others who lived within the marae precinct moved to town and abandoned their homes.

In 1972 a new generation of Ngāti Pareraukawa decided to return to the marae, to work towards the removal of sewage from the lake and to build a new whare tupuna and marae complex. Their memories of eeling, swimming, bathing and living at the marae galvanised them into action and fundraising and support from dozens of descendants of the original owners were successful in supporting a new complex. This generation wanted to pass on their knowledge and skills to the next generation before they too were lost.

The piggery was sold and developed into a large-scale commercial operation – ideally sited (ironically) beside a stream. The breeding sow population soon grew to 1,200, resulting in approximately 10,000 piglets twice a year, noting that the gestation period for pigs is 114 days and intensively managed sows can produce two litters per year. The new owners perceived that they lived in a rural area without neighbours. Their growing operation within fifty metres of the new whare tupuna, opened in 1978, began to impact seriously on the whānau who were increasingly using the marae for a range of activities. This coincided with the general renaissance of Māori activity that occurred in the 1970s. The marae committee had a policy of promoting good-neighbour relationships yet it became more difficult when each day the odour extractor fans blew massive waves of stench from the piggery buildings aided by the westerly breezes across the marae, through the dining room and meeting house. The flies were unbelievable. The marae became known among Māori for its smell, the flies and the heavy net curtains used to cover food and tables to prevent swarms of flies from landing all over crockery, cutlery and food. Every whānau bought large tins of fly spray with every grocery order brought to the marae. It was sprayed liberally in the kitchen and dining room during preparation of food and during serving of food.

After the Resource Management Act 1991 was passed, pig farmers required consent from regional councils to undertake pig farming activities. This change provided an opportunity for Ngāti Pareraukawa to be heard by decision-making bodies. A submission was carefully prepared asking for the elimination of odours offensive to the marae participants. Over the following years hapū members travelled to hearings and attended meetings with the neighbours seeking consultation.

We were asked if we would agree to a 'reduction' in odours. Te Maharanui Jacob, our kaumātua, was adamant that 'elimination' of odour was the bottom line. The marae committee minute books record the ongoing saga through the 1990s: "the smell and the flies are objectionable" (March 1996); "the Manawatu-Wanganui Regional Council are investigating the offensive 'odours' emanating from Biersteker's Piggery" (July 1996). Correspondence from the piggery owner refuted the hapū claims of "offensive" odours. They claimed that trees had been planted between the marae and piggery and this would "minimise" odour beyond their boundary (August 1996). In 1998, correspondence was received asking the Marae Committee to withdraw the objection to the "offensive odours". The Marae Committee resolution asked that the owner "commit to total elimination of offensive odours…" (August 1998). The following month the Marae Committee was invited to withdraw their objections. The resolution of the Marae Committee states, "That a group comprising Iwi Nicholson, Ran Jacob, Rachael Selby, Joe Paurini and Pātaka Moore meet with Mr Biersteker indicating that we are making the strongest possible objection to the odours and we seek total elimination of the odours" (September 1998). The following month the neighbours attempted to mitigate the concerns of the Marae Committee by offering to move their effluent discharge points further away from the marae.

A formal hearing resulted in the applicants being required to reduce the offensive odours. It was reported in June 1999 that a regional council consent had been granted for the piggery to continue operating until December 1999. In December the Marae Committee resolved to write to the Regional Council reaffirming that "the smell of the piggery had remained offensive during the consent period, request information on monitoring and seek a report from them" (December 1999). The Minute books are peppered with years of concerns and pain and requests to be heard by those in authority.

Over two generations the tangata whenua almost normalised the existence of the piggery, even when it expanded to an unacceptable size. We felt the shame of having a stinking marae, we apologised to manuhiri, we knew of kaumātua who chose not to visit our marae because of the smell, we felt powerless to effect any change, we avoided offending our neighbours yet our role as kaitiaki was compromised. High standards in terms of manaakitanga had always been promoted yet we were unable to prevent the smells and flies that emanated from the land adjoining the marae. We all regretted that the land had ever been sold, yet again there was little we could do to change that.

The new millennium dawned and we reflected that one hundred years earlier the first meeting house had been opened on Christmas Day 1900 (Selby 1999) in an environment where new settlers had made their mark upon the land and Ngāti Pareraukawa were well settled, maintaining their rangatiratanga over land and streams, lakes and the sea. On 1 January 2000 the group that had chosen to spend the final night of the passing millennium at the marae watched as the sun rose and pondered the future quite differently from their tūpuna one hundred years earlier.

In January 2000 when the Marae Committee met, it was noted that the smell was gone. The piggery was closed. The minutes record, "the marae is odourless and relatively free of flies" (January 2000). This is the status today – a marae almost free of flies and only the satisfying smell of food cooking.

The advice from our kaumātua that we maintain the request for 'elimination' of the odour was important because measuring 'reduction of odour' was impossible. Measuring 'elimination' was possible and in the end, in January 2000 when there was no stench, we realised progress had been made. Today when people refer hesitantly to the time when the marae stank, we celebrate over and over the efforts of our elders who stood strongly for many years, obstinately and stubbornly insisting on the 'elimination' of offensive odours. Our elders demonstrated that inoffensively we should hold fast to our principles forever. In this case we experienced the sweetness of success.

The Levin Rubbish Dump (aka Landfill)

In the 1950s a small local rubbish dump was established at Hōkio to cater for local rubbish disposal. It expanded in the 1970s for the growing Levin population. In the 1990s, following local government reform, there was pressure on the Council to manage a larger district. The result of these changes meant that the Council had to develop a district-wide landfill to cater for Foxton, Tokomaru, Shannon, and Levin. Ngāti Pareraukawa feared that Hōkio would become the site of the district-wide dump.

Two consultation hui were held at a neighbouring iwi marae across the lake (Kawiu) and the response from those who attended was that the Hōkio area could no longer be used as a landfill. As immediate neighbours and tangata whenua at Hōkio we were not consulted. Hōkio was chosen as the landfill site and this reflected again that Hōkio was seen as the general rubbish and effluent disposal area for the district. No suburb wants to have this reputation and no hapū wants to be surrounded by the district's waste. When Ngāti Pareraukawa realised that Hōkio was to be the site, there were varying responses. Some were furious, others were acquiescent. Whenever whānau travelled along the same road as those going to the rubbish dump located opposite the marae, it was clear that this was the pathway to a rubbish dump from the rubbish blown from vehicles travelling the road. As we were winning the battle of the pigs, the Council was developing a larger disposal site on our border.

Ngāti Pareraukawa spent the next decade monitoring the effects of the dump and opposing ongoing development. It came as a shock to the hapū to learn that the Horowhenua District Council had agreed to accept rubbish from other areas, beginning with neighbours Kapiti Coast District Council, whose last landfill at Otaihanga had a 6-month life-span. The landfill at Hōkio was closed and the Council was required to cap the landfill, manage litter, and monitor leachate bores surrounding the landfill. However, since 2004 there has been a history of non-compliance that included in 2004 and 2005 "inadequate capping of old landfill with quantities of refuse remaining exposed resulting in the forming of leachate. Leachate observed on the side of the old landfill, discharging to the stormwater drain, in breach of condition 19, consent 6010, and condition 5(b) of consent 6012 ... refuse being blown out of the landfill into surrounding vegetation ... leachate breakouts observed ... contaminated water in stormwater drain; source believed to be leachate runoff ... " (PCE 2008: 25). Following complaints made by local citizens, this non-compliance became the subject of an investigation by the Parliamentary Commissioner for the Environment from 2004 to 2008. To this date local and regional councils have yet to respond conclusively to these breaches of their own planning documents.

One of the responses by Ngāti Pareraukawa to the importation of waste from what could eventually be the lower North Island, has been to lobby the Kapiti Coast District Council to present our case for opposing Hōkio becoming the southern North Island Rubbish dump. This is in progress. The view that one large super dump is preferable to service the lower North Island is counter-productive to educating people to take responsibility for minimising waste. Super dumps fly in the face of local communities finding solutions to local problems. They may well provide income for the Council in whose area they are sited as waste disposal has become attractive as a business venture, but they are not sustainable. They are a liability to the local community and the environment.

Photo 4. Protest in Levin against Landfill expansion and importation of waste.

Ngāti Pareraukawa is committed to leaving our children and grandchildren a better environment than that which we received from our community in the 1970s. This is a massive task but it is one to which we are committed. We have initiated a strict recycling regime at the marae and encourage all whānau to extend this to their homes.

We are in the midst of another environmental disaster that potentially will be left to the next generation to clean up. Local councillors are elected to make decisions in the present and unless their values and beliefs include a long-term commitment to sustainability their values do not synchronise with ours. Closing the landfill to the public helps remove the unsightly landscape from the view of landfill users. Disposing of waste at a clean concrete pit changes the public perception of waste disposal. It removes any responsibility concerned citizens might otherwise have if they observed the size and site of the landfill.

Ngāti Pareraukawa will be here forever. Our Hapū Plan invites us to think ahead a thousand years. Long Term Council Community Plans (LTCCP), on the other hand, look ahead a mere 10 years, therefore relieving local government of any long-term responsibilities. The site of this landfill in an ecologically sensitive environment including sand dunes on a coast near lakes and streams and a community settlement above a ground water aquifer will surely be seen as irresponsible by future generations.

Photo 5. Whānau protest against Council landfill decisions 2007.

Conclusion

Over the course of 150 years Ngātokowaru marae has become surrounded by other peoples' waste on all sides. To the east, the lake was Levin's septic tank for over 30 years, while to the north the stream was heavily polluted during that time and for a further 25 years has suffered from the impact of that discharge. To the west, the piggery grew for 50 years and forced Ngāti Pareraukawa to spend over a decade fighting to have the offensive odours eliminated. To the south, the sewage effluent has been sprayed on to land for over 20 years and the rubbish dump or landfill has grown into a site that the Council proposes should be able to receive the southern North Island's refuse. Our protests to the Parliamentary Commissioner for the Environment resulted in a review that began in 2004 and a report that was finally released in August 2008. In 2009, after years of failing to do so, the Regional Council is finally reviewing the consent conditions. The Report of the Parliamentary Commissioner for the Environment found, among other things, that in 2007 the "Council was found to be non-complying with conditions 33-34, not having convened an NLG [Neighbourhood Liaison Group] meeting since 2005 and having failed to provide an annual report" (PCE 2008:17).

When the Horowhenua District Council opened its new premises in 2007, Ngāti Pareraukawa stood opposite the building as one community group voicing on-going dissatisfaction with the Council. A focus was their recent negotiations with the Kapiti Coast District Council (KCDC) to bring KCDC household rubbish to Levin. The perception that Hōkio is Levin's rubbish tip is repeatedly confirmed by the Council's decisions. It often appears that this is also accepted by the wider community, who may be relieved the dump site is 'out of site, out of mind'. Ngāti Pareraukawa has exercised kaitiakitanga for decades, making submissions to Council by presenting respectfully and professionally at dozens of hearings, by joining neighbours to discuss issues and find solutions, by conducting research into alternatives, and by reporting on various options. We have a long-term hapū plan for future generations that includes enhancing kaitiakitanga and rangatiratanga over Papatūānuku and her children, our land and environment. Central to this is a deep commitment to kaitiakitanga at Hōkio. This is in part demonstrated by the hapū continuing to develop the marae and environment for future generations. The commitment made by

Ngāti Pareraukawa to improve our environment at Hōkio over the past 30 years is unrelenting and supported by whānau from throughout the world. As global citizens, our hapū members link via internet and hapū websites back to their marae on the banks of the Hōkio Stream supporting innovative solutions to problems created by short-sighted 20th Century decisions. This generation wants to reverse the damage done and to ensure our role as kaitiaki is reflected in the progress in returning our land, waterways and ground water to a pristine state.

The Foreshore and Seabed Act: Five years on, where to from here

Tracey Whare

Introduction

One of the most politically galvanising periods for Māori in recent times was the lead up to and eventual enactment of the Foreshore and Seabed Act 2004 (FSA). The FSA bought Māori from across the political spectrum together, united with a concerted voice to reject the government's heavy handed approach to Māori concerns and, the extinguishment of Māori property rights in the foreshore and seabed.

Ngāti Porou has negotiated a deal for their foreshore and seabed rights within the confines of the FSA. How did their claim fare and what exactly have they achieved? In order to answer this, it is necessary to briefly canvass the history of the infamous FSA, including the government's and Māori response and consider the future of Māori rights within Aotearoa.

Terminology

The words "foreshore" and "seabed" in law refer to two distinct areas within the coastal region. The foreshore is that area between the mean high and low water tides, that is, the area of land that is dry during low tide and wet during high tide. The seabed is the area from the mean low tide out to the boundary of New Zealand's exclusive economic zone.

How it all came about

Iwi from the north of the South Island were prevented from undertaking commercial aquaculture activities on the foreshore and seabed lands of the Marlborough Sounds. In 1997, they went to the Māori Land Court (MLC) seeking a declaration that the foreshore and seabed within the Marlborough Sounds was Māori customary land as defined in Te Ture Whenua Māori Act 1993.

The MLC decided that it had jurisdiction to consider whether the foreshore and seabed was Māori customary land. The Crown and other parties appealed the decision. The case made its way through the judicial system and was eventually heard by the Court of Appeal in July 2002.

In June 2003, the Court of Appeal (Ngāti Apa) decided that the MLC had jurisdiction to consider whether the foreshore and seabed were Māori customary land and that Māori customary title to the seabed and foreshore had never been legally extinguished.

Whilst the Court of Appeal had positively answered the question of whether the MLC had jurisdiction, Māori customary title to the foreshore and seabed would still need to be established before the MLC. The Court of Appeal indicated that may be difficult.

At that point, the foreshore and seabed issue could have taken two different legal routes. The government could have appealed the decision to the Privy Council or, it could have accepted the Ngāti Apa decision. If the government had allowed the Ngāti Apa decision to stand, Māori would have applied to the MLC to inquire into whether defined areas of the foreshore and seabed had the status of Māori customary land. If the answer was yes, Māori could then apply to have the land converted from Māori customary land to Māori freehold land. The MLC would have considered each application on the evidence. The onus of proof would have been on Māori applicants to show that defined areas of the foreshore and seabed had the status of Māori customary land. There was never any guarantee that Māori property rights in the foreshore and seabed would be granted. The Ngāti Apa decision simply stated that Māori had the right to apply to the MLC to see if such rights existed.

However, as we know this is not the path the government chose to take. Whether it was the perceived need to protect third party rights, the assumption that the Crown already owned the foreshore and seabed or, the need to protect potential economic opportunities in the seabed area, the government was quick to act against Māori.

Government response

When the Ngāti Apa decision was released, the government responded with three separate strategies, a media campaign, formulation of their own policy and, because they were legally obliged to, an analysis of the FS Bill in light of the Bill of Rights Act 1990.

The government publicised their assumptions that they had always believed they owned the foreshore and seabed. This was a feeble rationalisation as the government or at least their legal advisors should have been aware of the legal inconsistencies that existed in relation to the ownership of the foreshore and seabed. (Brookfield, 2003) (Boast, 2004)

The government did nothing to correct the misinformed view of the public right to beach access, in fact they added to it. In allowing this concern to fester, the real issues of the Ngāti Apa decision and Māori property rights within the foreshore and seabed were swept aside. With the release of the Ngāti Porou Bill, Ngā rohe Moana o Ngā hapū o Ngāti Porou Bill (the Bill), this fixation on the public right to beach access has again raised its ugly head. (Fisher, 2009)

The government also formulated a policy that the foreshore and seabed would be vested in the Crown because they had always assumed that they owned it. This policy became the basis of the FSA. The policy was quickly toured around the country. Māori consistently rejected the policy. It was obvious to Māori that the consultation process was rushed and that the policy was not a proposal open for discussion and amendment but was the actual direction the government was going to follow.

In May 2004 the Attorney-General analysed the Bill in light of the Bill of Rights Act 1990. She concluded that the Bill was discriminatory against Māori but that such discrimination was "demonstrably justifiable in a free and democratic society". Much of the reasoning supporting the discrimination rested on the government's perceived need for legal certainty.

Whilst the government steam rolled ahead, they also managed to criticise anyone who they perceived was challenging them. They broke with convention by publicly criticising the judiciary. When MLC Judge Caren Wickliffe opened the way for applications to be heard, the Prime Minister,

Helen Clark, accused her of bias. The Prime Minister even suggested the MLC might have better things to do with its time. The government also criticised Māori who engaged in the United Nations (UN) as well as bodies of the UN who made critical findings against the government such as the Committee on the Elimination of all forms of Racial Discrimination (CERD) and the Special Rapporteur on the situation of human rights and fundamental freedoms of indigenous people (Special Rapporteur).

Māori response

There are four responses of Māori in relation to the FS Bill that particularly stand out, national Māori hui, the successful application to the Waitangi Tribunal, the hīkoi takutaimoana and the use of UN fora.

Māori national hui

A number of Māori national hui were held throughout the country from mid 2003 onwards. The resolutions of these hui are numerous but all focus on the fundamental belief that the foreshore and seabed belong to hapū and iwi under tino rangatiratanga and the final decision on the foreshore and seabed rests with whānau, hapū and iwi. The hui resolved that hapū and iwi be able to confirm their rights through the courts and also called on all Māori MP's to oppose any legislation which proposed to extinguish or redefine customary title or rights as well as the need for a constitutional review.

Waitangi Tribunal

In August 2003, Māori applied for and were granted an urgent hearing before the Waitangi Tribunal in relation to the government policy. In March 2004, the Tribunal found that the policy breached not only the principles of the Treaty of Waitangi but also the actual terms of the Treaty. The Tribunal held "the policy clearly breaches the principles of the Treaty of Waitangi. But beyond the Treaty, the policy fails in terms of wider norms of domestic and international law that underpin good government in a modern, democratic state. These include the rule of law, and the principles of fairness and non-discrimination." The Tribunal urged the government to reconsider their position. Whilst the government said it would consider the

Tribunal's report, it was in fact ignored. (Report on the Crown's Foreshore and Seabed Policy, 2004)

Hikoi takutaimoana

As always, Māori ability to organise and rally around issues of importance came again to the fore. As well as discussing the issue through national hui and taking the government's policy to the Waitangi Tribunal, Māori joined together for the hīkoi takutaimoana. This hīkoi besides being an incredibly well organised logistical feat clearly showed the government the level of discontent amongst Māori for the FS Bill as well as the government's handling of the issue. The Prime Minister refused to meet with the 35,000 strong hīkoi participants calling the organisers "haters and wreckers" and stating that she preferred the company of the celebrity sheep Shrek.

International law

Iwi and Māori organisations used a number of UN fora to bring the FS Bill and FSA to the attention of the international community. In doing so the NZ government was forced to explain their actions and were held accountable by the international community.

The Permanent Forum on Indigenous Issues

In May 2004, a delegation of Ngāi Tahu with the support of Treaty Tribes coalition addressed the UN Permanent Forum on Indigenous Issues. Whilst this forum cannot hold the government to account, Ngāi Tahu gained the support of other indigenous peoples attending the forum and brought the foreshore and seabed issue to the attention of the international community.

Convention on the Elimination of all forms of Racial Discrimination

In July 2004 the Taranaki Māori Trust Board, Te Runanga o Ngāi Tahu and the Treaty Tribes Coalition requested the CERD invoke its early warning and urgent action procedure to review the Foreshore and Seabed Bill (FS Bill). In March 2005, CERD determined that the FSA discriminates against Māori under the Convention on the Elimination of All Forms of Racial Discrimination (the Convention).

CERD stated in its report "the legislation appears to the Committee, on balance, to contain discriminatory aspects against the Māori, in particular in its extinguishment of the possibility of establishing Māori customary titles over the foreshore and seabed and its failure to provide a guaranteed right of redress".

CERD was concerned with the haste with which the FSA was enacted and that the Government gave insufficient consideration to alternatives more acceptable to Māori and all other New Zealanders. CERD urged the government to resume a dialogue with Māori to lessen the legislation's discriminatory effects, including through legislative amendment. (Decision 1 (66) New Zealand Foreshore and Seabed Act 2004, 2005)

CERD's finding that the FSA racially discriminates is a finding that the government is in breach of the Convention. It is a breach of international law.

Special rapporteur

When the Special Rapporteur came to Aotearoa in November 2005, Māori raised their concerns about the FSA with him.

In his report on New Zealand, the Special Rapporteur stated "the (foreshore and seabed) Act can be seen as a backward step for Māori." The report concludes that the Crown has "extinguished all Māori extant rights to the foreshore and seabed." The Special Rapporteur recommended that the FSA "should be repealed or amended." (Stavenhagen, March 2006)

Where to from here

The FSA has clearly shown us that Māori rights are extremely vulnerable. The constitutional arrangements of NZ give Parliament unfettered power and there are little if any checks and balances when the law makers are determined to push through legislation despite overwhelming rejection by the people it concerns as well as substantial legal decisions against the proposed law. Without constitutional protections we will face new confiscations and discrimination and relations between Māori, the general public and the government will continually be thrown into disarray.

The implementation of the FSA – the Ngāti Porou case

The outcome of the negotiations between the Crown and hapū of Ngāti Porou has resulted in a Bill that is currently before Parliament awaiting its first reading. The Bill has 121 clauses. It contains a summary of the negotiations between the parties as well as the new proposed legal frameworks for the recognition of the mana of Ngāti Porou within the foreshore and seabed. Given that Ngāti Porou were one of the many iwi to reject the FS Bill, it unsurprisingly also contains a caveat that Ngāti Porou do not endorse the FSA.

Whilst some would lament the Bill's development, it must be remembered that Ngāti Porou had commenced discussion with the Crown regarding the foreshore and seabed after the *Ngāti Apa* decision, but before the enactment of the FSA. With the government's response to the *Ngāti Apa* decision, they had to decide whether to continue with their negotiations. Some hapū chose to continue in the knowledge that any outcomes would now be framed within the confines of the FSA.

The Bill defines a number of terms. The *hapū of Ngāti Porou* are those hapū who have signed the Deed of Agreement with the Crown. Ngā rohe moana o ngā hapū *o Ngāti Porou* means the foreshore and seabed within the rohe of the hapū that have signed the Deed of Agreement. A territorial customary rights area referred to in the bill as a *TCR area* is an area of the public foreshore and seabed within ngā rohe moana o ngā hapū o Ngāti Porou in relation to which the Governor General has made an Order in Council. *Accommodated matters* are existing activities within ngā rohe moana o nga hapū o Ngāti Porou.

The objective of the Bill is set as follows:

- to recognise the unbroken, inalienable, and enduring mana of the hapū of Ngāti Porou in relation to ngā rohe moana o ngā hapū o Ngāti Porou, which is held and exercised as a collective right and
- to provide legal mechanisms that support the expression and protection of the mana of the hapū of Ngāti Porou generally and in those specific areas where territorial customary rights are recognised and

- to recognise that the Crown has a responsibility for public access in, on, and over the public foreshore and seabed, and a role in regulating the public foreshore and seabed and
- to provide certainty about the use and administration of ngā rohe moana o ngā hapū o Ngāti Porou.

These objectives are all based on the legislated assumption that the ownership of the public foreshore and seabed is now vested in the Crown. This means that any legal mechanisms created by the Bill will be of a lesser nature than exclusive property rights.

The truism of public access continues to be upheld by the government as one of its main justifications for imposing the FSA regime. Public access is not a right in law yet it has been bandied about by the government and the media as some sacrosanct principle that cannot be interfered with. Sadly, the same level of passion has not been brought to bear on Māori property rights.

The Bill does provide certainty however, as this chapter will explain, that certainty will exist for the current decision makers such as the Gisborne District Council (GDC) and the Department of Conservation (DOC) not the hapū of Ngāti Porou.

The Bill contains 9 instruments and mechanisms

1. Statutory overlay
2. Environmental covenant
3. Protected customary activities
4. Wāhi tapu
5. Fisheries mechanism
6. Conservation mechanism
7. Place names
8. Relationship instruments
9. Territorial customary rights

1. Statutory overlay

This part of the Bill contains four areas. Firstly, the Bill provides for a map that identifies the area that is ngā rohe moana o ngā hapū o Ngāti Porou to be prepared by the GDC, DOC, and the Ministry of Fisheries (MOF). These maps are to be attached to the public planning documents which each agency is responsible for. The purpose of the maps is for public notice only.

Secondly, the GDC must provide a copy or, give notice of receipt of a copy of a resource consent application to relevant hapū for an activity within, adjacent or impacting directly on ngā rohe moana o ngā hapū o Ngāti Porou, this includes both notified and non-notified resource consents. The relevant hapū also have the right to appear before the Environment Court in relation to such resource consent applications.

Thirdly, if a proposal of national significance is filed with the Minister for the Environment (MFE) or the Minister of Conservation and the proposal is within ngā rohe moana o ngā hapū o Ngāti Porou, the Minister can direct that a board of enquiry be set up. The Minister must give a copy of the direction to ngā hapū o Ngāti Porou and consult with them as to the terms of reference for the board of enquiry. Ngā hapū o Ngāti Porou can nominate one person to the board.

Finally, ngā hapū o Ngāti Porou must be treated as persons directly affected by a decision of, or the exercise of a power by, the New Zealand Historic Places Trust (HPT) if the decision, or the exercise of the power, relates to ngā rohe moana o ngā hapū o Ngāti Porou.

These mechanisms give greater awareness of the relationship of Ngāti Porou with the foreshore and seabed as well as greater legal standing for Ngāti Porou within existing decision making processes. The maps record the special status of the foreshore and seabed to nga hapū o Ngāti Porou. Important gains have also been made through the clear direction to GDC regarding resource consents, the standing of Ngāti Porou before the Environment Court, the ability to have input into the terms of reference of a board of enquiry as well as representation on that board as well as a clear direction to the HPT that nga hapū o Ngāti Porou are directly affected by the powers and functions of the HPT.

All of these mechanisms are small but significant gains; however they only tweak existing decision making processes by including Ngāti Porou in these processes. The RMA has caused Māori much grief. Whilst it contains references to iwi and iwi planning documents, such references are only in relation to planning documents of territorial authorities. The real and ongoing concern for Māori is the daily processing of resource consent applications and the difficulties and expense involved in appealing to the Environment Court. The Bill does address these concerns but how will these gains fare in relation to the upcoming RMA and FSA reviews? Did the parties consider a stronger role in decision making for Ngāti Porou such as a transfer of power under section 33 of the RMA allowing Ngāti Porou to make decisions on resource consent applications within nga rohe o nga hapū o Ngāti Porou?

2. Environmental covenant

An environmental covenant (the covenant) is a planning document that covers two areas, firstly, the sustainable management of the natural and physical resources of ngā rohe moana o ngā hapū o Ngāti Porou and secondly, the cultural and spiritual identity of nga hapū o Ngāti Porou within ngā rohe moana o ngā hapū o Ngāti Porou. The covenant is prepared by Ngāti Porou and must be signed by the Attorney General and the Minister of Māori Affairs. Ngāti Porou must review the covenant every 10 years.

The GDC must take into account the covenant in their planning documents and, if the covenant covers a TCR area, the GDC must recognise and provide for those matters in the covenant that relate to resource management issues. Also, when GDC are making a decision that relates to ngā rohe moana o ngā hapū o Ngāti Porou, they must consider the covenant.

As part of the standard review of their planning documents, the GDC must decide whether such planning documents need to be amended in light of the covenant. The Minister of Conservation, when considering an application for a resource consent for a restricted coastal activity wholly or partly within, or directly affecting, ngā rohe moana o ngā hapū o Ngāti Porou, must have regard to the matters in the covenant that relate to resource management issues, and, for an application within or directly affecting a TCR area, the Minister must recognise and provide for the matters in the covenant that relate to resource management issues.

Once the GDC has completed their review they can decide that changes are required to the planning documents or, they can decide that no changes are required. If they choose the former, a public submission process must be undertaken. If GDC decide the later, Ngāti Porou can request the GDC to reconsider its decision. Ngāti Porou can also appeal to the Environment Court.

Apart from the GDC, the Minister for the Environment must consider the covenant when considering the scope of a proposed national environmental standard and, a board of inquiry set up to inquire into a proposed national policy statement that impacts directly on ngā rohe moana o ngā hapū o Ngāti Porou must treat the environmental covenant as a relevant matter.

Lastly, the HPT must have regard to the covenant when they are processing an application for an authority to destroy, damage, or modify an archaeological site.

The covenant sounds very similar to an iwi planning document however it requires government officials to sign off on it.

The Bill sets out the status of the covenant for the GDC in relation to their planning documents. Firstly, the same legal standard that applies to iwi planning documents, that is "take into account" is to be used. However, a higher standard is set for TCR areas, here the GDC must "recognise and provide" for the matters in the covenant that relate to resource management. These same standards apply to the Minister of Conservation when they are considering an application for a restricted coastal activity.

Other decision making processes must consider the covenant. An application for a national environment standard "must consider" the covenant, a proposal for a national policy statement must consider the covenant as a "relevant matter" and the HPT "must have regard" to it in relation to applications to destroy, damage, or modify an archaeological site.

The GDC must review its public documents in light of the covenant. They can decide to change their public documents or not. If they decide to change, a public submission process is entered into. The general public can make submissions on the covenant which may not be favourable to Ngāti Porou. If the GDC decide no changes are to be made, Ngāti Porou must decide whether to request reconsideration or go to the Environment Court.

The review process and its outcome create no certainty for Ngāti Porou. The process could become costly and drawn out, especially if there is objection from the public. As a result of that objection, the GDC could decide not to include the covenant in any changes they make to the public documents. Potentially Ngāti Porou may not have standing to appeal to the Environment Court if they are not a submitter to the process. If the GDC decides no changes are required, Ngāti Porou must decide whether a costly court appeal is necessary. Inclusion of the covenant in the GDC public documents could be an expensive and unclear process and there is no guarantee of a favourable outcome.

3. Protected customary activities

In order for a protected customary activity within ngā rohe moana o ngā hapū o Ngāti Porou to be recognised and protected, agreement must be reached between Ngā hapū o Ngāti Porou, the Attorney General, and the Minister of Māori Affairs. The agreement must be in writing and must include a description of the activity, the scale, extent, and frequency of the activity, the hapū that will carry out the activity, and the location of the activity within ngā rohe moana o ngā hapū o Ngāti Porou. Notice of the agreement must be gazetted.

The hapū will determine how the activity will be carried out and by whom. They can also commercially benefit from the activity. The activity may be carried out without a resource consent but will be limited by the determinations of the hapū and any controls agreed between Ngāti Porou and the Minister of Conservation.

At any time, the Minister of Conservation can determine whether a protected customary activity has or will have a significant adverse effect on the environment. The Minister must consider the views of a number of parties including ngā hapū o Ngāti Porou and prepare a significant adverse effect report. The report is to be made publicly available.

The GDC must not grant an application for a resource consent for an activity that the GDC has determined will, or is likely to, have a significant adverse effect on a protected customary activity. Exceptions to this include accommodated matters or, where the hapū agrees. In order to determine whether a proposed activity will have a significant adverse effect on a protected customary activity, the GDC must have particular regard to the views of the hapū affected as well as the covenant. The GDC must also consider other factors such as the effects of the proposed activity on the protected customary activity and whether any conditions could be included in a resource consent for the proposed activity that would avoid, remedy, or mitigate any significant adverse effects of the proposed activity on the protected customary activity.

In order to have protection, protected customary activities must be agreed to by the government and their details must be publicly notified through the gazette process. Whilst the hapū can decide where and by whom these activities can be undertaken, the government still retains control by determining whether such an activity will have a significant adverse effect on the environment. This is unnecessary given that protected customary activities will be carried out within the confines of tikanga and kaitiakitanga.

Whilst resource consents that will have an adverse effect on a protected customary activity must have hapū approval in order to be granted, it does not cover resource consents that the GDC determines will not have an adverse effect on a protected customary activity. Again this creates a level of uncertainty for Ngāti Porou.

4. *Wāhi tapu*

For a place or area sacred to ngā hapū o Ngāti Porou in a traditional, spiritual, religious, ritualistic, or mythological sense to be a wāhi tapu, agreement must be reached between Ngā hapū o Ngāti Porou, the Attorney General, and the Minister of Māori Affairs. The process follows the same as for a protected customary activity, the agreement must be in writing and notice of the agreement must be gazetted. The gazette notice must contain details of the location, the restrictions imposed, the reasons for the restrictions and any exemptions.

Access to wāhi tapu can be changed by the Minister of Conservation and the Minister of Māori Affairs via a gazette notice; however the written consent of the relevant hapū must be obtained first.

The GDC must take positive steps to protect wāhi tapu sites for example, erecting fences. If a person fails to comply with restrictions on a wāhi tapu, they can be charged with an offence, the maximum penalty being $5,000.00. Wardens can be appointed to promote compliance with wāhi tapu.

The same concerns that exist for protected customary activities also apply here. In order for a wahi tapu to be protected, details of its location, prohibitions and reasons must be made publicly available. This may not sit well with hapū who do not want to disclose wahi tapu sites, and it is in complete contrast to the ability of a local authority to protect disclosure both orally and written of wahi tapu information during a hearing. Also, the ability of Ministers to change access to wahi tapu is unnecessary.

The duty now imposed on the GDC in relation to physically protecting wahi tapu is a positive step, as are the financial penalties for those who fail to comply with a wahi tapu. However, offences of destroying or damaging archaeological sites under the Historic Places Trust Act carry a far greater financial penalty of $100,000 and $40,000 respectively.

5. Fisheries mechanism

The Minister of Fisheries must consult with Ngāti Porou and recommend to the Governor General the creation of regulations regarding customary food gathering within ngā rohe moana o ngā hapū o Ngāti Porou and the special relationship between TCR hapū and places of customary food gathering in TCR areas. The regulations can include amongst other things the establishment of fisheries management committees and fisheries management plans.

Regulations made under this Bill are the same as if they had been made under the Fisheries Act 1986.

A person, when performing a function or exercising a power must recognise and provide for a fisheries management plan, if the function or power affects the area within ngā rohe moana o ngā hapū o Ngāti Porou.

The creation of regulations for customary food gathering as pointed out in the Bill can be achieved through the Fisheries Act, was this part of the Bill therefore necessary? The reference to fish management plans is however new and does provide an opportunity for Ngāti Porou tikanga to be recognised and provided for by those exercising power under the Fisheries Act.

6. Conservation mechanism

Particular regard must be had to the views of the relevant hapū when the following applications are made to DOC – marine reserve, conservation protected areas, concessions, marine mammal sanctuaries, marine mammal watching and stranded marine mammals. Applications for these activities within a TCR area, must be consented to in writing by the TCR hapū. If an application is received that does not contain the written consent of the TCR hapū , the application will be referred to them to accept or decline. If the TCR hapū do not reply within the specified timeframes, they are deemed to have consented.

A wildlife or marine mammal matter application can only be considered if DOC determines in their opinion that such an application is essential to achieve conservation management or, the relevant hapū has consented to the application. Alternatively, if the application is not determined to be essential, and the hapū has neither accepted nor rejected the application, the application is referred to the relevant hapū to either consent or decline. If the hapū do not reply within the specified timeframes, they are deemed to have consented. Ngāti Porou cannot charge a fee for their involvement in this process.

A written register of all wildlife or marine mammal matter that Ngāti Porou possesses must be kept. Access to the register and the material must be made available to DOC. Ngā hapū o Ngāti Porou have first right of refusal over wildlife or marine mammal matter that has been obtained by DOC within ngā rohe moana o ngā hapū o Ngāti Porou.

This section provides for greater participation in the decision making processes of DOC. However, there is the strange position where, if the hapū do not reply to an application in the specified timeframes, they are deemed to have consented. Surely no response should mean no? Ngāti Porou also cannot charge for their involvement in these processes even though this may take considerable resources and effort for small and ill-resourced hapū to deal with.

7. Place names

The following two place names are changed – East Island/Whangaokeno to Whangaokeno/East Island and Hicks Bay to Wharekahika/Hicks Bay. The changes are to be gazetted and certain parties notified.

The explanatory note includes a reference to pouwhenua instruments that will give the hapū of Ngāti Porou the right to erect pouwhenua at culturally significant sites. These are not mentioned in the body of the Bill but there is mention of them in the Deed of Agreement.

8. Relationship instruments

Ngāti Porou has entered into a number of written agreements with Ministers of the Crown. These agreements are with the Minister of Arts, Culture and Heritage, Conservation, Environment, Fisheries and Energy. A summary of the instrument plan affecting ngā rohe moana o ngā hapū o Ngāti Porou must be noted on certain planning documents administered by the DOC, the MOF and Ministry of Economic Development. None of these agreements create any property rights. Their attachment to the respective planning documents is for information purposes only.

These agreements formalise the relationship between the respective parties and highlight the special status of Ngāti Porou to ngā rohe o ngā hapū of Ngāti Porou.

9. TCR hapū permission rights

A proposed activity in a TCR area must be treated as having significant adverse effects on the relationship of the TCR hapū concerned with the environment of the TCR area if the activity is a new structure, an aquaculture activity, a reclamation, a discharge of industrial waste or sewage, extraction of shingle.

A resource consent application or an aquaculture management request within the TCR area can only be considered by GDC in one of three instances, if the TCR hapū have given their written permission or, if it is an accommodated matter or, if it is not one of the named activities set out in the preceding paragraph and the GDC has determined it will not have a significant adverse effect on the relationship of the TCR hapū with the environment of the TCR area. Ngāti Porou cannot agree to only a portion of an application for aquaculture activities, any activities that they have been made aware of in writing are consented to if consent is given.

The Bill also provides for an application for a proposed activity in a TCR area where hapū have not consented, it is not an accommodated matter and there are no significant adverse effects on the relationship of the TCR hapū with the environment of the TCR area. In this instance, the GDC must determine whether there are significant adverse effects and advise the TCR hapū that they are making this determination.

If an application for an activity which is listed in the Bill for example, an aquaculture activity or, an activity of which the GDC has determined that the activity will have a significant adverse effect on the relationship of the TCR hapū concerned with the environment of the TCR area, the GDC must refer the application to the TCR hapū. The TCR hapū must decide whether to consent or object. If they do not reply within the specified time frame, they will be deemed to have consented.

When GDC are making a determination, they must have particular regard to the views of the TCR hapū as well as any environmental covenant. The hapū or the applicant can object to the GDC's determination and appeal the matter to the Environment Court. Ngāti Porou cannot charge for their role in these processes either.

In order to create a TCR area, the Governor General must make an Order in Council after the High Court has confirmed that the requirements for establishing territorial customary rights as set out in the FSA have been met.

Whilst Ngāti Porou are being included in these decision making processes, given the special nature of TCR areas, would it not be more appropriate for Ngāti Porou rather than the GDC to make decisions regarding resource consent applications in these areas? As stated previously this could be achieved by a transfer of powers under the RMA.

Full and final settlement

The Bill states that Ngāti Porou cannot apply to the Māori Land Court nor the High Court to have Customary Rights Orders made in relation to the foreshore and seabed covered by the Bill. Further, that no Court, Tribunal or other judicial body has jurisdiction to inquire into either the Bill or the Deed between Ngāti Porou and the Crown except for the purposes of interpretation.

This part of the Bill clearly sets out that these negotiated outcomes are the final word on the matter. There is no mention of compensation, nor resources for Ngāti Porou to carry out their functions under the Bill.

Conclusion

Given the FSA premise that the public foreshore and seabed is vested in the Crown and that Māori have no right to compensation, is this Bill the best that could be achieved? Does the tweaking of existing decision making processes simply mean business as usual? If so, then all the concerns around the FSA continue to be played out in this Bill. Given the government's previous negotiation processes, it also sets the precedent for future negotiations with iwi and hapu. With the government's decision to review the RMA, the FSA and the promised constitutional review, it remains to be seen what effect those reviews will have on this Bill. If the Bill is enacted, its implementation will be closely monitored by all even more so by its supposed beneficiaries.

Rāwaho: In and out of the environmental engagement loop

Veronica M. H. Tawhai[1]

Following on from the Resource Management Act 1991, the requirements of the Local Government Act 2002 and the increase in local authority efforts to engage Māori[2] have, to a certain degree, cemented recognition of the rights of mana whenua in local environmental management. In particular, the growing number[3] of co-management arrangements between iwi and local authorities are sought to herald a newfound maturity in the relationships between iwi and local government in managing environmental resources (Local Government New Zealand 2007; Taupo District Council 2009).

What is not so clear, however, is the role for Māori who live outside their tribal areas; who have an interest both in the environmental integrity of their tribal regions, and the local environment in which they live. In the tribal area of another, the manner in which Māori individuals can express their interests as Māori is unclear. Similarly, there are concerns about the extent to which Māori living far from their tribal homelands can effectively be involved in the management of tribal and public environmental resources. This uncertainty arises from a statutory context in which customary environmental management practices are being acknowledged[4] but continue, particularly with regards to democratic participation, to employ processes based on assimilationist notions of citizenship.

Rāwaho is a term loosely applied in certain contexts to those Māori living outside of their own tribal region. It reflects their position as Māori who are (1) resident 'guests' in relation to the mana whenua of their residential area, and (2) iwi members living afar in relation to their iwi ahi kā. Other common terms associated with this state of being are taura here and mātāwaka.[5] The purpose of this chapter is to highlight some of the issues raised by rāwaho/taura here/mātāwaka in a research project about Māori engagement with local authorities. The chapter highlights their questions, concerns and aspirations in relation to their particular position as rāwaho regarding the environment and its management, maintenance, and protection for future generations. It explores the legislative context within which these questions have arisen, and gives voice to the concerns and hopes raised by the research participants about involvement in environmental management, both where they whakapapa to and where they live, and hopes to stimulate discussion on the implications, opportunities and new understandings for Māori engagement that the notion of rāwaho raises.

Māori and their local environments

I've lived here for seven years now and I have three homes, [place] here as my home, [place] where I was born and raised, and my ancestral home, my tūrangawaewae, [place].

Local government engagement with Māori

Local government in New Zealand comprises two main types of authorities: regional councils and territorial authorities (city/district councils). There is also a sub-local tier of local government called community boards, which are not mandatory but are growing in popularity (see, for example, Richardson 2008). The general term used in political science to refer to people's involvement in the decision-making processes of these local bodies is 'local political participation'. Political participation to date has focused on narrow conceptualisations of what constituted 'political' activity, such as voting, group membership, signing petitions and attending demonstrations.

Engagement, on the other hand, reflects the distinct nature of political interaction between Māori and local government. It signifies not only Māori participation in local body processes, but also the need for local bodies to become active participants in Māori processes. Engagement thus further reflects the need of local bodies to connect with Māori not only for the purposes of local political decision-making, but also for formulating in the first instance what shape those decision-making processes will take. This is stressed in the Local Government Act 2002, which states local authorities must:

> (a) *establish and maintain processes to provide opportunities for Māori to contribute to the decision-making processes of the local authority;*
>
> (b) *consider ways in which it may foster the development of Māori capacity to contribute to the decision-making processes of the local authority; and*
>
> (c) *provide relevant information to Māori for the purposes of paragraphs (a) and (b).*

Attention to the specific views of rāwaho, Māori who do not have a genealogical link to their area of residence, is an increasingly important aspect of enhancing Māori engagement over environmental issues. This is because Māori are not only more likely to live in urban areas, but are also increasingly more likely to be mobile. Currently, 84.4% of Māori live in urban areas, compared with 35%[6] in 1956 (Statistics New Zealand, 2007a). In addition to this, in the 2006 Census 60.3% of Māori were living somewhere different from where they had resided during the 2001 Census (Statistics New Zealand, 2007b). Of all New Zealanders, the 25–29 year olds were the most mobile age group, eight in every ten having moved at least once since 2001 (ibid). The current median age of the Māori population is 22.7 years (Statistics New Zealand 2007a), suggesting that in the near future a significant proportion of Māori electors will become even more mobile as they shift into this age group.

Addressing the growing number of Māori who are not mana whenua to their residential area thus poses specific questions for local governments: (1) what is the basis on which to engage Māori who are not mana whenua, but Māori residents and (2) what is the level of engagement of Māori who belong to mana whenua, but reside in another region? Representation of Māori interests through iwi authorities whose internal political structures will determine participation by their members, including those outside the region, in iwi affairs renders the latter an issue for local bodies to be aware of but not necessarily one for which they have any responsibility. The former, however, particularly as it addresses individual Māori citizens, is.

As stated by the Cabinet Policy Committee (2001: 3) in considering the content of the Local Government Bill, a central goal was to 'provide clarity as to the relationship between local government and the Treaty of

Waitangi'. The role of the Crown under Article One, kāwanatanga, and the subsequent guarantee to Māori of full exclusive and undisturbed possession of their resources under Article Two, is an important starting point to growing local authorities' understanding of their responsibilities to actively protect Māori environmental sites and resources. Even more so is the issue of Partnership: the need to balance the role of kāwanatanga in Article One with Māori rights to continued rangatiratanga in Article Two. Arguably, these issues are gaining more clarity as Māori persevere in their relationship-building with local authorities, and the body of 'good practice' literature on Māori-Crown authorities expands (Harmsworth 2005).

What is less clear is the relationship between local government and the Treaty of Waitangi based on Article Three, and the rights of Māori to equal citizenship. In receiving all the rights and privileges of British Subjects, the principle of equality means that Māori on an individual basis should not only have a say equal to that of other citizens, but should also be able to expect equal outcomes from their participation. It is widely acknowledged that culturally inappropriate processes have acted as significant barriers to effective Māori participation (Harmsworth 2005). Quite apart from the responsibilities to engage mana whenua then, is that individual Māori can expect to be engaged in a manner appropriate to their cultural preferences. The fact that Māori are over-represented in many measures of social exclusion (Ministry of Social Development 2006) is further evidence why local government need to become more responsive to what can constitute successful engagement of Māori.

Overall, citizens' participation in decision-making forums is an important measure of legitimacy for local democratic institutions (Lijphart 1997). A review of local government legislation following the 2000 General Election recognised that Māori participation in local government is not high, which results in low participation by Māori in local government decision-making (AC Neilson 2001). A later review by Alliston and Cossar (2006) of literature, information and research produced by and for New Zealand government departments about the participation and engagement of Māori in their decision-making processes expressed a limitation in data that addressed non- and low participation. They note:

> *While a significant amount of literature was provided by agencies on approaches to addressing low engagement and participation, there is*

very little produced by these groups that address the questions of why levels of participation are lower than desired. (Alliston & Cossar: 9)

As indicated in a recent report on Māori engagement with local government, for many Māori a lack of participation can be directly attributed to a lack of confidence in local government processes (Cheyne & Tawhai 2007). This can in part be associated with the current statutory and policy environment, which provides little guidance as to engagement of different Māori groups, and the basis of that engagement.

Mana whenua, Māori, or citizens?

Reference to Māori in the Local Government Act 2002 is consistent with previous legislation, such as the New Zealand Public Health and Disability Act 2000 (s. 4), which provides for mechanisms to enable 'Māori' to contribute to decision-making. The provisions of these Acts are, on one hand, a step up from past legislation, which provides for recognition of 'the principles of the Treaty of Waitangi' but cites no specific commitments to Māori communities. The Resource Management Act 1991, on the other hand, is somewhat more explicit in cementing the place of groups such as mana whenua by providing for the specific cultural traditions of Māori groups to their specific 'ancestral lands, water, sites, wāhi tapu and other taonga' (s. 6e), including regard to kaitiakitanga (s. 7a). The use of the term Māori in the Acts of 2000 has thus left a wide berth for local governments to engage all Māori in their region, and many employ a range of different avenues to engage wider Māori communities in addition to those of mana whenua (for example, see Local Government New Zealand 2004). Some local authorities, however, have expressed caution in treating differently the many stakeholder groups they need to engage with (Harmsworth 2005). This has led in many instances to processes that still neglect Māori values, realities, and cultural preferences for engagement.

Currently under New Zealand local government and local electoral legislation, Māori and non-Māori are treated the same in terms of voting and standing for electoral office, aside from the recent provision for Māori constituencies and wards. The Local Electoral Amendment Act 2002 provides for territorial authorities (city and district councils) and regional councils to be divided into wards (in the case of territorial authorities) and constituencies (in the case of regional councils) for electoral purposes. In the 2007 local elections, however, only one council, Environment Bay of

Plenty, had used this provision to provide Māori with the opportunity to elect Māori candidates. Therefore, for all intents and purposes, Māori have the same experience of participating in local elections as non-Māori.

Citizens are entitled to vote in the local government election held where they live, as well as in the local government election held where they own a property if that is different from where they live. To vote in a local government election one must be:

- enrolled as a parliamentary elector, at an address in the district or city where one lives;
- enrolled as a ratepayer elector for a property one owns that is in a different district or city from where one lives.

Ratepayers who own property in a different local body area from where they live can apply to go on the ratepayer roll for that area and have an additional vote for that local authority where their property is located. Thus, the roll of electors is comprised of those who meet the residential qualification (and as such is sometimes referred to as the residential roll). In addition, following the long-standing political principle of 'no taxation without representation', property owners who are not on the residential roll may apply to be listed on the non-residential ratepayer roll. Thus, Māori who are rāwaho who own land in their tribal areas may vote: (1) as a residential elector in their area of residence, and (2) as a rate-payer elector in their tribal area. Many factors make participation as a ratepayer elector problematic, however, including the restrictions based upon communally-owned land.

The rating of Māori land in particular represents the need for differential treatment of Māori land, to address the long-term historical impacts of ratings, and which manifest in continued and current inequities for Māori land owners (Dewes & Walzl 2007; Panel 2007). These impacts are a key part of Treaty of Waitangi violations by local government affecting the environment, along with allocation of 'waste-lands'; excessive surveying and settlement of Māori land for reserves and public works; the degradation of Māori land and water resources through pollution from waste and other hazards, and; disregard of other Māori resources values, such as protection of 'wahi tapu' (sacred and restricted places) (Rikys 2004). Thus, a primary problem is the engagement of Māori from an assimilationist model of citizenship, and not upon a basis that is culturally appropriate or recognisant of the disadvantaged socio-historical position that Māori bear when engaging with local authorities.

Thus, the mana whenua/Māori/citizen split is a particular challenge for local governments to address. Primarily because there is much development yet to be had with regards to effective engagement between local bodies and mana whenua, the incorporation on one hand of the views of those who are mana whenua but reside outside the region, and on the other of Māori who reside in the region but are not mana whenua, are yet to be addressed. As argued above, that these areas of engagement are addressed is both important under the Treaty of Waitangi and in improving the democratic legitimacy of local authorities. The findings of this research, which engaged the views of rāwaho on involvement and participation in environmental management, come some way to fleshing out the issues from which these developments might begin.

Engaging Māori voices: the research project

'There's a lot of Māori staying away from their iwi, staying in other towns and areas, so, you know, where does that link us? As manuhiri to be involved?'

Focus groups with Māori

The research undertaken in which the views and concerns of rāwaho arose as a distinctive element of Māori perspectives about environmental management was part of a larger project that explored New Zealanders' local political participation and engagement with local government. Gathering data on citizens' knowledge and interactions with local government, and in particular citizens' recommendations on how local authorities can improve their engagement of citizens, was a primary goal of the project. Data collection employed in this larger project incorporated a telephone survey of 400 voters in one region of New Zealand, focus groups with Māori, and focus groups with young people of voting age (18–24 years) (see Cheyne 2006).

Focus groups were employed to explore with Māori their knowledge, experiences and perspectives about local government, including engagement on environmental issues. Seven focus groups were held with different groups of Māori; 18–24-year-olds in tertiary study; 18–24-year-olds in the workforce; people 25 years old and over residing in rural areas, and; people 25 years old and over living in urban settings. Observing Arohia Durie's (1998) ethical framework based on mana,[7] focus groups were deemed an appropriate method for research with Māori as they allowed for observation of tikanga in the process of data collection, and through successive review hui ensured a high level of accountability to participants, including participants' right to veto and amend any research findings.

A key question in research where Māori are the focus of the inquiry asks what benefit the research is to positive Māori development, and more specifically, to the population group being researched (Smith 1999; Stokes 1985: 27–48; Teariki 1992). The central purpose of this research was to contribute to Māori development through the provision of data to local governments to: (1) assist their efforts to engage Māori in local decision-making, and; (2) stimulate further research about engagement by local authorities with particular Māori communities in their respective areas, such as mana whenua and rāwaho/taura here/mātāwaka. The review by Allison and Cossar (2006: 10) of government literature on Māori engagement states that current data possessed by government bodies do not touch on 'all that Māori think and feel about democracy, representation, participation, and consultation'. The use of focus groups provided a space within which Māori could explore these issues and fill some of the gaps in current understandings about Māori engagement on environmental management.

New knowledge generated about engagement

As mentioned previously, the meaning and significance of non-participation is an area of local political participation about which there is little evidence. For example, voter turnout data for local authority elections do not provide any information on reasons for abstention from voting (see Department of Internal Affairs 2006). Currently, it is unclear whether non-participation reflects contentment or apathy or other factors such as lack of information about participation or alienation from participation processes. Thus, another specific objective of the research project on Māori engagement with local government was to gather data explaining the factors that contribute to non-participation. The findings of discussions with participants about non-participation went some way to answering these questions, revealing particular perspectives and insights into non-participation from the position of rāwaho for local governments to address.

The research findings of the project of Māori engagement with local government included clear messages for improved engagement of Māori in their communities by local authorities. Their messages focused on views and perceptions of (1) their knowledge about local government, (2) information from local government, (3) contact with local government, (4) representation of Māori concerns, (5) participation by Māori, (6) engagement of Māori (by local government), and their recommendations for: (a) improving the information flow from local authorities to citizens; (b) enhancing Māori participation in local authority decision-making processes; (c) means to improve the engagement of Māori by local authorities; and (d) improving local authority accountability to Māori (see Cheyne & Tawhai 2007).

The voices of rāwaho, shared below, bring particular perspectives and angles to these recommendations. The success of focus group research often relies on the degree to which participants are able to connect to each other, and stimulate each other's thoughts and comments. How thoughts and comments are supported in a focus group context is a key way that qualitative research of this kind can show the strength, validity and support for ideas. It was therefore critical to include in the data recording and reporting these aspects of group interaction. When data were entered into the database software,[8] a conscious decision was made to identify these aspects. A comment in parentheses below indicates a second and sometimes third speaker's interjections. Names of iwi and places have been omitted for anonymity.

Rāwaho: Concerns, views and aspirations

The perspectives of rāwaho/taura here/mātāwaka that were particular to engagement with local government about environmental issues, including environmental management, focused on (1) involvement in environmental decision-making, (2) a local versus a generic focus on Māori issues, and (3) being engaged as Māori by local government.

Involvement in environmental decision-making

For all participants, environmental management was an issue of interest, and, for many participants, the sole reason for engaging with local government. Maintenance and protection of the environment from further degradation was of particular concern, and arose as a motivating factor for people who would not have been interested in engaging in political processes otherwise:

> *'If they're gonna throw raw sewerage out onto the land and they're gonna pump raw sewerage into the lakes where you get your eels and all that kinda stuff, course you're gonna [participate].'*

> *'Look at all the rivers now, like (yes) you look back, like maybe ten years ago, they were all fine to swim in, now, you know, we go to jump in the river and you're wondering what you're gonna get?'*

> *'I'd get them to do a replanting programme on both sides of the [name of river] all the way down to the city (oh good one) (replant) (yup).'*

Despite this interest, a general confusion over the processes of local government exacerbated participants' concerns. This confusion included where to participate, and emphasized the need for comprehensive information as the basis for engagement:

> *'Like, I still don't know, do I vote here or do I vote at home?'*

> *'See, I didn't know that; that once you're on the national roll that's how you get on your local roll.'*

> *'What do you mean by "wards"? I don't get that.'*

Many participants expressed a desire to somehow be involved in local decision-making in their tribal area, as opposed to their area of residence. This desire arose particularly out of concern for tribal environmental resources. Participants who were residing both short term and long term in a city outside their tribal area shared this perspective:

> *'You still take a bit more interest in your iwi, what's going on in your iwi, or what's going on where you do consider home (yeah).'*

> *'Tūrangawaewae…like your awa, those rāhui, those kinda things, marae, that sort of thing, urupā, all of that.'*

> *'Vote for our council back home (yeah).'*

This went some way to explaining the low participation rates and non-interest of some Māori communities in the participation processes of their local authorities. Other participants stated clearly that they felt it was not their place to be involved in the environmental management issues, as that was the place of mana whenua:

> *'I'm not voting for any local government yet, 'cause, why should I? My home is back there. . . I'm not from [local iwi], I'm not going to vote for (not our whenua) yeah, well, that's it, it's not our whenua, so that's that.'*

> *'Maybe that's why our stats are so low, because you have a lot of Māori living in other iwi around Aotearoa, some who are just sort of temporarily staying in a certain town like [town], like myself and other people who are from [iwi region], from somewhere else, you know?'*

> *'Cause it's their decision, eh? I probably would have thought the iwi, the local iwi...?'*

Others wished to explore further their possible role in decision-making about local environmental issues, especially those who felt they had made a long-term home in their area of residence. Thus, although they did not belong to mana whenua, many participants did feel compelled to participate in local environmental issues:

> *'There's a lot of Māori staying away from their iwi, staying in other towns and areas, so you know, where does that link us? As manuhiri to be involved?'*

> *'I believe while I'm here, te wairua o [iwi] has helped take care of me, because I reside here, so those things are important to me.'*

> *'It's about people dumping rubbish under the bridge, and for me I have five children… for my whānau we live at rivers and beaches and picnics, you know?'*

A local versus a generic focus on Māori issues

Of particular interests was the tension participants identified as existing between local Māori and national Māori issues, and the particular problems this raised for their awareness and engagement in local environmental management. As a result of media exposure about environmental ownership and other issues that drew attention to the Māori-Crown conflict, many participants said their own attention about Māori issues was focused at the national level:

> *'Issues like that aren't connected with local body government... local body for me personally is more about, um, what day*

*my rubbish is being collected and you know, whether or
not they're chopping down thirty trees in the [place].'*

*'It doesn't really register in my head that quickly. If I think
Māori issues, I think of the government taking care of
them rather than the council, it's not intentional.'*

Because of a lack of clarity about their role in environmental management,
both local and in their tribal area, some participants felt it was easier to
engage about Māori issues on a national level, primarily because they had a
clear role in terms of participation:

*'We all went down to the hīkoi and it wasn't just because our beach
was gonna get taken off us, it was because it was happening all around
the country, it was an issue for all Māori to get involved in.'*

Some participants' observations of local bodies were that they too were
more comfortable dealing with Māori issues than issues particular to
mana whenua. This generic approach, however, raised concerns among
participants about the identity and knowledge of individual iwi:

*'[Councillor] was more comfortable towards issues to do with
Māori, not necessarily issues to do with [local iwi].'*

*'Gone is every iwi because we are now generalised,
that is why we become just Māori, we're not iwi, we're
Māori, and we're becoming New Zealanders.'*

Following this was a concern that some local authorities are uninterested
in local knowledge; that it is sufficient to be aware of things 'Māori' as
opposed to knowledge of mana whenua. The participants saw tokenistic
attitudes towards aspects such as local tikanga:

*'Too often— "We do the noho marae, we do the week's hui, okay I
know all about Māoridom because I've done it for a week".'*

*'"I've just been educated by some Māori and now have permission
to speak on behalf of the tikanga of all Māoridom.'*

Participants were therefore keen to support recognition of mana whenua,
for mana whenua knowledge and views to be paramount in local decision-
making, and to engage themselves with mana whenua on how to support
their environmental goals. Many participants were concerned that lack of

contact with mana whenua could result in the ignoring of the specific goals of mana whenua for environmental management and/or development:

> *'Those people that get elected they have to do noho with the local rangatira that are here in this particular iwi, sit down with them, understand them, so they know where they are coming from – at least one every two months or something, just so they don't lose that contact.'*

> *'Do they have an iwi authority on the council? Like (yeah?) how it comes under the Treaty, like so that you have an iwi representative within the council?'*

> *'I don't have the same connection here, but I still tautoko the whanau and the iwi that are here, respect what they have going on.'*

Being engaged as Māori by local government

For many Māori who do reside outside their tribal area, although they do not expect to be afforded the authority of mana whenua, they still expect to be engaged in a way that is congruent to their cultural preferences. Participants stressed that this includes the maintenance of meaningful relationships:

> *'They don't turn up here, they don't go and hui with their people.'*

> *'If those reps on a regular basis held meetings for their constituents in an appropriate base, could be a marae or could be, you know, somewhere like that, and just report what's happening and then get some feedback?'*

> *'I s'pose if out on the marae, they might catch my interest. (Yeah, if they put on a feed or something)…(It's about a process, about building of relationships).'*

In particular, participants expressed frustration that due to lack of clear information and communication from local bodies, their environmental concerns were not as well met as they could be:

> *'Cause the rivers and that, they're regional council, eh?'*

> *'They've been passing her off to the regional council and they're trying to dispute it… it's the city councils, so yeah, you think they'd go and clean it up, but they're trying to pass it off, and the regional council is going "nah, nah, nah", it's the city council.'*

Further to this, failure to be heard on environmental issues was a particular factor that discouraged participants from further involvement with local government:

> *'They can't do anything about it unless the guy actually got the fire going when they came around, and I was like, I gave up in the end, I thought "Right, well, obviously I'm not going to get any help here", so I said "Thank you very much for your time" and hung up.'*

> *'A council member will come out; they will assess the situation and see whether or not it is actually causing any pollution or whatever on the environment. But I thought that's a bit, you know, crazy really.'*

> *'It's really discouraging to read and to see that there was a [place] preservation group, and that there was a [place] action group, and you know…its really discouraging to see both those groups fail because the council didn't listen, and that discourages participation.'*

Thus, as well as encouraging a greater presence and authority for mana whenua, participants also believed there should be greater numbers of Māori in general working for local bodies dealing with environmental issues:

> *'This issue with the land – that could have been another issue, if there were even numbers, there could have been the issue of the land not being sold. (I reckon).'*

> *'I reckon if we did see more Māori in there then it's like a motivation thing.'*

An ultimate concern for participants regarding involvement in environmental decision-making, however, was that engagement is still on the Crown's terms, as opposed to genuine meaningful relationships where Māori views are taken into account:

> *'You get the people in so there's an equal agreement, but that's not an agreement when the local government determine the deal.'*

> *'Let's make a decision, send a word out, get the input. "Too late, we've already made the decision, but we'll accept your whakaaro." That's consultation really isn't it?'*

> *'I still think if they have an idea it's already sorted before they send everything out. (Really?) (Yeah) (It's true).'*

The concerns, views and aspirations of rāwaho as described above provide particular insights into the nature of contemporary Māori engagement with local government on environmental issues. Involvement in environmental decision-making, tension over a local versus a generic focus on Māori issues, and securing engagement as Māori by local government are challenges facing Māori living outside their tribal areas today. The focus group data thus provide some interesting material for consideration of the future directions for further development of Māori engagement on the environment.

Shaping a future for Māori engagement on the environment

'It is really about recognising the diversity of our communities.'

The use of the term Māori in the Local Government Act 2002 has left wide scope for local authorities to engage all Māori in their respective area. In addition to mana whenua, Māori living away from their tribal areas are voicing a desire to be better informed on the opportunities for their involvement in environmental management, both in their tribal area and in the place where they have made residence. This presents both local and iwi authorities new opportunities to look again at our understandings and frameworks for Māori engagement.

Although welcome to participate on the basis of individual citizenship rights, many Māori, as illustrated in the research findings, prefer to engage only with local authorities about the environmental sites and resources to which they are tribally connected. This is evidence that, for many Māori, their collective identity overshadows their individual one, at least with regard to environmental management. Other participants, especially those who were long-term residents, expressed a keen desire also to be involved in contributing to the environmental protection and maintenance of the area in which they reside. Participants expected that, as rāwaho, their views would be secondary to that of mana whenua, but recognised an importance in this secondary role in regards to supporting the recognition of Māori values and perspectives in local environmental management.

Local governments thus need to re-conceptualise the frameworks currently employed in the engagement of Māori. In particular, engaging with rāwaho/taura here/mātāwaka in a manner that is culturally appropriate, to ensure effective participation of this group, is essential to addressing current low and non-participation of Māori in local government decision-making processes. The table below can be considered a first step in fleshing out the issues of engagement that the particular position of rāwaho presents.

Entity	Local Authority Relationship	Basis of Relationship	Nature of Relationship
Mana whenua / Ahi Kā	Local Authority (the area being both that of residence and tribal homeland)	Treaty of Waitangi Article Two – collective rights as hapu/iwi entities.	Partnerships, authority in formulating appropriate decision-making processes, dual weight in decision-making, local tribal knowledge drawn upon in environmental management, etc.
		Treaty of Waitangi Article Three- citizenship rights as individual Māori.	If not one and the same with collective engagement, could also involve authority in deciding appropriate processes for engaging Māori individuals/ rāwaho in the area.
Rāwaho/Taura Here/Mātāwaka	Local Authority in area of residence	Treaty of Waitangi Article Three – citizenship rights as individual Māori.	Not responsible for deciding upon the shape of processes, but still an expectation that those engagement/participation processes will be appropriate to Māori cultural practices. Potential relationships with mana whenua to support local environmental protection.
	Local Authority in tribal homeland	Treaty of Waitangi Article Two – collective rights as hapu/iwi entities.	An expectation that participation processes will cater for their role as a part of mana whenua (internal political issue of iwi, but one that local governments will be drawn to as issues of mandate are explored).

Table 1: Engagement between 'Māori' and Local Authorities.

These new perspectives on the basis of Māori engagement also provide iwi authorities with a mandate to engage with local authorities over environmental management about some issues, including: (1) effective engagement of taura here/iwi members living afar in environmental decision-making involving tribal sites and resources; (2) appropriate forms of engagement for rāwaho in their area, that mana whenua would find acceptable; and (3) communication processes between mana whenua and other Māori in their area. In particular, the degree to which some rāwaho/taura here/mātāwaka wish to support mana whenua goals, and the new relationships that could be formed with these entities to advance these goals within the decision-making forums of local government should not be underestimated.

Conclusion

This chapter is based on several assumptions. It assumes that now and in the future, whakapapa is a central principle around which Māori society is and will continue to be organised. It assumes that, for environmental sites and resources, including lands, forests, seas, waterways, Māori will continue to be drawn to those elements to which they have an ancestral connection – the bases on which they seek to engage over the management of environmental resources where they live primarily being out of respect for and desire to support the environmental goals of mana whenua.

This paper has therefore not intended to ignore the circumstances of urban Māori authorities who are not whakapapa-based, but rather acknowledges the difficult position of these groups as a result of historical alienation from traditional kinship groups. The discourse on new forms of collective rights that urban Māori groups are developing is not something this chapter addressed. Further research needs to be done in this area as part of the wider research with rāwaho/taura here/mātāwaka on improving the engagement of local government with Māori.

Thus, although there is still much work to be done, the widespread impetus to establish relationships between Māori and mana whenua has led to another sphere of local government–Māori relationship analysis: that of rāwaho, of Māori whose engagement in their area of residence is based on individual citizenship rights, but whose citizenship, when perceived as the right to equal outcomes, requires that they be engaged through Māori-appropriate processes. Processes based on assimilationist notions of citizenship must be abandoned as they are neither culturally appropriate nor recognisant of the disadvantaged socio-historical position that Māori bear when approaching engagement with local authorities.

The questions, concerns and perspectives of rāwaho regarding the environment and its management thus raise specific implications, opportunities and new understandings about Māori engagement for consideration by local authorities and Māori alike. As indicated by the recent increase in co-management agreements, the time is right for Māori and local authorities to advance their relationships over environmental engagement to a new level.

END NOTES

[1]Acknowledgement is given to Associate Professor Christine Cheyne of Massey University for her leadership of the Marsden Fast-Start project through which the research data in this chapter were generated, and for her input and advice in the drafting of this chapter.

[2]For example, in 2004 80% of councils had established formal processes for consultation with Māori, in comparison to 25% of those who reported in 1997. See Local Government New Zealand, (2004).

[3]The most recent of these being agreed to between Ngāti Tuwharetoa and Taupo District Council, January 2009. See Taupo District Council, (2009).

[4]Such as *kaitiakitanga* in section 7a of the Resource Management Act 1991.

[5]Each reflecting a particular position depending on the point of reference. For example, *taura here* suggests a continued connection to one's tribal area, thereby making it distinct from what can be considered other rāwaho entities such as urban Māori authorities that are not whakapapa-based.

[6]Approximately – source describes the number as just over a third.

[7]Specifically, Durie (1998: 259–265) cites: Mana tangata, observing the dignity, safety, mutuality of participants; Mana Whakahaere, issues of collaboration and control; and Mana motuhake, the emphasis on outcomes and evidence of benefit to Māori communities.

[8]Microsoft Access™ was used to build a database for data entry and analysis.

Ka mate kāinga tahi, ka ora kāinga rua. Tūhoe and the environment – The impact of the Tūhoe diaspora on the Tūhoe environment

Rangi Mataamua and Pou Te Rangiua Temara

> *Ka horo, e!*
> *Ka horo, e!*
> *Ka horo koa te tihi o Maungapōhatu ka horo.*
> *Tēnei a Tūhoe ka hiki i te ara,*
> *O riri whakauaua,*
> *O riri whakanekeneke.*
> *Kumea mai a Ruatahuna ki raro ra.*
> *Ka whakarārā koa te waha o Tūhoe ki te kopua wai,*
> *Ki Whakatāne, ki Rangitaiki e!*
> *E kume nei te whenua,*
> *E kume nei te tangata,*
> *Aue! Aue! Aue! Ha!*

Elsdon Best once described Tūhoe and their environment in the following way:

> *A lone land, a wild land of rough bush ranges; nor plain, nor pasture breaks the ever present forest. A land to breed a rude people, a fierce proud, and warlike tribe of mountaineers. They are here. The sons of Toi and of Potiki hold the savage bushlands. They are the descendants of the Celestial Child, and of Hine, the Cloud-born. They are the offspring of Toi, the Wood Eater; they are the Children of the Mist (Best 1972: 1).*

The language of this twentieth century ethnologist might be deemed too Shakespearian for the modern historian/anthropologist. Yet if we consider the mindset of the author and the period in which it was written, a closer examination of this passage shows us that in many ways Best's description of Tūhoe and their environment is rather accurate. In essence, Best creates an image of a rugged, harsh and inhospitable environment, which is occupied by a hardy people, bred to exist and even flourish in such conditions. Best insinuates that these often hostile people did not migrate from distant lands to occupy the bush and fern clad valleys, but rather descended from the environment itself. While this suggestion may seem somewhat far-fetched, it is in actual fact an accurate description of how Tūhoe understand their traditional relationship with their environment.

Photo 1. A view of Maungapōhatu and the surrounding bush. Photo: Rangi Mataamua 2008.

Tūhoe often refer to their boundary and their environment as Te Urewera, a name that can also be used to describe the people who dwell within this area. Te Urewera remains one of the last wilderness frontiers of New Zealand. It is a vast expanse of primordial bush and forest-covered hills, dissected by numerous small streams and a few large rivers. This ecological treasure chest of flora and fauna is set against the backdrop of formidable mountains and peaks that have risen in unison to form the ridges and spurs that criss-cross Te Urewera. The most significant of all these high points is Maungapōhatu, the sacred mountain of Tūhoe where the human remains of generations of ancestors have been entombed just below its apex. To the east of Maungapōhatu is Lake Waikaremoana, an immense body of water, nestled beneath the shadow of surrounding hills and the giant precipice of Panekire. To the west flows the picturesque Whakatāne River, gently winding its way past the majestic landscape towards Ruātoki and onward to the ocean. This is Te Urewera. This is Tūhoe.

Many Pākehā authors and poets have attempted to capture the splendour and magnificence that is Te Urewera. Yet perhaps the most alluring passage comes from Katherine Mansfield, who in 1907 journeyed from Tarapounamu to Te Umuroa in Ruatahuna, and in her notebook wrote:

> *From this saddle we look across river upon river of green bush then burnt bush russet colour – blue distance – and a wide cloud flecked sky – All the people must doubtless have gone shearing – I see no one…at the head of the great valley the blazing sun uplifts itself – like a gigantic torch to light the bush – it is all so gigantic and tragic – and even in the bright sunlight it is so passionately secret…We begin to reach the valley – broad and green – red and brown butterflies – the green bush. The sunlight slanting in to the trees – and island – then a river arched with tree fern – And always through the bush the hushed sound of water running on brown pebbles – It seems to breath the full deep bygone essence of it all (Mansfield 1978).*

Traditionally, Tūhoe believe they are the direct descendents of their environment. The mountains and rivers are their ancestors and the forest inhabitants their kin. As a tribal group Tūhoe trace their origins to the ancient union between Te Maunga (the mountain) and Hinepūkohurangi (the mist maiden). This archaic marriage is personified in the mist that settles on the mountainous abode of Tūhoe (Melbourne 1998), which gave rise to the saying 'ngā tamariki o te kohu' 'the children of the mist'. Hinepūkohurangi and Te Maunga begat Pōtiki, eponymous ancestor of the people known as Ngā Pōtiki, who eventually became Tūhoe.

Photo 2. The Whakatāne River flowing through the heart of Te Urewera. Photo: Rangi Mataamua 2007.

To Tūhoe, all manners of tree, plant, rock, fish, eel stream, pool, lake, bird, rodent insect and environmental force, have a genealogy and are related either directly or indirectly to the people. For instance, in Ruātoki, a particular wind that blows down the gorge of the Whakatāne River is called Te Hau Ōkiwa (Best 1972: 235). This supernatural being, Ōkiwa, is personified as a pond, a dog, and also as the wind that has a primeval connection to the people of this region. Further upstream towards the settlement of Ōhauaoterangi is a hill called Te Kōhuru. Situated on this hill is a hinau tree known as Te Iho o Kātaka, which is said to have the power to cause barren women to conceive (Orbell 1985: 169). Childless couples are escorted to this tree where they embrace its trunk and undergo various ceremonies. The subsequent result is usually the birth of a new generation of Tūhoe descendants.

*Tūhoe identity is encapsulated by its environment. The way Tūhoe
understand themselves, the manner in which Tūhoe interact with
each other and express themselves has, since the foundation of the
tribe, been influenced by the environment. Simply put, Tūhoe
are the environment, and the environment is Tūhoe. This idea
was noted by John Rangihau when he stated, 'And for me and for
others the mountains seem to look down...sometimes benignly...
sometimes with anger...You feel the different moods of the very hills
that surround you because it is part of you' (Stokes 1986: 11).*

*Hōhepa Kereopa of Waimana expands on this connection
between the environment and Tūhoe, saying, 'So in the end
we need to think of the land as ourselves, and treat it like how
we would want to treat ourselves' (Moon 2003: 140).*

For centuries Tūhoe have maintained a constant relationship with their environment, a bond that connects the people to the hills, the rivers, the trees and to all that surrounds them. No physical task was undertaken without consulting the appropriate deity and reaffirming the relationship with the environment. Each year during the rise of Matariki (Pleiades) in the eastern sky, Tūhoe tohunga invoked the te mata o te tau ceremony where new shoots of growth were taken from the forest and burnt on an altar to ensure a plentiful harvest (Best 1972). Tūhoe have always preserved a deep, rich and meaningful interconnectedness with their environment.

Evidence suggests that Tūhoe are connected to the land and to their traditional environment in both a physical and metaphysical manner. Furthermore, Tūhoe derive their identity directly from the environment that surrounds them and the environment in which they interact. This interconnected, multi-faceted relationship has been preserved for centuries, moulding Tūhoe into the unique people they are today. However, in the last fifty years Tūhoe have undergone a diaspora of sorts. There has been a mass exodus of Tūhoe from their homelands to distant urban areas. So how has this diaspora affected the relationship between Tūhoe and their traditional environment?

It could be argued that presently most Tūhoe have an estranged relationship with their traditional environment. In fact, 81% of all Tūhoe live outside their tribal boundaries, with the vast majority populating urban centres (Nikora 2000: 39). Today most Tūhoe individuals would be more familiar with the locations of the best coffee shops and label clothing outlet stores in downtown Auckland and central Wellington, as opposed to historical sites and landmarks of Te Urewera. Tūhoe have become global, with members of the tribe travelling to all corners of the earth, working abroad, and experiencing the various flavours of the globe. A high proportion of these same urban-dwelling, new-age Tūhoe have never set eyes on Maungapōhatu, or ventured to Waikaremoana, or walked the Whakatāne River to Ōhauaoterangi and on to Te Pūtere. Only fifty years ago, a common lifestyle for Tūhoe members was living on and around the marae, being part of a wider whānau and hapū collective, utilising the forest and its natural resources to survive. Today's Tūhoe members visit the marae infrequently, and if they do it is only to attend the funerals of very close family. These same individuals live in nuclear family units, have little to do with hapū affairs, and if they ever found themselves lost in the forest with no food, would either starve to death or die from exposure.

While these comments may seem unkind, no malice is intended. Tūhoe are only victims of circumstance with the consequences of urbanisation, globalisation, privatisation, market forces, and government policy combining to alienate them from their own environment. Still questions must be posed: "Are we now becoming Tūhoe by name and not by nature?" Is the mystique that surrounds Tūhoe, proclaiming a mysterious and proud tribe living in harmony with Tanemāhuta nothing more than a myth? Is it now time for Tūhoe to re-define their identity as they evolve into a new group with diminishing knowledge of their natural environment? These questions are extremely difficult to pose and even harder to answer. However, what needs to be understood is that the overwhelming majority of Tūhoe descendants no longer live in traditional Tūhoe settlements. Very few members live near their marae and interact with the environment. In fact, most Tūhoe are not even born close to their tribal strongholds. Today Tūhoe are urban, becoming more educated, technologically capable, more politically aware, and dare I say it, middle class.

So what about Tūhoe and the environment in this present day and age? I suppose it is possible to stereotype Tūhoe people into various categories and attempt to define the relationship each group has with their Tūhoe environment. While this exercise is not scientific in its approach, has no methodology, and does not take into account the interests and uniqueness of the individual, it may help explain how and why Tūhoe have particular views about their environment.

The first stereotypical group are those Tūhoe members who were born and bred within Tūhoe, who grew up around the marae, attended Tūhoe schools, are fluent speakers of Māori, and have knowledge of the forest and the environment. Most people in this group are aged over 50 and can recall occasions when they harvested kereru, when each marae had their own gardens, when people lived in various settlements along the Whakatāne River, and when the forest and the environment were vital to their survival. It was an age when the hills were alive with deer and pigs, when you could drink from the river, when most Tūhoe lived in Tūhoe communities, and when the marae were true focal points. Many in this group often reminisce about an era of iconic Tūhoe characters and a time when Tūhoe had reached a cultural zenith. Even if we remove the rose-tinted glasses and all the selective romanticism, some truths remain evident. This group of Tūhoe members maintain a deep seated affinity to their land, to their community and to their environment. This relationship is a primal connection they inherited at birth and that was reaffirmed throughout their lives. It was instilled into these individuals on a daily basis, as they moved within the communities of Tūhoe and interacted with their environment. As children, the bush was their playground, the rivers were their aquatic centres, and important landmarks were their global positioning system coordinates. As they aged they became hunters and gathers and the environment provided their sustenance. They know how to 'live off the land', they recall the pains of hunger, they remember the taste of native wood pigeon, and they understand what it means to be Tūhoe and part of the environment.

This group of Tūhoe were eventually divided by the urban drift, which saw most members move to urban centres, while a few remained at home. At various stages in their lives they went between their urban homes and their rural hinterlands. Most established themselves within the cities, building careers, having families, and settling down. A few, drawn by a longing for their homeland, left the towns and cities and relocated back into their traditional settlements, often with family in tow. Yet the vast majority opted to remain urban where they could make a living and provide for their families. Still this group understands the environment in which they were raised. While perhaps only a small number of them still occupy Tūhoe hamlets, all of them have an affinity to their Tūhoe environment.

The second group are the children and grandchildren of the first group. However, they are split into two distinctive clusters. There are the descendants of those who moved and stayed in the urban centres, and the offspring of those who remained within the Tūhoe strongholds. Those who where born and raised outside Tūhoe make up the majority of the 30,000 registered Tūhoe members. This group is the new-age, modern, common Tūhoe, usually aged less than 40 and existing as urbanites. Their environment is one of concrete, motorways, fast food, text messages, internet, play station, and instant gratification. While some of this group might speak Māori and have knowledge of Tūhoe customs and traditions, most do not. It would be fair to say that their knowledge of the traditional Tūhoe environment would at best be average. This group are seen mostly at funerals of their close relatives, where they spend the mandatory two or three days mourning a parent, an uncle, an aunty or other close relatives. This prototypical tribal member will then try to catch up with all and sundry before having to rush back to work to deal with the inevitable pile of tasks that await them. They do not have memories of the environment, and while they might spend time taking photos and gazing in awe at the visual splendour of the bush clad mountains, they do not venture far from the marae. It is not to say that these individuals do not feel a sense of identity, but their actual relationship and interaction to the environment is very limited. The next cluster is made up of the children and grandchildren of the first group who have been raised within Tūhoe. Like their parents, they have an understanding of their environment. While they are perhaps more worldly and do not spend as much time in the forest as their predecessors, they have a bond and unique link to the land and the environment, even if this just means living within a Tūhoe community.

So what does this all mean? In essence it shows us that the more than 30,000 Tūhoe members can be loosely divided into two categories, rural and urban, or ahi kā and taura here, or wealthy and impoverished, or even educated and uneducated. Yet the vast majority of Tūhoe fall into the urban, taura here, educated and relatively wealthy section. It is this group who have little to no understanding of their traditional environment. It would also seem inevitable that as they themselves mature and have families, a new generation of Tūhoe will become further alienated from their tribal environment. Therefore in actual fact only a small portion of Tūhoe maintain significant and regular contact with the Tūhoe environment. One could even suggest that as few as 5% of the tribe actively reaffirm their relationship with Te Urewera.

Most Tūhoe have therefore become somewhat disconnected from their environmental origins. This realisation might go someway to justifying some of the questions already posed. Have most Tūhoe now become Tūhoe by name and not by nature? Is the mystique that surrounds Tūhoe, proclaiming a proud tribe living in harmony with Tāne mahuta nothing more than a myth? Are Tūhoe now at a crossroads where they have to redefine their own identity within the context of a completely new environment?

These questions become even more important as Tūhoe enters a new era of its history; the treaty settlement era. In 2008, Tūhoe undertook a series of historic meetings with the Crown, working towards settling historical grievances. More than 150 years of hostility and distrust were, for a day, set aside, when on 31 July 2008, Tūhoe and the Crown signed the Terms of Negotiations for the Treaty of Waitangi claims. During this event, Tūhoe declared its intentions, as part of the settlement, to have the Urewera National Park returned to the tribe (*Dominion Post,* Friday August 1 2008: 1). Essentially this means the disestablishment of a National Park, and the complete return of the Tūhoe environment into Tūhoe hands. While for Tūhoe this will seem a simple and fair request, no doubt many other sections of New Zealand's society will be outraged and demand that the natural resources of the country be held in Crown ownership for all New Zealanders.

This potential debate aside, the Urewera National Park faces considerable issues that must be addressed and fully understood before any party, including Tūhoe, can move forward. The forest is not in the healthy state it was once in. Just over a decade ago Ruatahuna elder Wharekiri Biddle remarked, "Kei te mate haere te ngahere … The forest is dying". A strong sentiment indeed for someone who had spent a lifetime in and around the bush, and evidence would suggest this comment is correct. The Urewera National Park faces threats on a number of fronts, mostly from introduced animals and plants. Opossums have a significant impact on native trees devouring massive amounts of foliage every day (Beven et al. 1999). Stoats, magpies and rats kill native birds and breed at an alarming rate, and even feral pigs and deer damage much of the native bush (DOC 2003:25). In addition introduced plants like blackberry, ragwort and barberry have taken hold in many parts of the bush. A number of the waterways, including the Whakatāne River, are affected by farm run off and sewage, which has managed to leach into the watertable (Titchmarsh & Blackwood 1997). It is now unsafe to drink directly from the many rivers and streams because of Giardia. Even the smallest inhabitants of the bush have been affected. No longer is the bush alive in the summer months with the hum of native bees pollinating flowering trees, but rather wasps that pester native birds and sting anything that happens to disturb them (Scott 1984).

Photo 3. Tūhoe hunters, (left) Raymond and (right) Hekenoa Te Kurapa, stop at a clearing for a rest while hunting pigs in Te Urewera. Photo: Rangi Mataamua 2007.

A natural suggestion would be to propose a series of programmes to eradicate introduced problems, combined with breeding programmes for native species. The problem is that these programmes have been in operation for many decades (DOC 1994: 3), yet still the problems remain.

The Department of Conservation (DOC) has been responsible for the management of the Urewera National Park for many years, yet if you were to ask Tūhoe elders who grew up in the 1950s and 1960s about the state of the forest, I have little doubt they would all comment that the forest is now in a significantly worse condition than in their childhoods. This chapter does not seek to assign blame for the state of the forest, but serious discussion and major investment are needed to preserve the Urewera National Park.

This is where the problem begins to get complex. If Tūhoe are to have the Urewera National Park returned, who will be responsible for the many environmental issues that exist? Perhaps the Government is only too willing to return the park, problems and all? As an example, if we examine the issues surrounding introduced pests in the forest we might ask how do we eradicate our pests? Do Tūhoe have the ability to mobilise a unit large enough and capable enough to deal with the issues, or are there other means? Should I even mention 1080 poison and the battles that currently exist between DOC and other interested groups? It should also be noted that for a number of Tūhoe living in Tūhoe settlements, the opossum fur trade is their main source of income. In addition, it is these Tūhoe opossum hunters who frequent the forest more than any other. If we remove the opossum, and for argument sake the pigs and deer, even fewer Tūhoe would venture past the marae. The opossum, pig and deer hunters maintain a true and regular link to the Tūhoe environment. One could even argue that it is the opossum, the pig and the deer that ensure Tūhoe maintain its relationship with the forest, and that without them there might be more Pākehā trampers traversing Te Urewera Forest than Tūhoe. The point being raised here is that the issues surrounding the Urewera Forest are very complex and interconnected. Any decisions that are made will most likely produce positive results for some and negative ones for others. Most importantly, Tūhoe needs to take an honest account of its situation before making any decisions in relation to the environment and its cultural heritage.

No doubt many Tūhoe relations will be somewhat annoyed by the questions raised in this chapter, perhaps even incensed by the way in which we have stereotyped them, challenged their relationship to the environment, and questioned their identity. If this is the case, then I am pleased to some extent, because this chapter was intended to provoke a response and to stimulate Tūhoe to examine their identity and their relationship with the Tūhoe environment. It is better for Tūhoe to have the courage to ask these questions of themselves, than to wait for others to pose them. Tūhoe are not alone in this regard. Most tribes and their members have become isolated from their traditional environments. Circumstance and fate have dragged Māori into the 21st century, with many traditions, beliefs, practices, values and ideas discarded and replaced with new ideals and modern methods. Whether we accept it or not, Tūhoe has been part of this shift and a casualty of the change has been the Tūhoe relationship with their environment. Tūhoe need to be honest about their identity and accept that fact that most Tūhoe no longer live within the Tūhoe boundary and even less have a relationship to the environment. This is nothing to be ashamed of. Change happens to all people and all societies. History has shown us that numerous civilisations throughout time have risen and fallen, others have evolved and morphed into new entities, and maybe this is what is happening to Tūhoe. Tūhoe are in many ways like their environment. Both Tūhoe and Te Urewera have been affected by change, by colonisation, by introduced perils, by new technologies, by government, by law, by privatisation, by money, and by the same factors that affect every society in the world. Tūhoe are not unique in this circumstance, nor are Tūhoe able to hold back the inevitable tide of change that forces all people either to evolve or to become extinct.

The purpose of the chapter was not to belittle any of my fellow Tūhoe kin, or to divide sections of Tūhoe from one and other. Rather this chapter seeks to explore how Tūhoe related to their environment in a traditional context and to discuss this relationship in its present form. I would propose that most Tūhoe believe their relationship to the Tūhoe environment is more profound than it actually is. Furthermore, if we remove the romanticism, clear the mist from the surrounding hills, and ask Tūhoe members to reveal their interaction with their environment openly and honestly, we would see that it is rather limited. Yet I can understand the reluctance to explore these issues, least we be labelled less Tūhoe than our relations. These issues aside, Tūhoe have always had a relationship with Tāne-mahuta and Te Urewera. It is from this environment that Tūhoe emerged and subsequently flourished. While the winds of change have impacted on this bond, there still remain

Tūhoe descendants who maintain this attachment on a regular basis. One must also take into account the unique Tūhoe connection of matemateaone that binds us together as kin to our environment. These bonds are in many ways perpetual and it is through our extended relationships that we connect to our environment and reaffirm our identity. We must not forget our obligation to our traditional environment and how important the preservation of this relationship is for our cultural wellbeing. This belief is best reflected in the Tūhoe proverb, 'E hoki ki ngā maunga kia purea koe e ngā hau o Tāwhirimatea' (Return to your mountains and let your soul be cleansed by the winds of Tāwhirimātea) (Karetu 1991).

Photo 4. The untamed splendour of Te Urewera. In the background stands the Huiarau range as seen from Manawaru in Ruatahuna. Photo: Rangi Mataamua 2008.

Climate change implications for Māori

Lisa Kanawa

Climate change is one of the most debated topics of the millennium. Whether in business, science, policy, economics, land development, politics, or kaitiakitanga, the issue of climate change has infiltrated New Zealand life. Debates rage on the certainty of the science and the accuracy of the data. Debates are even more aggressive on the appropriate mechanisms New Zealanders should implement in response to the issue. Questions continue to be tossed to and fro about whether New Zealand should be a world leader in response to climate change. While these are interesting debates and discussions, literature and research in the climate change space are failing to address in simple terms what climate change may mean for Māori individuals, whānau, hapū, marae and iwi. Few Māori understand the implications of climate change and such knowledge is invaluable if Māori are to move forward on this issue. Their expertise and contribution to the Māori understanding of climate change should be valued by the wider Māori community.

This chapter contributes to the debate on what climate change may mean to Māori. It reinforces that climate change needs to be considered when exploring Māori aspirations. Whether those aspirations are social, economic, environmental or cultural, climate change has the ability to straddle the spectrum. This chapter is not constructed as an expert opinion but offers a Māori view. Information has been collated and deconstructed to find relevance and build a Māori perspective that incorporates the idea of adaptation to climate change and contributes to planning for the future.

Climate change: definitions and regional projections

It is important to get a basic understanding of the difference between weather and climate and how that contributes to our understanding of climate change. Climate is not weather. Weather is the condition of the atmosphere at a particular place and time measured in terms of such things as wind, temperature, humidity, atmospheric pressure, cloudiness, and precipitation (rain, snow, etc.) (USCGCIRO 2009). In most places, weather can change from hour to hour, day to day, and season to season, usually in the short term. By comparison, climate is the average pattern of weather conditions and the extent to which those conditions vary over the long term (USCGCIRO 2009). In taking into consideration weather and climate, when we look at climate change this can be described as "a significant and persistent change in an area's average climate conditions or their extremes" (USCCSP 2009). Therefore, climate change in the context of this chapter is the significant and persistent increase in New Zealand's average surface temperature and the frequency and intensity of extreme weather events that occur because of human activities. Extreme weather events include floods, landslides, droughts, storm surges, heat waves, and fire risks (MFE 2007). There is widespread scientific acceptance that human activities that release 'greenhouse' gases into the atmosphere are altering the earth's climate, which contributes to climate change (MAF 2009). Human emissions of methane and nitrous oxide together contribute almost half as much warming as carbon emissions. Some human activities that contribute to greenhouse gas release are the burning of fossil fuels (coal-fired power stations), emissions from transport, methane from ruminant animals (cows and sheep), electricity generators, and deforestation (as carbon stores are released) (MAF 2009).

In preparation for a changing climate Māori need to know how we may be affected in our rohe so that we can plan for the future. The Ministry for the Environment has compiled generic information by region which is depicted in Figure 1. This illustrates at a high level what the likely climate change impacts will be in New Zealand.

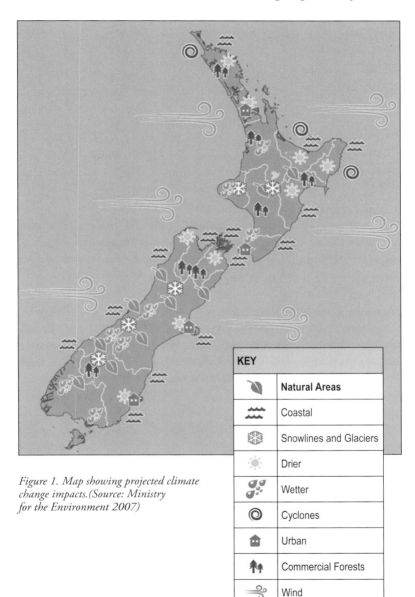

Figure 1. Map showing projected climate change impacts.(Source: Ministry for the Environment 2007)

KEY	
🌿	**Natural Areas**
〰	Coastal
❄	Snowlines and Glaciers
☀	Drier
💧	Wetter
◎	Cyclones
🏠	Urban
🌲	Commercial Forests
🌬	Wind

Regions will be affected in different ways as a result of climate change projections. Over the whole of Aotearoa there will be rising temperatures, increasing average rainfall in the west of the country, decreasing annual average rainfall in Northland (and other areas), reduction in frosts, increasing risk of dry periods or droughts in some eastern areas, increasing frequency of heavy rainfall events, and rising sea level (MfE 2008). In understanding the impacts on our rohe, as kaitiaki, preparation and planning can begin by identifying the potential impacts and the opportunities for adaptation.

Te Ika a Maui, the North Island, could be 3°C warmer over the next 70–100 years, while Te Waipounamu, the South Island, could be warmer by 2.5°C. The following are regional projections.

Te Tai Tokerau

There will be less rainfall in drier periods, increased drought for already drought-prone areas, increased intensity of cyclones (with increased rainfall, wind, waves and storm surges associated with those events), increased sea level rise, increased storm surges, and an increase of coastal erosion (MfE 2008).

Hauraki/Tāmaki Makaurau

Less rainfall in drier periods is expected, increased drought for already drought-prone areas, decreased run-off to rivers, and increased irrigation demand. In the urban environment there will be decreased electricity use in winter (less heating) and increased electricity use in summer (more air-conditioning) (MfE 2008).

Tainui

By 2070 the area could become up to 20% wetter, with more varied rainfall patterns and flooding up to four times more frequent, with increased precipitation, intensity in weather events, flooding for already flood-prone areas, slips, and soil erosion (MfE 2008).

Tauranga Moana /Te Arawa waka/Tūwharetoa

Coastal areas can expect reduced rainfall in drier periods, increased drought for already drought-prone areas, increased intensity of cyclones (with increased rainfall, wind, waves and storm surges associated with those events), a rise in sea level, increased storm surges, and an increase of coastal erosion. There could also be a change in the distribution of species, changes to or loss of habitat and increased pressure from pests, animals and plants. Tongariro National Park and the surrounding ranges and area could experience changes in the lengths and area of glaciers, rises in snow line, and a possible increase of snowfall and avalanches (MfE 2008).

Mataatua/Te Tai Rāwhiti

This area could be up to 20% drier but with more varied rainfall patterns (dry periods interspersed with very heavy rainfall) and flooding could become up to four times more frequent by 2070. The East Coast can expect less rainfall in drier periods, increased drought for already drought-prone areas, increased intensity of cyclones (with an increased rainfall, wind, waves and storm surges associated with those events), and increased sea level rises, storm surges and coastal erosion (MfE 2009).

Hauāuru

This area could be up to 20% wetter with more varied rainfall patterns and flooding that could become up to four times more frequent by 2070. The area could experience an increase of snowfall, precipitation, intensity in weather events, flooding for already flood-prone areas, and increased slips and soil erosion. The coastal areas can expect a rise in sea level, and increases in storm surges and coastal erosion (MfE 2008).

Te Moana o Raukawa/Whanganui ā Tara

The area could be up to 20% wetter, with more varied rainfall patterns and flooding that could become up to four times more frequent by 2070. The area will experience increased precipitation, intensity in weather events, flooding for already flood-prone areas, slips and soil erosion. In the urban environment a decrease in electricity use in winter (less heating) and an increase in electricity use in summer (more-air conditioning) is likely (MfE 2008).

Te Tau Ihu

Most of the region could be up to 10% wetter, while coastal areas could be up to 10% drier. Overall, the rohe is likely to experience varied rainfall patterns and flooding could become up to four times more frequent by 2070. There would be less rainfall in drier periods, increased drought for already drought-prone areas, a rise in sea levels, and increased storm surges and coastal erosion (MfE 2008).

Te Waipounamu/Murihiku

The West Coast could be up to 25% wetter with more varied rainfall patterns and flooding that could be up to four times more frequent. The Southern Alps could experience changes in the length and area of glaciers, a rise in snow line, and a possible increase of snowfall and avalanches. The area should also expect increased precipitation, intensity in weather events, flooding for already flood-prone areas, increased slips and soil erosion, a change in the distribution of species, changes to and loss of habitat and increased pressure from pests, animals and plants. There could also be a rise in sea level, and increased storm surges and coastal erosion. The east coast of Te Waipounamu can expect less rainfall in drier periods and increased drought for already drought-prone areas (MfE 2008).

Throughout Aotearoa there will be significant and noticeable changes in climate and weather patterns that will impact on the daily lives of Māori whānau, hapū and iwi. These changes will include higher rainfall than the present in some areas, which will result in more flooding, soil erosion, higher snowfalls, cyclones, storms, rises in sea level, and the associated impacts of such events. In other areas there will be more droughts, wind, sea surges, and waves. Associated with these changes will be the need to adapt to changes in the design of homes and where they are located. Other impacts will be on home heating and cooling, clothing, the food grown, and on general health and well-being. There will be rohe variations. These will demand that Māori reconsider the ways in which significant events such as flooding and soil erosion impact on farming activities, biodiversity, and the management of risks to people and the environment.

Toitū te whenua, whatungarongaro te tangata – The land remains while the people pass on (Mead and Grove 2001).

As kaitiaki of precious resources, Māori have a responsibility to prepare for future generations. When taking into consideration how Māori can respond to climate change, there is an obligation to be prepared and to focus on future planning. This is tied to our intergenerational obligations; obligations in the sense that Māori need to be aware of future risks and opportunities that may affect future of generations. Adaptation offers the greatest opportunity for Māori.

Adaptation to climate change is about preparedness and reducing the vulnerability for Māori. In particular, adaptation means addressing and responding to the physical impacts arising from:

-   gradual changes in the climate over longer time periods
-   changes in weather extremes, including increased droughts and floods
-   opportunities presented by a changing climate as well as increasing resilience (MAF 2008; Stroomenberg et al. 2008).

Adaptation is not mitigation. Mitigation in terms of climate change is the practice of implementing human measures that help reduce greenhouse gas contributions to the atmosphere. An example of mitigation would be the introduction of New Zealand's Emissions Trading Scheme, specifically targeted at reducing greenhouse gas emissions by using legislation and a price-based mechanism to force change and reduce the effects of an issue.

This idea of adaptation/preparedness is not unusual for Māori and historically we have whakatauki that guide us on the importance of preparation:

-   He tau hāwere tētahi, he tau tukuroa tētahi – One is a season of plenty another is a season of famine. This was a reminder that weather or other factors could have extreme effects on a food source and therefore food must be stored in preparation for years of a restricted supply.
-   Mā te kai ora ai te tinana, e hinga ai te hoariri – By food the body is sustained and the enemy defeated.
-   For warriors to perform well in battle they must be kept well-fed. Today this saying is applied to making adequate preparations for any major undertaking.
-   Ka whaia te wahie mō takurua, ka mahia te kai mō tau – Firewood for the winter is gathered, food for the year is prepared. This is a lesson in being well prepared (Mead and Grove 2001).

Adaptation to climate change will help Māori prepare for a changing environment. The lessons learned by tūpuna are left to us as whakatauki and these can prepare us for adaptation to climate change and the associated changes that are anticipated.

Adaptation and resilience

While there may be scepticism about the science of climate change and the policy decisions being made by the government of the day, climate change is an issue that requires Māori to fulfil an inherent role as kaitiaki, proactively responding to the issues. Māori have an ability to influence all future decision making. A Māori response to adaptation can be by individuals, whānau, marae, hapū, iwi, and various organisations established to manage Māori resources (see Figure 2). This figure illustrates the relationships of different interests of Māori. There is not only interest in climate change from individuals but also from whānau, marae, hapū, iwi, and many Māori organisations. These organisations overlap with whānau, marae, hapū and iwi. Māori organisations also consider the accountability of their decisions to this collective set of interests. What the figure also depicts is that due to our diverse interests it is likely that our responses to climate change will also reflect that diversity, and therefore a 'one size fits all approach' will not be suitable.

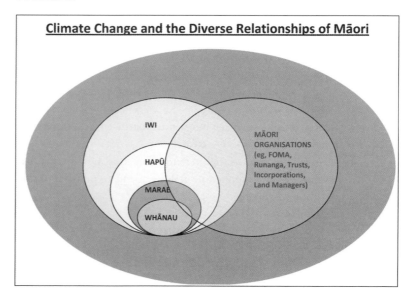

Figure 2. Diagram outlining the diverse relationships of Māori in relation to climate change.

Adaptation to climate change projections is important for our resilience as Māori. Resilience has three defining characteristics: the amount of change a system can undergo while maintaining its functions and structures; the degree of self-organisation; the capacity for adaptation and learning (Milestad 2003). Climate change has the potential to disrupt our systems and lower our capacity to absorb change, so it is important that Māori consider adaptation as a way of maintaining resilience. The adaptation ideas below are intended to be cues to trigger thinking of what can be done by Māori to prepare for a changing climate and moving out of reactive mode to a proactive approach to a future of adaptation to climate change.

Marae and papakainga

Marae and papakainga located in the coastal regions that are likely to experience rises in sea level, need to consider options to protect their buildings and communities from the potential impacts of rising sea levels and variations in climate. Relocation may be an option for those marae and papakainga located not only in coastal regions, but also on flood prone areas and/or those areas that have a high risk of erosion. The spiritual and whakapapa links Māori have with ancestral land and buildings will make this process challenging and as such needs to be discussed at whānau and hapū level to identity appropriate tikanga that will be used, particularly if there is a high risk to whānau. Retrofitting marae and homes with better insulation to deal with changing temperatures, thinking about the types of building materials used; considering the projected changes in climate, are all opportunities to be explored.

Land use

A general adaptation will be required from farmers and growers, considering the projections in climate change across Aotearoa. Those likely to experience warmer weather and droughts on farms need to consider the following: collecting rainwater in dry periods for crop irrigation and drinking water for livestock; improving soil structure to increase water uptake and reduce erosion by adding organic matter; altering irrigation systems for efficiency and repairing any leaks; if possible, spraying crops at night to reduce evapotranspiration; introducing drought-resistant varieties of crops or alternative livestock breeds; and applying manure or compost to improve soil water availability. All these are adaptation options for drier periods (Farming Futures 2009).

For extreme weather events the following adaptations will need to be considered: planting shelter belts to protect crops and livestock; ensuring buildings are maintained and prepared for stormy weather; adjusting growing practices to take account of soil erosion events; improving field drainage and soil water retention; promoting and undertaking good soil management; reducing run-off by planting riparian margins; and considering increasing investment in infrastructure to prepare for more intense weather events (Farming Futures 2009).

For flooding events landowners could improve drainage capacity by digging drainage ditches where appropriate and collecting excess rainwater for use in drought periods (Farming Futures 2009).

Adaptation means developing plans for farms that are flexible and optimise the current land-use options but also take into account the future projections of climate change. Planning for the future of farming is important for the sustainability of whānau and, at a collective level, the marae, hapū or iwi.

Taonga species

With changing climate conditions, the habitat of taonga species will also change. For example, those areas that are likely to experience droughts and drier periods need to consider the effect this type of condition will have on taonga species that are suited to wetter environments. Pest management may also become an issue. Climate change may threaten biodiversity and affect ecosystems. Species that are already under threat or at the limit of their climatic range may not be able to survive. New diseases and pests may take hold. Tropical pests and tropical diseases like malaria may become established in areas where they currently do not exist (Environment Waikato 2009). Therefore, continual vigilance with pest management will be important for the protection and enhancement of taonga species.

Maintaining kaupapa Māori within adaptation

While undertaking environmental work with whānau and hapū in Te Tai Tokerau, I was constantly reminded by kuia and kaumātua that, '…this is not how the fishing used to be…', '… this is not how the environment use to be…', '…we don't get that kind of kai here anymore…'. These comments are occurring throughout Aotearoa. However, Māori have always adapted to the environment, adapted practices to suit conditions, and adapted to the ever-changing landscape created by development and other external pressures. Māori may recognise that twentieth century economic development, including various farming, fishing and forestry practices, have contributed to environmental degradation. However, the impending climate changes associated with global warming have encouraged Māori to reconsider the role of kaitiaki and lessons of tupuna that may guide a Māori response.

Adaptation incorporates tikanga and enhances identity as Māori, while maintaining the teachings and lessons of the past. It also provides an opportunity to express mātauranga Māori as a way of building capability to respond in a meaningful way to climate change. Anecdotal historical accounts of weather, climate, and environmental indicators (NIWA 2008) can be used as a platform for decision making into the future. These anecdotal accounts and evidence are bases for understanding of the past, the present and the future. They will be starting points for a Māori adaptation approach. Developing a framework that incorporates an opportunity for a Māori approach to adaptation could be simple or complicated depending on the interests and the complexity of accountability structures. A plan for adaptation is no different from any other type of planning process that prepares groups for all possible future scenarios. This highlights the tools Māori have to adapt to climate change and to promote resilience in communities. This idea of adaptation is not new to Māori and has in the past been embraced to create new paths.

Adaptation is an opportunity for Māori to engage in climate change debates, to be proactive in future planning for climate change, and to provide a sustainable future for future generations.

WAI MĀORI

The death of the Manawatū River

Malcolm Mulholland [1]

Ko Manawatū te awa o te ora, ko Manawapouri te awa o te mate.

Photo 1. Lisa Christiansen and child at the "Save our river march", October, 2006.

Ko Manawatū te awa,
Ko Rangitāne te tangata!
Nāna ko Kopuparapara,
Nāna ko Tokatumoana,
Nāna ko Te Puehu,
Nāna ko Te Aweawe,
Nāna ko Maiao,
Nāna ko Wharekohu,
Nāna ko Moeteao,
Nāna ko Mahangatikaro,
Ka puta ko Ngāti Moe, ko au anō hoki tēnei,
Tihei mauri ora!

Introduction

This chapter provides a historical overview of the systematic failure of councils to protect the Manawatū river from being polluted by both regional councils and industries that border the main waterway of the Manawatū region. The chapter offers a brief overview of Māori history regarding the river, the polluting of the river by the various authorities and industries, the effects of pollution on the river, Māori concerns regarding the pollution, and the reaction of the regional authority in addressing the pollution of the river.

Much of the debate surrounding the pollution of the Manawatū river relates to how much pollution is caused by certain industries. As Horizons Regional Council *Managing our Environment* pamphlet (2006), states, 'Climate, soil, geography and land cover can influence the water quality in rivers, as well as damage that an urban population can cause through waste disposal and urban development. Mostly however, poor water quality is a result of our agricultural practices'.

From Horizons' estimations, point source discharges into the Manawatū river causes only 4% of the pollution experienced by the river. This figure has been disputed, with some scientists arguing that pollution from industry accounts for 20% of the pollution. Regardless of what pollution industry causes to any river, any reduction in the pollution of rivers should be the aim of Regional Council.

The state of the Manawatū river was summarised by Horizons Regional Council in their State of the Environment Report of the Manawatu-Wanganui Region (2005). Of the four categories used to assess the health of rivers referred to the report, the Manawatū was recorded as being in poor health regarding suitability for contact recreation, very poor regarding turbidity, and the main issue confronting the health of the river in which it was registered as being very poor again was nutrient enrichment. The following is a definition of each category (Horizons Regional Council: 26–27, 29):

1. Suitability for Contact Recreation: Suitability is assessed via the presence of elevated concentrations of pathogens from human and animal faecal matter. The matter can enter the freshwater environment from urban and rural run-off or from the discharge of untreated or poorly treated sewage, agricultural or industrial waste.

2. Nutrient Enrichment: Being too nutrient-rich causes algae and weed to grow on the surface of the river substrate. This can be caused from the discharge of treated wastewater and run-off from agricultural land.

3. Turbidity: High turbidity results in low water clarity and large amounts of sediment suspended in the water, which in turn adversely affects the aquatic life in the water. This is caused by land erosion, run-off from agricultural land, and the discharge of stormwater and industrial wastewater.

The approach from both central and regional government to rectifying poor farming practices that see stock urine and faeces, along with pesticides, go into adjoining bodies of water, was the 2003 Dairying and Clean Stream Accord, which was agreed to by Fonterra, the Minister for the Environment, the Minister of Agriculture, and regional councils across the country. The Accord seeks to achieve healthy water, including streams, rivers, ground water and wetlands, in dairying areas.

Despite the best intentions by authorities and the farming industry, Accord results have been poor, as Horizons note 'However, the results of these voluntary approaches are not being seen as lower nutrient or faecal levels in the rivers and further improvements are needed' (Horizons Regional Council 2007: 75).

Traditional history

The relationship between Rangitāne, Ngāti Raukawa, Muaūpoko and the Manawatū river is much like other relationships between iwi and their main waterway; they are deeply connected through hundreds of years of interaction. Ngāti Kahungunu and Rangitāne claim mana whenua status over the upper reaches of the Manawatū river, whilst Rangitāne also have this status over the central section of the river. Ngāti Raukawa and Ngāti Kauwhata assert their claim to the river from Rangiotū to the mouth of the river. Muaūpoko and Ngāti Raukawa are also affected by the health of the Manawatū, as their kaimoana beds, which lie at Hōkio Beach, receive the pollution emitted from the river.

Rangitāne marae are situated at Rangiotu, the marae being Te Rangimārie and servicing the needs of Ngāti Rangitepaea and Ngāti Hineaute, and at Palmerston North with the Te Hotu Manawa o Rangitāne o Manawatū marae providing a facility for the same two hapū that are affiliated to Rangiotu, as well as to Te Rangiaranaki, Ngāti Mairehau and Te Rangitauira. For Ngāti Raukawa, Poutū marae stands at Shannon under the auspices of the hapū, Ngāti Whakatere. Further west on the northern banks of the Manawatū at Foxton, stand Motuiti and Paranui marae, which, combined, house the hapū of Ngāti Te Au, Ngāti Rākau Paewai, and Ngāti Tūranga. Ngāti Takihiku, Ngāti Ngārongo and Ngāti Parereukawa all maintain ahi kā on the southern side of the Manawatū from Porokaiaia to Kōpūtaroa.

As McEwen (1986: 1) explains in the tribal history, Rangitāne, the creation of the Manawatū river is due to the exploits of a massive tōtara tree from the Puketoi range, in Hawke's Bay. The tree, under the influence of a supernatural being named Okatia, headed towards the Manawatū region, forging a deep channel, only to be stopped by the ranges of Ruahine and Tararua. On reaching the obstacle, the tree turned west and created what is now known as the Manawatū Gorge. From there, it crossed the plains and reached the sea. The path of the tree is what we now know to be the Manawatū river – a river that spans 182 kilometres. The naming of the Manawatū river is attributed to the famed Māori tohunga and explorer, Haupipi-a-Nanaia. The wife of Haupipi-a-Nanaia, Wairaka, eloped with another man by the name of Weku. Haupipi-a-Nanaia chased the couple down the West Coast of the lower North Island, eventually ending his journey at Lake Wairarapa. Most prominent Māori place names in this region are attributable to Haupipi-a-Nanaia. When he arrived at what we now know as the Manawatū river, he stood in awe of the waterway that was so deep, wide and cold, and the site made his breath 'stand still' (McEwan 1986: 16).

As of 1855 it was estimated that 3400 Māori resided along the banks of the Manawatū river (Hannigan 1982). The table below records the pā sites situated along the banks of the Manawatū river and their populations in 1874:

Hokowhitu	18	Te Wi	6
Te Motuiti	35	Te Awapuni	36
Matakarapa	56	Tiakitahuna	19
Moutoa	47	Ngāwhakaraue	22
Te Karaka	51	Puketotara	12

Table 1. Pā sites situated along the banks of the Manawatū river and their populations in 1874.

Apart from local Māori using the river for cultural and social purposes, the main use of the Manawatū river centres on the collection of tuna (eel). As Pātaka Moore stated (2006: 3)

The Manawatū river was so rich with quality eel that it was not uncommon for entire hapū to relocate their people to areas closer to the Manawatū river in the fishing season for no other reason than to fish for eel...Eel became the staple diet for many Māori in the Horowhenua and Manawatū, and their reliance on this food source made it devastating when the number of eels began to dwindle.

Pollution of the Manawatū river

Pollution of the Manawatū river first occurred with the disposal of untreated sewage from the residents of Palmerston North in 1890 (White 2007). Despite instant protests being lodged by communities, such as Foxton, which were affected further downstream, it took the threat of bubonic plague for Palmerston North authorities to act and treat the waste of their community in 1905.

After 50 years of expansion of Palmerston North, the Palmerston North City Council recognised that the sewage treatment disposal process was outdated and in need of urgent attention. A study was undertaken by the City Engineer in 1958 to determine the level of pollution in the Manawatū river and thus the cost of a new treatment plant could be justified (White 2007). Despite the results being unsatisfactory by today's standards, a new treatment plant would not be opened until 1968 to cater for the needs of 100 000 people.

In 1957 a report was compiled by central government's Health and Marine departments, as concern mounted over sewage disposal from PNCC and Feilding (Ministry of Works 1957). According to the report, the pollution of the Manawatū river was being caused by sewage and waste disposal from Palmerston North, Feilding, Foxton, Linton Military Camp, and Mangahao Village; by the tipping of rubbish at Palmerston North and Mangahao Village; by meat wastes from freezing works at Feilding and Longburn and an abattoir at Feilding; by wastes from a wool scour and boiling down works at Feilding; and by dairy factory waste.

Some excerpts of the report follow:

Gasworks: The wastes include 1000 gallons daily of ammonia water. Ninety percent of this is disposed of in a soak pit; the remainder, along with floor washings and clean condenser water, is culverted beneath the highway to the open roadside drain, which it follows for a few yards, and is then piped across fields to the Manawatu river 1957: 29).

Kairanga Co-op Dairy Co. Ltd: '...discharges its wastes into a natural lagoon in the bed of the Manawatu river. When the river is in flood the lagoon is submerged and thus the discharge is then made directly into the river. The factory produces butter and casein, sending to waste 8 or 9 thousand gallons of casein whey plus floor and can washings to total from 30 to 40 thousand gallons daily' (1957: 31).

Tokomaru Dairy Co: 'The whey is piped to two pig farms and the wash is a grease trap in the washwater pipe. The pipe discharges in the grass at the edge of the old course of the river...The liquid trickles through the grass for about 100 yards before falling into the river' (1957: 34).

Results from all the testing stations along the Manawatū deemed the river to have an abundant supply of green algae and sewage fungus, bacteria originating from faecal matter, and a consistently high count of dissolved oxygen. As a result of these findings the report recommended that people should be banned from swimming in the Oroua river as it was being used as an open sewer, and that swimming at Foxton Beach should also cease. The response from the PNCC was that the report greatly exaggerated the situation and the various local authorities did not meet to discuss the issues raised (The Times, 1958 in PNCC, 1/5/5, Ian Matheson Archives).

In July 1977 the Manawatū Catchment Board wrote to the City Engineer of the PNCC, informing him that the quality of river water was not satisfactory in terms of the Water, Soil and Conservation Act (Hannigan 1982). In the same year, the findings of the most comprehensive survey to date regarding the pollution of the Manawatū river, The Manawatū Catchment Board's Report on Water Quality Management in the Manawatū river below Palmerston North was released. The report concluded that the river was badly polluted and in dire need of being restored to full health. It noted that the Biochemical Oxygen Demand needed to be reduced by the three biggest polluters of the Manawatū river; by three quarters by the PNCC and by one sixth by the Manawatū Dairy Company and the Longburn Freezing Works. The river was of particular concern during the lower flow months of summer. The lowest level of oxygen recorded was 5.7 parts per million; at the time, the lowest level permitted was five parts per million. The maximum limit for safe swimming is 200 faecal coliforms per 100 ml of water; again, it was noted that in the river below the discharges, between 33 000 and 700 000 faecal coliforms per 100 ml of water were being reported.

The author of the report and the Board's Water Resources Manager, K.J. Currie, concluded that the river was not grossly polluted yet ('Board has Big Plans' 1977). He did, however, report that certain stretches of water were unsafe to swim in, that no water in the Manawatū river was fit for consumption, that trout and other species of fish were "stressed" (adding that there were worrying signs that should the level of ammonia rise more fish would die), and that a sewage fungus did appear from time to time at the river. The following year, Board members viewed the pollution for themselves during a jet boat trip through the river" 'The odour could be smelt from the time the six-boat fleet rounded the Opiki bend. By the time they reached the city the smell was overpowering, the river little more than an open sewer' (Stewart 1978:3). The flotilla also had to make some unscheduled stops, as green slime clogged their jet intakes.

In 1977 the Wellington Acclimatisation Society wrote to the Manawatū Regional Water Board regarding the discharge of treated sewage, industrial effluent, and stormwater into the Manawatū river (PNCC 1/5/5, Ian Matheson Archives), stating:

1. That the pollution is having severe effects on aquatic invertebrate fauna that form a major part of the diet of trout
2. That the alteration of pH, the reduction in dissolved oxygen, and the increase in ammonia levels is causing stress on the aquatic life of the river
3. That sewage fungus lining ten kilometres of the river bank is ugly and causes an unpleasant smell (PNCC: 1/5/5).

In January 1978 a major fish kill occurred in the Manawatū river (Manawatu Regional Water Board 1978). A fish kill occurs when there is not enough oxygen in water for fish to survive. The report noted that the condition of the river bed was poor with much sewage fungus growth, that the water smelt foul, and that "scum" (1978: 1) was resting upon the banks of the river. On one day of the fish kill over 100 trout were dead, as were hundreds of bullies and galaxids, and numerous freshwater shrimp and red chironomids. It was reported:

> *One trout was observed in a moribund state exhibiting the*
> *following symptoms; head directed to the river bed, disorientated,*
> *difficulties in maintaining depth, i.e. floating to the surface tail*
> *first, appeared to have spinal spasms, the fish appeared to alternate*
> *between periods of lethargy and violent activity. When the trout*
> *finally died its mouth and opercula were gaping and mud had*
> *collected in its mouth from its moribund activity (1978: 2).*

The fish kill of 1978 was attributed to polluted water fauna (sewage fungus). Another fish kill took place in February, 1984. It was attributed to a combination of factors, the only non-natural factor being a number of industries dumping their effluent. Although Borthwick-CWS were later exonerated from blame, authorities were angered to learn that the company had exceeded its correct discharge level at Longburn. The Wellington

Acclimatisation Society investigated the possibility of prosecuting the company under the Fisheries Act.

To rectify concerns about the pollution of the Manawatū river, the Manawatu Catchment Board introduced a new scheme (Watson 1980:2). What the scheme amounted to was closer monitoring of the river flow and informing the three major dischargers of the river's ability to process effluent. The rule followed was that if the flow was low, effluent would have to be treated; when the flow was high, less care was taken in treating the discharges.

Despite the new regulating process of pollution in the Manawatū river, only 3 months after it was announced by the Board, a Manawatu Catchment Board Water Resources Investigator, Phil Spencer, resigned, as a result of the Board's lack of action in not prosecuting those who openly polluted the region's waterways (Watson 1980:3). After citing several cases of pollution around the district, Spencer (1980) stated that the "big three polluters" were still offloading untreated effluent into a short stretch of the Manawatū river at the rate of 30 million tonnes a year.

It was not until 1985 that secondary treatment of Palmerston North sewage began (White 2007). Aerated lagoons, however, did not deal adequately with the issue of stormwater infiltrating the sewerage system, thus leading to raw sewage escaping onto city streets. A temporary and unsatisfactory solution was found by the City Council – by-passing the treatment plant and dumping sewage straight into the river. This occurred until the treatment plant was upgraded and the old pipes were replaced.

In 1993 the PNCC applied to the Manawatu-Wanganui Regional Council to enable them to discharge from two city sewerage lines at times of overloading during flood peaks ('Staff Reporter 1993:2). Despite protests from the Chairman of the Manawatu River Pollution Free Group, George Paton, that it was illegal to allow raw sewage to be disposed of in open water, the permit was allowed.

The most recent example of poor management of the Manawatū river regarding sewage was in October, 2007, when the Horowhenua District Council allowed between 10 000 and 100 000 litres of raw sewage into the Mangaone Stream, which feeds into the Manawatū river (Chapman 2007:1). Containing such items as used sanitary pads and condoms, whitebaiters became alarmed as the Manawatū was being fished for the delicacy during the discharge. At present, sewage from Dannevirke, Woodville, Pahiatua, Eketāhuna, Ashhurst, Foxton, Longburn and Feilding accompanies that of Palmerston North City. The permits granted to the various local authorities to discharge sewage into the Manawatū total an allowed maximum of 74 870 cubic metres per day.

Another point of concern for some members of the Manawatū community is the allegation of leachate discharging from the Awapuni Landfill to the Manawatū river via the Mangaone Stream.

In 1999, coal tar, one of three types of creosote that can cause cancer, was removed from central Palmerston North and disposed of at the Awapuni Landfill (Nash 2002:1). Some 100 cubic metres were first uplifted from the current Spotlight site, with the remaining coal tar being mixed with lime and sawdust and then put into a capsule at the landfill. The coal tar was sealed in heavy plastic, against the advice of the Regional Council. Those concerned are worried about the 100 cubic metres that were not treated.

Concerns were raised by a neighbour of the landfill, Tony Kaye, after his dog drank water from the Mangaone Stream and became temporarily paralysed (Nash 2002:3). In reply, former Chief Executive of the PNCC, Paul Wylie, stated that Council investigations failed to find any evidence of the leachate (Nash 2002:3). The Council also threatened to sue Kaye and Tex Schwass of New Plymouth, if they continued to make public allegations of the leachate (Nash 2002:3). Schwass is the owner of a chemical recycling business and was first involved with coal tar from Palmerston North when he was called to identify the substance when it was first discovered.

In October, 2006, the TV3 show Campbell Live investigated the Schwass claims, showing filming conducted by the pair of a black substance leaking from the Awapuni Landfill into the Mangaone Stream (Wilson 2007:5). The substance was sent to Chemical Engineer Wolfgang Janata who successfully tested for coal tar. The PNCC took 13 samples of groundwater bores from the Mangaone Stream, the Manawatū river and the stormwater infiltration pond and had them tested by Wellington-based consultants Tonkin & Taylor (Wilson 2007:5). While the results were deemed by the consultants not to contain traces of coal tar, they did find toluene and phenolics, contaminants associated with coal tar. Tonkin & Taylor's senior scientist attributed the find to other materials disposed of at the site. Janata disagreed that the results did not prove that the coal tar was leaching (Wilson 2007:5).

During the sitting of the Hearing Committee to determine whether or not to allow the PNCC to extend the current permit granted regarding the Awapuni Landfill in 1994 (Decision of the Hearing Committee, Application by the Palmerston North City Council for Resource Consents relating to Awapuni Landfill 1994), and despite some of the consequences of the leachate being noted in the report, the permit was granted to the PNCC.

In October, 2007, the *Manawatu Standard* reported that the PNCC had been fined \$750 by Horizons Regional Council for spilling Awapuni landfill leachate into a drain that discharges into the Manawatū river (Chapman 2007:1). Tests undertaken stated that the leachate was not coal tar, but the toxins being released from the leachate were not any better than the properties contained within coal tar.

Killing the river: The effects of pollution

Science and Ecology Lecturer at Massey University, Dr Mike Joy,[2] has been the most vocal critic of the management of the Manawatū river. Prompted by the decision of Horizons Regional Council to allow Fonterra to discharge their waste into the Manawatū river, in 2006 Joy wrote an open letter to the then Environment Minister, David Benson-Pope, the Parliamentary Commissioner for the Environment, and local Members of Parliament. Signed by a collection of scientists, academics and environmentalists, Joy alleged:

1. That the biggest dischargers into the river have all failed to comply with at least one of their five resource consent conditions for more than the last five years. There have been no prosecutions over this matter since 1998.

2. That eight of the ten State of the Environment sites in the river's catchment have shown significant increases in nitrogen and dissolved reactive phosphorus for more than the past ten years.

3. That the migratory native fish species shortjaw kokopu, banded kokopu, koaro and redfin bully are no longer found in approximately two-thirds of the Manawatu catchment (2006).

Reaction to the letter from Horizons was provided by their Science Manager, Dr Royguard. He stated that the letter raised 'valid issues' and that nutrient pollution had increased over the past ten years, while the number of discharges had dropped over the same period of time (Cummings 2006:1). Concerns over the Regional Council not prosecuting industry and local authorities over mismanagement of the Manawatū river are nothing new.

Two cases in 1991 highlighted this fact: the burst of 34 000 cubic metres at the Linton Oxidation Pond and the overflow of sewage onto Palmerston North streets (Manawatu Evening Standard, 26/7/91 in PNCC, 1/5/5, Ian Matheson Archives). No prosecutions were laid by the Council.

Fonterrorism: The community fights back

On 14 October 2006, a number of concerned Māori individuals formed 'Te Roopu Huirapa' to voice their concerns about the permit granted by Horizons Regional Council to Fonterra Cooperative Group (Decision of the Hearing Committee 2006), to allow the company to discharge their 8500 cubic metres of effluent per day, between May and October, into the Manawatū river for 15 years. The effluent was divided into two categories – low and high strength. The low-strength effluent consists of condensate and cooling water, the high-strength effluent consists of wash water and flushing water used to wash Fonterra's machinery.

Photo 2. Some of the 500 people marching through Palmerston North over Horizon Regional Council's decision to allow Fonterra to dump their waste into the Manawatū river, October, 2002.

Approximately 500 people from the community attended, marching through the central business district of Palmerston North under the banner of 'Save Our river'. The march issued an ultimatum to Horizons Regional Council not to allow any more businesses to dump their waste into the Manawatū river from 2010 onwards.

The decision to allow Fonterra to dispose of waste into the Manawatū was met with widespread disapproval. Organisations that lodged submissions against the consent included the Department of Conservation, Wellington Fish and Game New Zealand, Foxton Community Board and Horowhenua District Council, the Manawatu Estuary Trust, Muaūpoko Tribal Authority, the Public Health Unit, MidCentral Health, the Horowhenua Branch of the Royal Forest and Bird Protection Society of New Zealand, and the Waitarere Environment Care Group (Decision of the Hearing Committee).

On appeal to the Environment Court, mediation resulted in an agreement being reached between the Waitarere Environment Care Group and Fonterra (Terms of Agreement 2007). Fonterra was to reduce the amount being disposed, as well as improve the treatment process of their effluent.

The Chair of the Consents Committee for Horizons Regional Council, Annette Main, considering the committee's decision, reflected that the river was not in a pristine state and 'so when you add to that the effects of the discharge by Fonterra, it's no more than minor. Personally, I don't believe it's good for any river to have these kinds of discharges' (Cummings 2006:1). The PNCC Water and Waste Services Manager, Chris Pepper, asked by the Manawatu Standard to comment on the decision, stated, 'When you're looking at taking your opportunities to increase water quality over time, it doesn't really fit with that, does it?' (Cummings 2006:1). The following week, former PNCC Chief Executive Paul Wylie phoned Horizons, apologising for what he labelled 'miscommunication' in the article (Cummings 2006:1). Wylie then distanced the PNCC from the comments made by Pepper, saying that the PNCC had never had a stance regarding the discharge from Fonterra.

Māori concerns ignored: Mauri is degraded

Hapū opposed to the Fonterra discharge included Ngāti Te Au, Ngāti Manomano, and Ngāti Pareraukawa; iwi opposed to the discharge included Rangitāne, Ngāti Raukawa, and Muaūpoko (Decision of the Hearing Committee 2006). Almost all Māori opponents highlighted the lack of consultation with Horizons Regional Council over the consent hearing process.

The main concern registered by Tanenuiārangi Manawatū Inc. (TMI) was that the mauri of the Manawatū river would be adversely affected by the discharge (Decision of the Hearing Committee 2006). The submission made by Pātaka Moore (2006), on behalf of Ngāti Pareraukawa and Ngāti Raukawa, encapsulated what many Māori who have an association with the Manawatū believe. He began by explaining the relationship he and his hapū have with the river; that the river fulfils social, recreational, cultural and spiritual needs. Moore paid particular attention to the fish stocks of the river, claiming that the Fonterra discharge would result in many species declining in numbers. He concluded his submission by citing the pollution of the Manawatū river as a breach of Article Two of the Treaty of Waitangi.

Kaumātua from Ngāti Raukawa voiced their concerns, recalling earlier years when they were able to swim in the Manawatū river and catch plenty of fish as opposed to today where they have noticed a steady decline in the river's resources. Alex Barnes of Hāpai Whenua Consultants cited the Hauraki Iwi Environmental Plan definition of Mauri as being '...the life energy or unique life essence that gives being and form to all things in the universe. Tikanga had emerged around this duty bringing with it an intimate knowledge and understanding of our local environments and a set of rules that guide our way of life, both spiritual and secular' (Barnes 2006). In response to claims that the Fonterra discharge would affect the mauri of the Manawatū river, councillors sitting on the Hearing Committee questioned iwi and hapū representatives about how best to negate the effect on mauri, while still allowing the discharge to continue.

Commissioner van Voorthuysen questioned Barnes as to whether or not he had ever experienced any tangible form of mauri (Decision of the Hearing Committee 2006). Van Voorthuysen continued by asking the Consents Manager of Horizons, Sarah Gardiner, whether or not Horizons had any rules for discharges that degrade the river and the mauri of that river, to which she responded they did not. Gardiner, in tabling her report, also argued that she believed Fonterra's discharge was no more significant regarding the status of mauri. The Committee's ruling on the effect the Fonterra discharge would have on mauri, stated that it could be managed as per the report submitted by TMI. The TMI report recommended:

1. that the low and high strength effluent be separated
2. avoiding discharging high strength effluent during the summer months
3. avoiding discharging high strength effluent during low river flows
4. setting a maximum limit for the high strength effluent discharge
5. basing allowable discharges on contaminant mass loadings (Decision of the Hearing Committee 2006).

Despite the committee recognising that the mauri of the Manawatū river is degraded and that the Fonterra discharge would add to the degradation of the mauri, they granted the permit.

New Zealand Pharmaceuticals (NZP) were granted a consent by Horizons Regional Council in January 2008, to discharge 240 cubic metres per day of process wastewater, 3200 cubic metres per day of stormwater, and 2400 cubic metres per day of cooling water into the Manawatū river for 25 years (Decision of the Hearing Committee 2008). NZP was initially founded to extract and purify biochemicals from by-products of the NZ meat processing industry. Recently, NZP have focussed on biochemicals and extracts from plant materials. The quality of the discharge is dependant on which processes are producing waste at any given time.

Māori concerns were also tabled. These included a lack of consultation, the lack of a Cultural Impact Assessment (CIA), the absence of a culturally appropriate outlet structure, and the potentially adverse effects on the mauri of the water. During the consent process it was stated that a CIA had been written by Tānenuiārangi Manawatū Incorporated and was discussed at a hearing from which the public was excluded (Decision of the Hearing Committee 2008).

The result from the private hearing was that a Memorandum of Understanding was to be reached between TMI and NZP. This occurred, despite pollution affecting Muaūpoko and Ngāti Raukawa further downstream. NZP also called the evidence of Buddy Mikaere who argued that cultural issues had been addressed and that due to the improvements made concerning the discharge of waste from NZP the mauri of the river would not deteriorate (Decision of the Hearing Committee 2008).

The consent was immediately appealed by the Water & Care Environmental Association (2008). At the heart of the appeal, WECA argued that Horizons had not properly considered the conditions imposed on the permit, as the effects of the wastewater and cooling water would damage the Manawatū river and that alternatives, such as land disposal, were not considered.

The report submitted by Good Earth Matters Consulting Ltd (2007: 4), on behalf of NZP during the consent process, stated, 'NZP's longstanding reputation as a reliable producer of high quality products is further strengthened by the international recognition of New Zealand's "clean green" and "disease free" status'.

Horizons Regional Council: The financial cost comes first

In 1995 when discussions were first held regarding how best to dispose of sewage from Palmerston North City, the two major arguments were articulated by the City Council against looking at alternatives to the current sewerage system. The first was cost. The second avoided blame regarding pollution of the river by attributing responsibility to run-off from farms surrounding the Manawatū river. Four years would pass before another Regional Council report, Measures of a Changing Landscape, would highlight the same issues of river pollution through the combined effects of farm run-off and the city's wastewater outfall (White 2007).

As time neared the expiry of the city's consent to discharge waste into the Manawatū river in 2006, the Council embarked, in 1997, on a project called 'WasteWater 2006' (White 2007). Subsequently a Wastewater Community Liaison Group took seven options regarding sewage disposal to the community: two involved land options for 'all seasons'; three involved part Manawatū river, part land options; and two involved disposal solely to the Manawatū river. The Wastewater Group recommended river discharge, as 52% of returns from the brochure outlining options to the community favoured this approach, compared with 48% who preferred a land-based option. The group was at pains to note that their decision would not be met with approval from Foxton and other downstream groups who were more affected by sewage disposed of at Palmerston North. The recommendation led to the Council agreeing to a $13 million river discharge system, including ultraviolet light disinfection and phosphorus removal (White 2007).

A collective of seven marae placed along various points of downstream Manawatū was formed (White 2007). "Te Ohu marae working party", made up of representatives from the marae of Te Rangimārie, Motuiti, Poutū, Aorangi, Paranui, Kererū and Kauwhata remained opposed to the discharge of wastewater going into the Manawatū river. Some of their fears were alleviated, however, as the Council agreed to the wastewater also having to travel through a new wetland and then through a rock land passage. While neither system has any scientific benefit to the discharge of wastewater, it was agreed that the marae would be more accepting of the discharge as Papatūānuku plays a role in cleansing wastewater.

The One Plan: A better management system?

The 'One Plan' is the policy document formulated by Horizons Regional Council by which they will manage the region's resources. At present in draft form, the plan is scheduled to be adopted by Council at the end of 2009.

In the document, Horizons have highlighted 'The Big Four' issues confronting the area, one of which is Surface Water Quality Degradation. Under this heading, the Council note that run-off from nutrients, and sediment and bacteria from farms, are now the largest threats to water quality in the Region, with some waterways considered risky for swimming or gathering food. The Manawatū river is used as an example of the problem.

To address the issue, the Council suggest (2007: 12):
1. Set water quality standards for ecosystem, recreational, cultural and water-use values identified for catchment water management zones.
2. Identify water management zones most affected by nutrient enrichment and/or bacterial contamination.
3. Use a mixture of persuasion, advice and rules to manage agricultural run-off in these water management zones.

A separate section of the 'One Plan' dedicates itself to point source discharges, proposing that such emissions conform to the strategies outlined under the 'Surface Water Quality Management' section. Water quality issues are raised again in the 'Te Ao Māori; section. These concerns include (2007: 40):

1. Management of water quality and quantity throughout the Region does not provide for the special qualities significant to Māori.
2. Hazardous substances and nitrate run-off need to be better managed to avoid contaminants entering waterways.
3. Access and availability to clean water to exercise cultural activities such as food gathering and baptismal rituals have diminished.
4. Sewage disposed to waterways, in treated form or otherwise, is culturally abhorrent. Land-based treatment is preferred.

Regarding the protection of mauri of waterbodies, the Regional Council propose to involve iwi and hapū in resource management and restrict and suspend water takes at times of low river flow.

Conclusion

It remains to be seen how effective the new management regime will be under the 'One Plan', as iwi and hapū concerns were dismissed by Horizons Regional Council under the provisions of the Resource Management Act. What is obvious about the health of the Manawatū river is that one problem has been substituted for another.

Whereas during the late 1970s/early 1980s the river lacked oxygen, the river is now nutrient-rich, leading to the growth of algae that suffocate aquatic life. Despite strong objections to the discharge of waste to the river by both the local community and tangata whenua, it still remains to be seen if the latest efforts by Horizon Regional Council to clean the river are genuine. As of August, 2006, Horizons Regional Council had allowed 194 discharges to be made into the Manawatū river (Cummings 2006:1).

END NOTES

[1]Malcolm Mulholland is from Ngāti Kahungunu. He was the leader of Te Roopu Huirapa, a group that has been involved in raising awareness regarding the health of the Manawatū river. The author would like to acknowledge the assistance of Barry Gilliand of Horizons Regional Council, Michael Cummings of the Manawatū Standard, Pātaka Moore, and Dr Rangi Mataamua. The author stresses that the opinions expressed within this chapter may not reflect those of the people who offered assistance.

[2]Dr Joy is an expert on native fish and freshwater bioassessment. Since 1999 Joy has sampled over 400 fish and invertebrate communities from freshwater sites in the Manawatū Region, including the Manawatū river.

Ngā Wai Pounamu: the state of South Island waterways, a Ngāi Tahu perspective

Craig Pauling

Te Whakatūwheratanga introduction

Water is a taonga of the utmost importance to Māori. For Ngāi Tahu, water plays a central role in the culture, traditions and ongoing identity of the iwi, particularly in relation to the custom of mahinga kai. As Tau et al. (1990: 4–12) explain "water is held in the highest esteem because the welfare of the life that it contains determines the welfare of the people reliant on those resources". Water is therefore not only a source of food and physical sustenance, but a source of mana and spiritual sustenance, being intricately linked to, and reflective of, the well-being of tangata whenua.

Through the customary gathering of food and other resources from rivers, lakes and estuaries, Māori have historically collected, and continue to collect, a range of valuable environmental information in relation to waterway health and well-being. This information, however, has not traditionally been recorded in a form that is readily accessible, useable or defensible in a modern context, and is therefore often under-utilised in resource management decision making (Tipa & Tierney 2003, 2006).

In response to this, Te Rūnanga o Ngāi Tahu have been developing the State of the Takiwā tool, which is aimed at allowing tangata whenua to systematically record, collect, collate and report on the cultural health of significant sites, natural resources and the environment within their respective takiwā, and in turn play a greater role in environmental management. In 2007 over 100 freshwater sites from over 20 catchments throughout the South Island were assessed using the Takiwā tool, to test and refine the method for wider application, and to develop a report on the health of freshwater resources of Te Waipounamu from a cultural perspective. This paper presents the results of this study, along with an overview of the Takiwā tool and its methods.

Tāhuhu Kōrero background

The 1997 State of New Zealand's Environment Report highlighted a number of significant issues facing the health of freshwater, including widespread pollution from both point and non-point sources, and the loss of natural character and habitat quality from drainage, flood control, removal of riparian vegetation, waste disposal, stormwater, and agricultural runoff (Taylor & Smith 1997: 7.6). A recent review of national water quality trends by Scarsbrook (2006) revealed that non-point source pollution has become an even greater concern.

Māori have long held such concerns about the degradation of New Zealand's water environments and the erosion of traditional relationships with water, particularly with regard to customary rights, access, ownership and management (Ellison 2007). Furthermore, Māori continue to raise water-related concerns under the Resource Management Act and to the Waitangi Tribunal, and both statutory monitoring and planning agencies, largely driven by conventional western science approaches, continue to struggle to adequately include Māori cultural values, such as freshwater food gathering quality and standards, in data gathering techniques, analysis, reporting, and the development of policy in relation to freshwater protection and management.

What is state of the takiwā?

State of the Takiwā is an environmental monitoring approach developed by Te Rūnanga o Ngāi Tahu as part of their Ki Uta Ki Tai – Mountains to the Sea Natural Resource Management Framework (Pauling 2003) and outlined in the tribal vision, Ngāi Tahu 2025 (Te Rūnanga o Ngāi Tahu 2001). Its development has been partly funded by the Ministry for the

Environment and supported by Environmental Science and Research, Manaaki Whenua - Landcare Research, NIWA, Envirolink Southern Community Laboratories, Environment Southland, and Environment Canterbury.

The major objective behind State of the Takiwā is to ensure tangata whenua can build robust and defensible information about the health of the environment, which can in turn be used to assess the effectiveness of both internal policy and practices and those of external agencies, including local councils who have statutory responsibilities to undertake monitoring and report on the state of the environment (Pauling 2004).

The takiwā database

Takiwā is a specially developed Microsoft Access 2002 runtime application linked to a physically separated database, and can be run on any computer by downloading from an installation CD-ROM. The primary aim of the Takiwā database is to facilitate data collection and make information available to tangata whenua, to help them identify and quantify the current or changing quality of a particular site, and to be able to report this data in an easy, clear and repeatable way. This is achieved by the inclusion of a site assessment module for storing, analysing and reporting data collected on particular sites, and a print centre where monitoring forms for data collection and standard reports can be produced.

Site assessment module

The Site Assessment Module identifies environmental monitoring sites and records details from both present day visits by participants, as well as historical information. Data gathered is in a combination of reasoned multi-choice evaluation of criteria (for example, access for harvesting: 1 = very poor, whereas 5 = very good), and comments of visitor impressions. Within this module, details based on Takiwā Monitoring, Cultural Health Index and SHMAK forms can be entered to describe a geographically defined site and the details of the visit, as well as being able to assess environmental and other qualities in a consistent fashion over time.

The Site Assessment Module also includes a section labelled 'journal', where important historical information and references about a particular site can be stored. A further feature is the image portal where an unlimited number of photographs or other diagrams (.jpg, .gif or .bmp format) can be associated with the site.

In order to grade and compare sites and visits, index calculations are incorporated within the database. These include an overall Takiwā site health assessment index, a species abundance index, and the Cultural Health Index for Waterways (Tipa & Tierney 2003, 2006). The Site Assessment module also includes a module to enter data from the Stream Health Monitoring and Assessment Kit (Biggs et al. 2000) and to produce scores for stream habitat quality, and invertebrate and periphyton health, as well as data from electric fishing and E. coli testing. All indexes can be recalculated for either the current questionnaire, or for all questionnaires in the database (Mattingley 2005, 2007).

Takiwā monitoring forms

Takiwā includes a series of specially developed monitoring forms that can be printed directly from the database, used to gather information about sites, and facilitate the storage and reporting of data from the field. These include the Takiwā Site Definition, Visit and Assessment forms. Takiwā also currently includes forms for the Cultural Health Index and Stream Health Monitoring and Assessment Kit.

The aim of the Takiwā monitoring forms is to record observations and assessments by tangata whenua for a particular site and at a particular time relating to key cultural values and indicators of environmental health, such as mahinga kai. The forms were developed and tested through discussion with, and use by, both tangata whenua groups and monitoring experts, and by reviewing previously developed monitoring tools (including Otaraua Hapū 2003; Tipa & Tierney 2003, 2006; Ogilvie & Penter 2001; Harmsworth 2002; Handford & Associates Ltd 2003; and NIWA 2003).

Feedback dictated that the monitoring forms needed to be simple, rather than being overly complicated or abstract, and that the forms should attempt to capture the cultural information and values about a site, which is normally internalised during mahinga kai (food gathering) or similar activities and often called 'anecdotal information', including:

- Heritage/Site Significance;
- Amount of pressure on the site from external factors;
- Levels of modification/change at a site;
- Suitability of the site for harvesting mahinga kai;
- Access issues in relation to the site;
- Overall health/state of the site;

- Presence, abundance and diversity counts for native bird, plant and fish species, other culturally significant resources as well as exotic (including pest and weed) species; and
- Willingness to return to the site.

Other details that were seen as being important to record were in relation to general visit and site details (date, time, weather conditions, site location, and legal protection). This was achieved by the development of two separate but interdependent forms – The Site Definition form and the Visit Details Form. The visit details form also includes prompts to ensure photographic references are recorded for a site.

Ngā kauneke methods

The major data collection undertaken within this study was conducted between March and November 2007. It was facilitated by a central coordinator from Te Rūnanga o Ngāi Tahu and involved working with members of Papatipu Rūnanga from around Te Waipounamu. In total, over 100 sites from over 20 catchments and across four regions of the South Island were assessed. The rūnanga monitoring teams were also supported by researchers and monitoring staff from ESR, NIWA, Manaaki Whenua - Landcare Research, Envirolink/Hills Laboratories, Environment Canterbury, Environment Southland, and the Otago Regional Council.

The data collection primarily involved cultural health site assessments using the Takiwā tool. This was further complemented by the use of the Cultural Health Index, Stream Health Monitoring and Assessment Kit, and electric fishing surveys and the collection and testing of water samples for the analysis of E. coli and antibiotic-resistant E. coli. From the total number of sites monitored, 17 reference sites were selected for final analysis and reporting. These sites were chosen to give a good geographical representation of the sites monitored and due to their significance as traditional and/or contemporary mahinga kai (food gathering sites and/or areas).

Kauneke arotake data collection & assessment

The process followed for the data collection at all sites involved the following steps:

- After arriving at the site, the monitoring team gathered together so that any appropriate mihi, karakia and/or kōrero could be given.

- The team then completed the Site Definition and Visit Details forms, including obtaining GPS coordinates and photographic records for the site.
- The team then completed the Takiwā site assessment form and gathered the water sample for E. coli testing. At all river/stream sites the team then undertook the various tests as part of the SHMAK kit, and completed the Cultural Health Index water quality form, before finally undertaking an electric fishing survey of the site.
- Before departing, a general kōrero/discussion was held about the site, and travel and other details about the next site and/or activity.

Data analysis

After the fieldwork was concluded, data from the completed monitoring forms were loaded into the Takiwā database, from which scores for the Takiwā, Cultural Health Index, and SHMAK assessments were calculated.

Scores from the 17 selected reference sites were then analysed and graphed using Excel and used to show the relative rankings of the sites from very good to very poor. Other data were also extracted from the database in relation to the presence and abundance of native and exotic species and how these related to the relative scores of each site. Individual indicator scores from each assessment tool were also isolated, totalled and averaged across the sites. This allowed an evaluation of the relative significance of different aspects of stream health to be undertaken.

E. coli and anti-biotic resistance test results were obtained from Hills Laboratories and the data entered into Excel spreadsheets. The data was then assessed against national drinking water, shellfish gathering and recreational standards for E. coli and graphed to show the number of samples that passed and failed the different standards, as well as the number that had anti-biotic resistance.

Ngā hua results

Takiwā site assessments

Takiwā assessment results across the monitoring sites ranged from good to poor, with the majority being of moderate health (47%). A further 35% of the sites were rated as poor, and only 18%, or three sites, achieved a good rating. No sites were rated as very poor or very good. Overall, the sites scored well on access, willingness to harvest and return indicators, but poorly on pressure, modification, and in particular native species abundance indicators. Māngai Piri (3.7), Arahura (3.4) and Ōnuku (3.4) were the highest ranking sites, while Waipapa (1.9), Mataura Falls (2.0) and Waikare (2.1) were the lowest scoring. Features of high scoring sites included intact native riparian buffers, and a lack of modification or pressure on the margins. Features of low scoring sites included a lack of native riparian buffers (or any buffer at all), high modification or intense pressure (both rural and urban land-use) on the margins, and often directly visible point source and/or non-point source discharges and pollution.

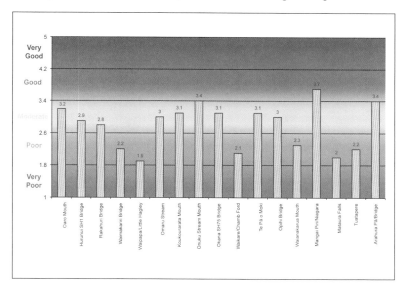

Figure 1. Ngā Wai Pounamu Takiwā Scores.

Native species abundance

Overall, native species abundance and in particular native vegetation dominance across all sites was poor. Of the sites, 46% had less than 15% of the site area dominated by native vegetation, with a further 24% having less than 35% dominance. Only two sites (Māngai Piri and Tuatapere) had greater than 50% native vegetation dominance.

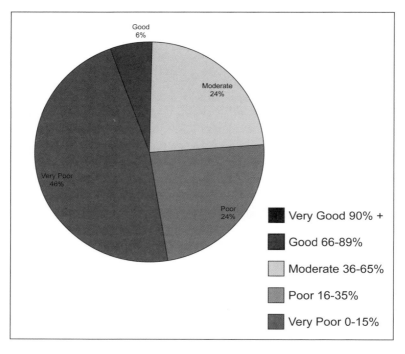

Figure 2. Native Species Dominance across Ngā Wai Pounamu Sites.

Of the native plants distributed across the sites, Ti Kouka (cabbage tree) was the most prevalent, being found at 11 sites. Harakeke (NZ Flax) (7 sites), Karamū (*Coprosma robusta*) and Koromiko (*Hebe salicifolia*) (both with 5 sites) were the next most common. Kāroro (Black backed gulls) were the most common native bird, being encountered at eight sites. These were followed by kāhu (NZ Hawk) and pīwaiwaka (Fantail), which were found at five sites each. Common bully (six sites) and Tuna/eels (five sites) were the most common native fish species encountered. The most common plant or animal encountered across all sights, however, were exotic pasture grasses and weeds (15 sites). Willow (13 sites), broom (nine sites), and gorse (seven sites) were the next most common exotic plant species. Rock Pigeons (four sites) and Cattle (three sites) were the most exotic animals encountered.

Kōrerorero discussion

When taking into account the results of all types of assessment undertaken, the cultural health of waterways within Te Waipounamu is considered to be moderate to poor. The assessments and analysis indicate widespread modification and degradation in the cultural health of South Island waterways, particularly with regards to native riparian vegetation and associated wildlife.

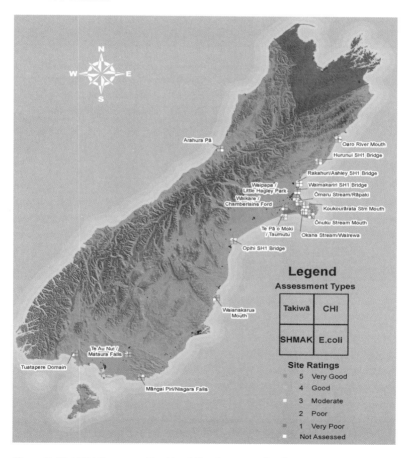

Figure 3. Ngā Wai Pounamu Combined Site Assessment Results.

Photos 1 and 2. A common view of riparian zones across the sites showing a lack of native riparian vegetation, the dominance of exotic species, and intense riparian land use. Left: Koukourārata, Right: Waianakarua

Photos 3 and 4. Signs of Promise. Left: Waikekewai Stream, Te Pā o Moki; and Right Ōmaru Stream – examples of native vegetation

While the waterways monitored were functioning in some form, they were highly modified and under continual pressure from surrounding land-use, particularly along the margins. Most strikingly, only three out of the 17 sites analysed received a good rating. Furthermore, all assessments point towards significant issues in the management of the riparian zone and the importance of this area as both a habitat for native plants, birds, fish and other wildlife, and as a buffer from the negative impacts of surrounding land use.

The lack of native riparian and wetland vegetation was apparent at the majority of sites. In most cases, such as the larger river sites of Rakahuri, Waimakariri, Waikare, Ōpihi, and Waianakarua, riparian areas were completely void of native vegetation, being replaced by exotic vegetation, such as willows, or gorse and broom. While such species may still provide a buffer from surrounding land use, in other cases no buffer exists at all, with pasture or other types of intensive land use being present right to the edge of the waterway. As well as the important ecological function that a vegetated riparian or wetland zone provides, native riparian and wetland vegetation is an important cultural indicator of health, providing significant habitat and breeding areas for native birds, fish and insects, and in particular mahinga kai species.

Takiwā, CHI and SHMAK indicators for margin condition, vegetation and the abundance of native species were particularly poor across all sites. The only sites that had healthy native riparian vegetation were Māngai Piri and Arahura, with Ōnuku and Tuatapere having moderately healthy margins. A number of other sites, including Waipapa, Ōmaru, Ōkana and Te Pā o Moki, did, however, show promise, with efforts being made to restore native riparian vegetation along these streams. These projects are mostly led by local marae.

The pressure on waterways from surrounding land use and the associated impacts of non-point and point source pollution was another feature across the majority of the sites. A number of sites had visible and direct discharges entering the waterway, while a number of others showed obvious signs of problems from non-point pollution and/or intensive margin land-use. This was supported by assessment data from both the CHI and SHMAK, which revealed significantly lower scores across all the sites for stream and river bed condition, bed deposits and sedimentation as well as conductivity. Periphyton results at a number of sites, including Ōaro, Waimakariri, Ōkana and Koukourarata, were also poor, a further indication of intensive land use and associated pollution discharge issues.

The assessments and analysis also identified that there are very few areas that remain unaffected by land use and discharge issues. Even the two highest rating sites, Arahura on the West Coast and Māngai Piri on the fringe of the Catlins, have intensive land use, including dairying and

Photos 5 and 6. Extreme modification: Top: Te Au Nui/Mataura Falls as it was in the 1800s and Bottom: The Falls today overshadowed by primary processing plants. Photo 5: Southland Museum & Art Gallery Collection.

forestry, within the lower catchment areas upstream of the monitoring sites. However, the most extreme example of intensive margin land use, modification and discharge issues was found at the Mataura Falls site. Surrounded on either bank by primary processing plants, this highly significant mahinga kai site for the taking of kanakana (lamprey eels) has lost its natural riparian zone and is subject to regular industrial discharges from the factories on the river margins. On a positive note, the local marae have been successful in gazetting a Mātaitai reserve to protect and enhance the management of the river along a ten kilometre stretch, including the Falls site.

The assessments also highlighted unacceptable levels of faecal contamination across the majority of sites. While most sites achieved the recreational standard for E. coli, only two sites passed the current national shellfish standard and three of the sites that passed the recreational standard contained E. coli that were resistant to human and agricultural antibiotics. From a cultural perspective, a major value of waterways is their ability to provide for kai. In this respect, the recreational standard is insufficient to protect the values of tangata whenua, as the expectation is that water should be clean enough to eat from, not just to swim in.

The assessment results therefore raise questions about the effectiveness of our management of non-point and point source discharges as well as the current standards for which waterways are monitored for and managed under. Investigation into an adequate water quality standard for freshwater food gathering is therefore urgently required. This would provide some protection and piece of mind to those who continue to practice the gathering of food and other resources from freshwater environments, as well as other users of freshwater.

Te whakamutunga conclusions

While water holds significant values for Māori and the wider community, many waterways have undergone dramatic modification and show obvious signs of degradation and stress. This chapter outlines the results of a cultural health study of South Island waterways undertaken by Te Rūnanga o Ngāi Tahu in conjunction with members of Ngāi Tahu Papatipu Rūnanga aimed at quantifying how tangata whenua view the current health of waterways.

Overall, the results of the study found selected South Island waterway sites to be in a state of moderate to poor cultural health. In particular, the assessments and analysis point towards significant issues with the management of the riparian zone and the importance of this area as both a habitat for native plants, birds, fish and other wildlife and as a buffer from the negative impacts of surrounding land use. The study also highlights significant issues with non-point and point source discharges and the failure of E. coli recreational water quality standards to protect customary freshwater food gathering practices and users. The majority of sites displayed a complete lack of native riparian or wetland vegetation, extensive modification of the riparian margin and often intensive land use right up to the edge of the waterway. A number of sites had visible and direct discharges entering the waterway. Although the overall assessment was moderate to poor, there were some sites and features that were seen as positive and provide ideas for how future management may be able to improve the cultural health of waterways. These included the presence and abundance of remnant and/or restored native riparian vegetation and the separation of waterways from intensive land use.

Protecting, enhancing and extending adequate native riparian and wetland buffers and other native vegetation patches within intensively used rural and urban catchments and continuing to deal with sources of contaminants, both point and non-point, will be the most important challenges for the future management of waterways in Te Waipounamu. Developing a national standard for freshwater food gathering quality and systematically recording and reporting on this will also be important into the future.

Cultural opportunity assessments: Introducing a framework for assessing the suitability of stream flow from a cultural perspective

Gail Tipa

Introduction

In a New Zealand context, Māori (the indigenous people) cannot divorce themselves from the challenges associated with setting flow regimes and water allocation as their culture and ways of life are closely tied to the lands and waters within their tribal territories. In the last two decades Māori have sought greater recognition of their cultural beliefs, values, and practices. However, barriers still limit their ability to convey to decision makers how allocative decisions affect their cultural interests since many of the existing methods of assessing flows are dominated by western science techniques that emphasise physical and biological values rather than specifically responding to cultural needs. This chapter introduces one tool – a Cultural Opportunity Assessment – that has been developed for Māori to assess their opportunities to engage in a range of cultural experiences in a catchment under differing stream flows.

Landscapes and societies are shaped, in part, by the quality, quantity and form of water movement. The course of settlement, cultural development and economies within nations has long been deeply affected by the availability of water. In many parts of the world, however, water is a scarce resource. Globally, changes in the quantity and quality of freshwaters represent a strategic threat to humans, environmental sustainability and the "vitality of human cultures" (Ecological Society of America 1998). Indigenous communities are particularly sensitive to the use and development of freshwaters as they hold distinct perspectives on water that concern their identity, attachment to place, knowledge, and custodial obligations to manage tribal lands and waters (Sheehan 2001; Flanagan & Laituri 2004; Jackson et al. 2005).

Within New Zealand, many regions receive insufficient rainfall to sustain contemporary land uses and meet the needs of communities dependent on streams, rivers, and groundwater for life-giving moisture. Consistent with international observations (O'Gara 2000; Knack & Stewart 1984) inadequate rainfall recognises no racial or cultural distinctions.

Māori have, for generations, voiced their concerns at the continual modification and manipulation of the waterways within their tribal territories (Waitangi Tribunal 1984, 1991, 1992, 1995, 1998). Many streams and rivers are degraded as a result of what Māori perceive as inappropriate use and development. Of particular concern are the level of extraction from waterways and the perceived inappropriateness of manipulated stream flows. In the last two decades Māori have become more vocal in seeking greater recognition of their cultural beliefs, values, and practices, fearing that a failure to recognise them will ultimately destroy many of the foundations of their culture and identity. The challenge Māori confront is to convey to decision makers how allocative decisions affect their cultural interests since many of the existing methods of assessing flows are dominated by western science techniques. If the needs of Māori are to be seriously considered and weighed alongside the needs of other populations, new techniques are needed to assess the appropriateness of flows in culturally sensitive ways. This chapter introduces one such tool – a Cultural Opportunity Assessment – that has been developed to assess the opportunities for Māori to engage in a range of cultural experiences in a catchment under differing stream flows.

This chapter first reviews existing methods for determining river flows. The usefulness of management techniques from other knowledge traditions (most notably the Recreational Opportunity Spectrum) are then discussed, before an integrated conceptual framework is presented. The chapter concludes by noting the implications resulting from the adoption of such an approach to freshwater management.

2. Existing techniques for assessing stream flows

There is considerable literature concerning environmental flow assessments, which are defined by King et al. (1999: 3) as 'an assessment of how much of the original flow regime of a river should continue to flow down it in order to maintain specified valued features of the river ecosystem'. Arthington et al. (2004) contends that this body of research confirms the level of global concern at the increasing hydrological alteration of rivers and their resultant deterioration. Until the mid-nineteenth century water quality had been at the forefront of issues arising from human manipulation of rivers (Tharme 1996). Then a range of new issues arose concerned with the reduced flow in rivers. Subsequently, as understanding of river changes resulting from flow manipulations has increased, a range of methods for calculating environmental flows has evolved. As Tharme (1996) explains, methodologies have evolved from ad hoc approaches for specific cases through to formal methodologies. Of particular relevance to this paper, however, King et al. (1999: p.3) cautions that

> *historically, and still today in many instances, the focus of environmental flow assessment was entirely on the maintenance of economically important freshwater (and hence associated estuarine and/or marine) fisheries... The inherent assumption in such assessments is that flows that aim to protect target fish populations, habitats and activities will ultimately ensure maintenance of the overall riverine ecosystem.*

More recently, assessments have also considered the flow needs for other biota. Many assessments now consider the flow needs of riverine invertebrates and birds, aspects such as channel form, riparian habitats, floodplain wetlands, and sometimes ecosystem processes like nutrient cycling and primary production (Tharme 1996; Harding et al. 2004).

Four basic groups of methodology are widely recognised: hydrological index methodologies; hydraulic rating methodologies; habitat simulation methodologies; and holistic methodologies (Arthington et al. 2004; Harding et al. 2004, Tharme 1996).

Methodologies geared towards specific ecosystem components are evolving. Several methods exist that explore other kinds of information such as riparian vegetation, the channel and its sediments, wetlands, floodplains and estuaries, groundwater, water quality, and wildlife (Harding 2004). Each methodology has inherent strengths, weaknesses and limitations that cannot be fully critiqued in this chapter. Furthermore, each to some degree is cognisant of and responsive to cultural values expressed by indigenous communities. As highlighted by Craig (2005) a common assumption has been that environmental flows are an acceptable surrogate for the protection of cultural values. But a factor common to all methodologies is their reliance on professional expertise for their implementation (King et al. 1999) and the predominance of objective, scientific philosophies and techniques that may serve to limit the engagement of indigenous peoples.

With reference to water management in New Zealand, Minhinnick (cited in Douglas 1984) challenges existing techniques and explains that

> *Great harm was done to Māori people and their relationship*
> *with their ancestral lands and waterways as a result of the mono-*
> *cultural law regime that prevailed prior to the passing of the RMA*
> *in 1991. Cultural offences could not be avoided where the law*
> *did not allow their consideration. The sole focus on biophysical*
> *impacts was particularly damaging to Māori spiritual values.*

The experiences of other indigenous communities were similar. As Burmil (1999: 106) explains 'The emphasis on technical standards has tended to place perceptual, cultural and spiritual values of water at a disadvantage in affecting water policy and management'. In New Zealand, however, the enactment of the Resource Management Act 1991 has resulted in managers being charged, pursuant to section 6(e) to recognise and provide for 'The relationship of Māori and their culture and traditions with their ancestral lands, water, sites, waahi tapu and other taonga'. But there remains a need for methodologies that enable Māori to assess what is a sustainable flow regime from a cultural perspective. This chapter thus seeks to highlight both relevant Māori relationships with freshwater and a proposed assessment of opportunity that could meet these methodological challenges.

3. Māori notions of freshwater

Māori maintain an appreciation and respect for the life-giving properties of freshwater. Protecting the integrity of valued freshwater resources is an important aspect of the responsibilities of those Māori who are mandated as kaitiaki.

Values associated with specific freshwater resources include: the role of particular freshwater resources in creation stories; the role of those freshwater resources in historical accounts; the proximity of settlements and/or historical sites in or adjacent to specific freshwater resources; the value of freshwater resources as a source of tribal identity, mahinga kai; the use of freshwater resources as access routes or transport courses; and the continued capacity for future generations to access, use and treasure the resource (Crengle 1997[1], 2002; Tipa & Teirney 2003). The Māori worldview does not separate spiritual and intangible aspects from the non-spiritual practices of resource management. In other words, Māori do not distinguish between the biotic and abiotic, or between the animate and inanimate. Consequently, it is the intangible values ascribed to freshwater by Māori that arguably become difficult for resource managers and scientists to accommodate within existing management regimes.

In assessing the impacts of a proposed flow regime for freshwater, the fundamental requirement for Māori is whether the mauri[2] of the waterway will be destroyed or defiled beyond redemption and reasonable utility as a result of the interruption of 'natural' flow and the substitution of human managed flow. In other words, Māori assess whether the mauri of the river continues to live and its values subsist. In forming an answer to this question, Māori will utilise a combination of traditional knowledge and direct observation utilising indicators which are the manifestations of a robust mauri life force.

Māori, in many forums,[3] have emphasised the necessity of considering a catchment in its entirety: from its source, the passage of its waters through a network of tributaries, onto lower floodplains, to its interface with saltwater along the coast. Holistic conceptualisations that emphasise integration, interdependencies and interrelationships rather than fragmenting and compartmentalising the environment are common to indigenous peoples (Posey 1999).

This section has introduced (albeit briefly) two of the foundations from which a culturally sensitive Māori-based methodology can be derived. First, it is recognized that the core values and practices of Māori need to be provided for. Second, the need for a catchment wide management perspective was introduced. Together these notions may be joined to create a meaningful tool for Māori to assess the appropriateness of flow regimes.

4. Framing a discussion of cultural values

From a management perspective, all issues associated with freshwater arise because of human values and the perception of risks to those values (Galindo & Rodriguez 2000; Gold 1980). The condition of freshwater resources can directly affect perceptions. The challenge for managers, however, arises because attitudes, perceptions and traditions can be resistant to change. This chapter is principally concerned with how cultural values are conveyed to water managers and subsequently represented in water management. It responds to the observations of Groenfeldt (2005) that the 'perspective embedded in indigenous views about nature and water is largely missing from the western toolkit on water management'. As previously stated, the difficulty confronting managers is to translate an articulation of cultural beliefs, values and practices associated with a resource (such as freshwater) into contemporary management practice.

Craig (2005) argues that requirements for environmental flows should be kept distinct from the cultural values associated with water because protection of cultural values is likely to require different considerations – different values, different spatial scales, and different geographic interpretations. This chapter proposes a new tool to facilitate participation by Māori in processes to determine stream flows. This requires first, identification of a process by which Māori can articulate the breadth and depth of their association with a river catchment. Second, the process of assessment should explicitly recognise and accommodate Māori conceptualisations; and finally, the process should be participatory and utilise accepted and proven methods of data collection and analysis (Rapport et al. 1998).

The Sustainability Assessment Method (SAM) has been promoted by the World Conservation Union (IUCN) as 'a method for measuring sustainable development, by treating the wellbeing of people and ecosystems together'

Explicit coupling of social and environmental values recognises that values influence an individual's or a community's assessment of impacts of change, while environmental science helps explain the biophysical processes affected by such change. The SAM provided a step-by-step progression that aided the definition of the multi-dimensional nature of the association of Māori with a river catchment. Importantly, the SAM process enabled explicit linkages to be drawn between the association of Māori with a catchment and issues of stream flow. The SAM assesses sustainable development by measuring specific indicators and aggregating these indicators into themes (dimensions). The process is intended to provide a comprehensive assessment by covering a broad range of themes (Guijt & Moiseev 2001). To assist with interpretation, Moiseev et al. (2002: p.9) explain that

A dimension is a broad theme, such as land, resource use or community... An element is a key issue or concern related to a dimension. An indicator is a measurable sign or signal of a phenomenon; a context specific measure of an element or sub-element. Indicators are combined to measure elements; elements are combined to measure dimensions.

While the IUCN has used SAM at global and national levels, it has potential for application at a sub-national, or catchment level (Moiseev et al. 2002). Figure 1 describes an assessment process comprising seven stages, including: defining Māori who will participate in the assessment process; documenting the cultural association with a catchment; defining the dimensions of that association; identifying dependencies of that association on stream flow; and identifying cultural indicators of flow appropriateness.

To develop this further in a New Zealand context, a review of literature enabled construction of the multi-dimensional relationship with a river catchment. Contemporary writings were examined as well as historical material. This was complemented by a series of interviews with Māori living in three catchments around the South Island of New Zealand as shown in Figure 2.[4] By applying an adaptation of the SAM process to data, a number of tables were constructed, each of which documented a belief, value or cultural practice. Table 1 lists the values, beliefs and practices for which tables were prepared.

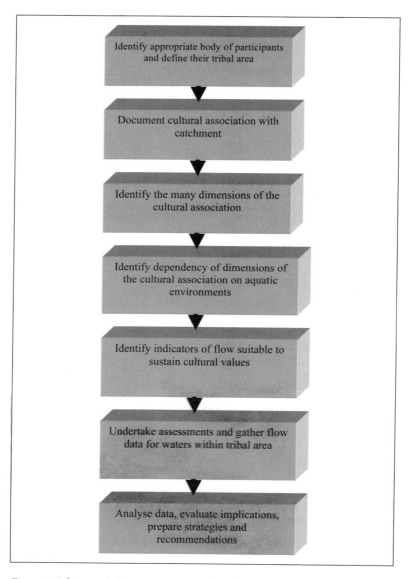

Figure 1. A framework for incorporating a cultural perspective in the determination of flow appropriateness.

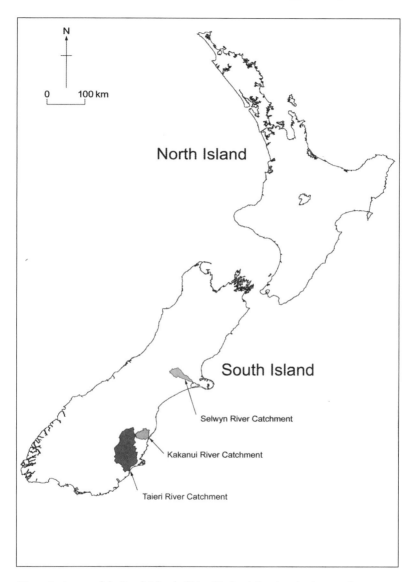

Figure 2. A map of the South Island of New Zealand showing the three study catchments.

A selection of cultural beliefs, values, practices	
Whakapapa (genealogy)	Waiata/whakatauki (songs/proverbs)
Taniwha (legendary serpent like creature)	Reserves/easements
Wai Māori – including puna (springs), repo raupo (wetlands) and water quality	Mahinga kai (places where foods are procured and or produced)
Hauora (health and wellbeing)	Wāhi ingoa (traditional place names)
Kainga (settlement, place of residence)	Ara tawhito (ancient trails)
Tauranga waka (canoe mooring / landing site)	Pā (fortification)
Mauka (mountain)	Urupā (burial place)
Whanaungatanga (kinship, familial relationships)	Recreation

Table 1: Cultural beliefs, values and practices for which dimensions, elements and indicators were defined. In total, sixteen tables were developed.

DIMENSIONS	ELEMENTS	FLOW INDICATOR / DISCRIMINATOR
MAHINGA KAI	Abundance and diversity of species	Valued species (fish, birds, plants) present
	Needs of species at all stages of life cycle a. Habitat b. Food sources c. Migration	Range of habitats • Breeding & rearing areas for valued species present • Quality edge habitat present • habitats of valued species inundated (e.g., eel burrows) Movement of species through catchment Food available for valued species
	Being able to access and use places and resources	Access to site Site safe for users
	Ability of Māori to use river	River clean and free of pollution Condition of species gathered healthy Compatibility with other users of the site Preferred method of fishing possible Preferred sites for fishing useable

Table 2: An example of how the SAM assisted analysis of mahinga kai (places where food produced or procured) data

In total, sixteen tables were developed. Table 2, one of the sixteen tables, provides a summary of the beliefs and practices associated with mahinga kai. With respect to the physical dimension, mahinga kai incorporates the bounty gathered from the river and requires consideration of the physical characteristics necessary, both within the river and on adjacent lands, to support terrestrial and aquatic species. However, mahinga kai is also important for sustaining the well-being of Māori. Finally the activities associated with gathering and use of the river resources, including harvesting, whānau interaction, and transmission of cultural practices between generations (Crengle 2002) are equally essential.

The values, beliefs and practices detailed in the tables confirm that the experiences of Māori interacting with a waterway are significant components of their cultural identity (Haggard & Williams 1992). It is important to note that there is not a separate table for 'mauri'. Focus group discussions and subsequent interviews confirmed that not all aspects of mauri can be captured in a resource management technique or process.

> *Mauri is the whole bloody lot – you can't break it up. It is just like the river – you've got to look at the whole catchment and not just bits of a river (Interviewee 3, Catchment 2).*

Importantly, the SAM process enabled a critical examination of flow issues because interviewees were challenged to identify how the different flows in the river impacts the nature and extent of each value, belief and practice they identified. In other words, they had to specify, during stage 5 of the SAM process (Figure 1), the indicators that they use to assess flow appropriateness.

While the SAM process and the data contained in the sixteen tables constructed (for example, Table 2) are important for identifying indicators of stream flow appropriateness, they did not provide a process by which the indicators could be applied. Thus a tactic, or framework, for applying the indicators was required. This was considered through attention to the opportunities afforded to Māori to interact with a catchment and the quality of their experiences when interacting.

5. Opportunities and connections – A cultural opportunity assessment

In this section of the chapter the reasons for developing a tool that examines opportunities and experiences are explained before the components from which the tool is constructed are detailed.

5.1 Reasons for concentrating on opportunities and experiences

As Māori and environmental managers continue to be charged with New Zealand stream management obligations, a framework enabling Māori to assess stream flow appropriateness can be of value.

An opportunity assessment has been developed rather than a tool that results in a definitive flow because it is through observation that Māori determine the suitability of river conditions for diverse activities or practices. In other words, they make a judgment based on observations. They may struggle to quantify definitively the flow necessary to enable their activities. Further, there may be inherent risks for Māori (and indeed other indigenous communities) to base assessment of cultural sustainability on an absolute numerical value. In proposing a 'cultural flow' as a mechanism for protecting the cultural values of Aboriginal communities in Australia, Craig (2005) similarly cautions that 'Determining how much water should be allocated to cultural flows is a difficult problem'. It is believed, however, that application of the cultural opportunity assessment will enable the articulation of cultural flow requirements. Cultural opportunities are also being promoted as a concept that is inclusive, safe and defendable.

A range of techniques for assessing opportunities have emerged in the last twenty years, including the Recreational Opportunity Spectrum (ROS), a Water Recreation Opportunity Spectrum, Tourism Opportunity Spectrum, and Forestry Opportunity Spectrum. Proposing an opportunity assessment builds on this body of literature and is consistent with the theoretical propositions of Kaplan and Kaplan (1977, 1982, 1989) that environmental judgments constitute an intuitive guide for human behaviour and determine whether an individual will utilise or avoid specific sites and areas. The application of an opportunities approach to freshwater via a Cultural Opportunity Assessment enables Māori to identify the flows that are conducive to their continued association with a river.

The engagement of Māori with a river catchment is experiential. Monitoring and assessment of environmental condition and flow appropriateness is sensory and perceptual (Crengle 2002). Conceptually, parallels can be drawn between the intent, design and application of the ROS and the monitoring techniques of Māori. The ROS is promoted as an experience based system that is spatially orientated and easily applied (More et al. 2003). Clarke and Stankey (1979) define a recreational opportunity as the combination of conditions and attributes that give value to a place. The experiences of users are fundamental as the ROS is predicated on the assumption that differing conditions will support different experiences. Quality outdoor recreation requires a diverse range of opportunities to be available to users thus recognising that a community comprises of individuals with diverse tastes and preferences (Clarke & Stankey (1979). Diversity is also to be found within Māoridom as different iwi, hapū and whānau interact with sites within a catchment in a variety of ways. Flow can impact the quality and condition of a site and consequently the opportunities afforded Māori. The purpose of the Cultural Opportunity Assessment is therefore to assess how flow attributes at a site of cultural significance influence the quality and condition of that site from the perspective of Māori.

5.2 Constructing the Cultural Opportunity Assessment

While the Cultural Opportunity Assessment is modelled on the ROS, its components are grounded in the worldview of Māori, integrating conceptualisations previously presented in this paper. Interviewees confirmed that:

- Māori want a river flow that affords them the opportunity to sustain their multi-dimensional cultural association with a river catchment with positive cultural experiences resulting.
- Adopting a catchment perspective is fundamental. Accordingly, sites are to be assessed across a catchment
- The suitability of flow is to be assessed using the indicators identified by Māori.

5.3 Future Application of the Cultural Opportunity Assessment

The Cultural Opportunity Assessment involves a broad-scale assessment (which can be completed through hui/focus groups and interviews) that is followed by detailed field assessments undertaken by groups of Māori, mandated as having the knowledge necessary to inform the stream flow appropriateness assessment.

Once the broad-scale desktop assessment is complete, field visits are necessary to assess the condition of sites and the appropriateness of stream flow as a contributor to sustaining the cultural values and affording the opportunities sought at each site. An assessment form should be completed by each member of the team at each site.[5] Māori are first to confirm significance of the site and its values, and then assess the extent to which the identified values of significance are affected by stream flow attributes, using the prescribed indicators. Finally, as part of the assessment, Māori are asked to provide qualitative data in response to three open-ended questions.

Once assessments are completed team members discuss their assessments. The facilitator records the group's assessment of opportunities and highlights any inconsistencies that need resolution before moving to the next site.

When there is agreement between the members within the team, the information from the assessment is graphically represented in three ways:

    (a) Through the compilation of a photographic record of site conditions, with photos taken from viewpoints looking upstream and downstream;

    (b) As a conceptualisation of low flow issues at the site – an example of such a model is presented in Figure 3;

    (c) On a map using a multi-part summary that registers cultural values, an assessment of flow attributes, and an assessment of whether first, the flow and second, the overall condition of the site sustain cultural values. This summary can be recorded as appears in Table 3.

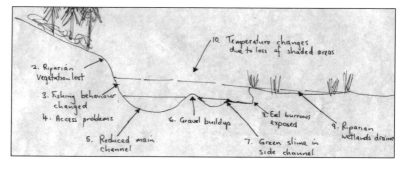

Figure 3. A conceptualisation of flow-related issues at a site of significance.

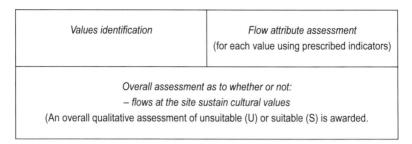

Table 3. The multi-part summary showing how the data collected from an assessment is presented.

Photo 1 shows a site from one of the study catchments. The assessment for this site, which is found in the lower reaches of the river, is summarised in Table 4.

This summary indicates that the site is valued for its mahinga kai, wahi kōhatu (its unique rock formations), and its popularity as an area safe for swimming.

Using a numerical scale (supported by qualitative statements), with 1–3 representing unsuitable flow attributes, 4 being suitable, and 5–7 being appropriate flow attributes, at the time of the assessment the mahinga kai values were sustained and considered to be appropriate but were starting to be affected by flow. In contrast, flow does not affect the rock formations. Although still being used for swimming, there were observable adverse affects that were partly attributed to stream flow such as changing patterns of sediment deposition and erosion affecting safety, and reduced assimilative capacity with respect to contaminants being carried downstream from intensive farmlands upstream. Interrogation of the qualitative data collected highlighted concerns about the quality of the site that potentially limit usage by Māori and not issues associated with stream flow. As a consequence, future discussions with resource managers will focus on initiatives to improve water quality. Overall it was determined that the flow provides opportunities for Māori to engage with the site and therefore the flow attributes do sustain cultural values. Cumulatively across a catchment summary matrices could be mapped onto topographic and GIS maps. Assessments will ideally be undertaken at different times of the year so that site is assessed under different flows.

Photo 1. A site found in one of the study catchments.

Mahinga kai	4
Wāhi kōhatu	7
Swimming	2
S	

Table 4. The summary of the assessment undertaken at a site found in one of the study catchments.

The Cultural Opportunity Assessment has the potential to be a valuable planning tool for water managers. The simplest application would see iwi record historical and contemporary associations with a catchment and, significantly, the opportunities they want to see afforded them. In other words, it would enable an inventory of significant sites, associations and opportunities sought within a catchment to be recorded.

The Cultural Opportunity Assessment enables a tribe to collect information specific to flows in a river and the potential effects river flows have on both the characteristics for which the river is valued, and on the continued ability of Māori to interact with the river and use sites. Because a catchment-wide perspective is utilised it is possible to identify the strategic sites within a catchment where flow related attributes cause concern. This information, in both written and graphic forms, will facilitate discussions with water managers. The data collected as part of each site assessment also enable Māori to identify their conceptual understanding of flow, ecological, and cultural associations and define their priorities and objectives for flow regimes. This structured approach is consistent with the propositions of King (2003) that a rigorous approach to the design of programmes assessing and monitoring flows is required.

As was discussed previously, existing environmental flow methodologies are seen as a surrogate for protecting cultural interests (Craig 2005). The data collected through the application of the Cultural Opportunity Assessment may provide an assessment of the appropriateness of existing flow assessment methods and enable more effective collaboration with scientists and technicians trained in their application. For example Jowett and Mosely (2004) explain that the in-stream flow necessary to sustain mahinga kai is likely to be similar to that necessary to sustain ecological values and consequently in-stream flow assessment procedures may be applicable. Jowett and Mosely (2004) also confirm, however, that other values, which are often considered to be intangible or reliant on anecdotal evidence, could be more problematic.

A related issue from the perspective of indigenous communities may concern the individual(s) who undertake the flow assessments. Having observed earlier that existing methods have the potential to marginalise Māori (and other indigenous communities) because they are applied by scientists and engineers, the Cultural Opportunity Assessment as a method depends on active engagement with Māori. Both the design of the Cultural Opportunity Assessment and the process by which it is applied explicitly recognise the custodial role of Māori as kaitiaki of their lands and waters.

6. Conclusions and implications

The Cultural Opportunity Assessment was developed in response to the perceived need for more comprehensive management techniques enabling water managers to respond to the broad array of cultural values and meanings attributed to water, particularly when allocative decisions were being made. The tool that examines opportunities and experiences was considered sensitive to the multi-dimensional and experiential relationship of Māori with catchments, as well as building on existing management techniques that evaluate opportunities and experiences. Research on the experiences of Māori under different flow scenarios can enhance understanding of how flow impacts on cultural beliefs, values and practices. Such research can contribute to the identification of stream flows necessary to sustain cultural associations with a catchment and specific sites within a catchment.

Acknowledgement

This research is funded by National Institute of Water and Atmospheric Research (NIWA) as part of its FRST funded research programme "Water Allocation: Protection of Instream Values".

END NOTES

[1]Crengle, D. 1997. Notes on Environmental Performance Indicators, unpublished.

[2]Mauri seems to be whatever it is in an ecosystem which is conducive to the continued good health of that ecosystem (Massey University 1990). The primary management principle for Māori is the protection of the mauri or life-giving essence of a resource from desecration.

[3]See Te Runanga o Ngai Tahu 1999, 2003 and Waitangi Tribunal Reports 1984, 1991, 1992, 1995, 1998.

[4]The study catchments were the Taieri catchment (in the Otago region), the Kakaunui catchment (in North Otago) and the Selwyn Catchment (in the Canterbury Region). Ten Māori living within each catchment were interviewed.

[5]This parallels similar practices of cultural stream monitoring such as the application of a Cultural Health Index for assessing overall stream health (Tipa & Teirney 2003, 2006a, 2006b).

Uncharted waters – recent settlements as new spaces for enhancing Māori participation in fresh-water management and decision making

April Bennett

Introduction

Recently two iwi – Te Arawa and Waikato-Tainui – completed or entered into negotiations with the Crown to settle claims related to fresh-water bodies, namely the Te Arawa lakes and the Waikato River respectively. Both settlements address the degradation and future management of these water bodies and open up new spaces for the claimants, and potentially other iwi and hapū, to participate in fresh-water decision making and management. In the context of increasing pressure being placed on fresh-water resources (Ministry for the Environment 2007) and the difficulties Māori still face in engaging in fresh-water planning (Benson-Pope 2006), these settlements have emerged as tools for addressing broader fresh-water management issues and building a vision for the future of fresh-water bodies that is more inclusive of iwi values and aspirations. This chapter first briefly considers Māori values relating to water and then explores the mechanisms used in the settlements, commenting on how these enable both iwi to participate more fully in the ongoing management of their ancestral waters.

Māori values for water

There is a significant body of literature related to Māori values for water.[1] In the context of the settlements concerned, the degradation of the natural and cultural values for the Waikato River and Te Arawa lakes was the principal component of the claimants' grievances and driver for their claims. Accordingly, the redress mechanisms that are used in each settlement attempt to restore these values.

In both claims, the main issues were the pollution of waterways and the loss of control over them. The claims highlight the tremendous impact these have had on the iwi concerned and the significant undermining of values such as mana (authority, power), mauri (life force), taonga (treasure, anything highly prized), mahinga kai (food gathering places), whakapapa (traditional relationships), and tikanga (rules, methods).

In providing for the recognition and expression of these values, the settlements also contribute to the sustainable management of the relevant fresh-water bodies. Notwithstanding the argument that Māori values for water, such as mahinga kai, are synonymous with natural values for water (cited in Bennett 2007), managing natural resources in a way that enables people to provide for their cultural wellbeing is an essential component of sustainable management.[2]

Te Arawa settlement

The Te Arawa Lakes Settlement Act 2006 settles the historical claims of Te Arawa in relation to fourteen lakes in the Rotorua district.[3] At the heart of these claims is the loss of ownership, use and control of the lakes through an agreement signed between the Crown and Te Arawa in 1922. Many of these lakes are now severely degraded as a result of increased nutrient inputs from activities such as farming, septic tank use and wastewater discharges (Parliamentary Commissioner for the Environment 2006).[4] This has also been a major source of grievance for the tribe and a motivating factor for their claims.

Background

The circumstances that led to the 1922 agreement for ownership of the lakes, and the consequences for Te Arawa, make for tragic reading.[5] As a tourist attraction and an essential source of food and other resources, the lakes were the backbone of the Te Arawa economy and way of life. The tourism value of the lakes was not lost on the government, which during the 1880s introduced trout into the lakes and a licensing regime to fish them.

There were two major implications of this for Te Arawa. First, the introduction of trout had the effect of virtually destroying the native fish species Te Arawa used for food, leaving them 'sometimes on the verge of starvation' (Mair cited in White 1998: 104). Second, if tribal members were found catching trout without a licence, even if the trout was a by-catch of an effort to catch native fish, they could be, and were, fined.

From 1910 to 1920, Te Arawa tried unsuccessfully to have their title to the lakes confirmed by the courts. Their efforts were stymied by the government, who refused to supply the relevant survey information to the Native Land Court to enable it to carry out its inquiry. The court's inquiry, which was further delayed by the outbreak of World War I in 1914, ceased after the death of the presiding judge in 1918. The government was not confident that it would win if the inquiry reconvened and convinced Te Arawa to enter into negotiations for ownership of the lakes. In the ensuing agreement, Te Arawa relinquished title to the lakes in exchange for an annual payment of £6,000, 40 trout fishing licences at a nominal fee, and recognition by the Crown of their traditional fishing grounds and burial sites. The annuity was not adjusted to inflation, despite counsel for Te Arawa requesting this during the negotiations. The effect of this was to reduce its value in real terms over time until it became insignificant as a source of income for the tribe (Office of Treaty Settlements 2004).

Redress mechanisms

There are three types of redress in the contemporary settlement: an official apology by the Crown for injustices committed towards Te Arawa; financial redress to compensate for economic losses; and cultural redress to recognise the tribe's relationship with the lakes. For the most part, the focus of the following discussion will be on those parts of the cultural redress that provide for Te Arawa to have a greater role in determining how the lakes will be managed in the future.

Under the settlement, title to thirteen of the fourteen lakebeds is vested in a governance body, the Te Arawa Lakes Trust (the Lakes Trust). As the owner of the lakebeds, the Lakes Trust can regulate certain commercial activities and the building of new structures on the lakebeds. Over time, these rights may encompass matters not anticipated in the settlement. For example, in late 2007, Ngāti Tūwharetoa – who have held legal title to the beds of Lake Taupo and its tributaries since 1992 – closed access to the upper reaches of the Tongariro River to prevent an incursion of the invasive algae didymo (*Didymosphenia geminata*) into the Lake Taupo catchment.

While the lakebeds have been vested in the Lakes Trust, the water in the lakes remains a public resource – that is, no one owns it *in situ*. As such, it continues to be managed by statutory management authorities under the Resource Management Act 1991 (RMA). Existing rights of public access and use are preserved. The space occupied by the water and the air above the lakebeds, referred to in the settlement as the Crown stratum, is owned by the Crown. The creation of the Crown stratum, and the exclusion of rights to own water and control its use from the settlement, has been labelled by a Māori Party member of Parliament as a ploy by the government to expand its ownership and control over specific resources and avoid answering the question of who owns water (Harawira, 13 September 2006). At a national level, Māori have urged the government to clarify the issue of who owns water in light of government proposals, and actions by commercial entities, to encourage transfers and trading of water permits (Bennetts 2006). It seems unlikely that water will be transferred to claimants through the Treaty of Waitangi settlement process (Gibbs & Bennett 2007). In the end, however, it may not matter. Water ownership may be a secondary issue if claimants have other priorities, such as securing a more meaningful role in fresh-water management and decision making. One iwi, Te Ātiawa ki Te Tau Ihu, have recently lodged a claim in the Waitangi Tribunal seeking such an outcome ("Statement of claim before the Waitangi Tribunal in the matter of the claim of Sharon Barcello-Gemmell, Harvey Ruru and Jane duFeu on behalf of Te Atiawa," 3 December 2007).

As well as vesting the beds of the lakes in Te Arawa, the settlement enables the tribe to influence policy for the lakes. It provides for the Lakes Trust to have representation as of right on the Rotorua Lakes Strategy Group, and for this group to be a permanent joint committee under the Local Government Act 2002. The purpose of the group is to 'contribute to promoting the sustainable management of the Rotorua lakes and their catchments for the use and enjoyment of present and future generations, while recognising and providing for the traditional relationship of Te Arawa with their ancestral lakes' (Office of Treaty Settlements 2006: 21).

To achieve this purpose, the group has several functions. These include providing leadership to the responsible organisations and the community on implementing the vision for the lakes,[6] and being involved in the preparation of local planning documents. Such documents include regional policy statements and regional plans, which (along with the resource consent process) are the means by which regional councils manage fresh water under the RMA (Water Programme of Action Interdepartmental Working Group 2004). For Te Arawa, therefore, participating in the process of developing these plans is critical to influencing the future management of the lakes.

Opportunities to participate in the plan development process are already available to Te Arawa under the RMA. However, the settlement strengthens the ability of the tribe to affect key stages in the plan development process – such as those before and during the development of a proposed regional plan – where policy for the lakes is being shaped. Participating meaningfully in these stages relies on good relationships being built with influential staff and politicians within the regional council. Given the composition of the Rotorua Lakes Strategy Group – comprising political and senior management representatives from the Bay of Plenty Regional Council and the Rotorua District Council, and key individuals within the Te Arawa Lakes Trust – it is potentially a valuable platform for Te Arawa to influence the content of, and outcomes from, policy related to the lakes.

The effectiveness of the tribe's involvement on the Rotorua Lakes Strategy Group and the extent to which their values for the lakes can be achieved will depend on the methods that the regional council uses to realise these values. Methods such as rules that give practical effect to these values are desirable. Developing such rules, however, may be very difficult in practice and is an area that requires further research.

Indigenous fisheries, or mahinga kai, were also an important component of the tribe's claims. To address these claims, the settlement provides for the Crown to make regulations that enable Te Arawa to manage the non-commercial fishing of certain indigenous species in the lakes. Also included is a sum of $400,000 to allow 200 fishing licences to be purchased each year for Te Arawa members.

Finally, the settlement includes financial redress of $10 million. Most of this amount ($7.3 million) realises the present value of the annuity granted to Te Arawa by the Crown in the 1922 agreement. The remaining sum ($2.7 million) is for economic and social development, recognising the economic losses suffered by Te Arawa as a result of Crown actions.

In addition to the settlement, Te Arawa is using other tools to maximise their influence in shaping policy for the lakes. One such tool is direct representation in local government. The Bay of Plenty Regional Council has established three Māori constituencies in the region, one covering the Rotorua Lakes area (Kohi constituency). The Rotorua District Council has not created Māori wards, but in the 2007 local government elections three of the twelve councillors (25 percent) elected were Māori. At 36.4 percent of the Rotorua population, however, Māori still remain under-represented at the territorial local authority level.

Waikato-Tainui Agreement in Principle

In December 2007, Waikato-Tainui[7] signed an Agreement in Principle with the Crown to settle their historical claims for the Waikato River.[8] The central issues in the claims were the poor state of the river and the lack of Waikato-Tainui involvement in decisions about and management of the river. The Agreement in Principle aims to address both issues.

Background

Waikato-Tainui consider the Waikato River to be their tupuna (ancestor) and as such, the source of their identity. The river is a physical embodiment of the mana and mauri of the tribe. The claims of Waikato-Tainui in respect of the river arise from the confiscation of tribal lands by the Crown in the 1860s. In 1995 the Crown and Waikato-Tainui reached a settlement that addressed those confiscations. The claims to the river were excluded from that settlement and set aside for future negotiation (Office of Treaty Settlements 2007a).

Waikato-Tainui assert that by virtue of the confiscations, the Crown assumed control of the river. To facilitate development and settlement of the surrounding lands, the river was used as a waste sink for effluent from towns such as Hamilton, industrial sites such as freezing works, and dairy farms (Environment Waikato 2008). It was also modified by activities such as the drainage of wetlands, the building of flood protection schemes and gravel extraction (Office of Treaty Settlements 2007b). Although the water quality of the river has improved since the 1970s, it is not pristine (Environment Waikato 2008). The degradation of the river has been a long-standing concern for the tribe and is the basis of their claims. Consequently, the over-riding purpose of the proposed settlement is to restore and protect the health and well-being of the river for future generations.

Redress mechanisms

The Agreement in Principle has been hailed as ushering in a new era of co-management between the Crown and Waikato-Tainui for the Waikato River. Co-management is defined in the Agreement in Principle as including "the highest level of good faith engagement and consensus decision making as a general rule, while having regard to the mana whakahaere [authority, rights of control] of Waikato-Tainui and other Waikato River iwi" (Office of Treaty Settlements 2007b: 8). The Agreement in Principle also recognises that co-management requires more than consultation and must be implemented by a range of agencies that manage and make decisions about the river.

The Agreement in Principle provides for Waikato-Tainui to have a key role in crafting and implementing a vision and strategy for the river. To this end, it establishes three bodies – the Guardians Establishment Committee, the Guardians of the Waikato River (the Guardians), and the Waikato River Statutory Board. Importantly, each body has equal representation from Waikato River iwi and other key parties. The Guardians Establishment Committee and the Guardians, for example, will each have 16 members – four from Waikato-Tainui, four from other Waikato River iwi, and eight representing the national interest (selected through a ministerial appointment process) and the regional community. The Waikato River Statutory Board will comprise an equal number of members from Waikato-Tainui and local and central government.

The vision is to be based on and incorporate the tribe's objectives for the river. Dominant themes in these objectives are: restoration, protection, enhancement and holistic management of the river, the adoption of a precautionary approach to decision making, the avoidance of adverse cumulative effects, and the use of science and mātauranga Māori (Māori knowledge) to achieve the objectives. The strategy must describe how the vision will be implemented and set out a programme for, among other things, improving water quality, customary rights and responsibilities, public use and access, and commercial use. The Guardians Establishment Committee will be responsible for developing the vision and strategy.

Both the Guardians and the Waikato River Statutory Board (the Statutory Board) will have crucial roles in implementing the vision and strategy. The purpose of the Guardians – which will be a permanent, statutory body – will be to promote and work to achieve the overarching purpose of the settlement, assist each river iwi to exercise mana whakahaere over the river, work to achieve a holistic and coordinated approach to the management of the river, and act consistently with the vision. This will involve promoting the inclusion of the strategy in relevant policies and plans, monitoring progress towards the vision, and regularly reviewing the strategy to ensure that it remains relevant. The Guardians will also be a link between the vision and strategy and the community. For example, they will be required to develop co-management arrangements with statutory bodies and share information about the health of the river.

The purpose of the Statutory Board will be to ensure that relevant statutory management authorities give the vision and strategy the highest level of recognition. Like the Rotorua Lakes Strategy Group, the Statutory Board brings key people from the regional council and claimants together, creating a forum in which relationships between the two parties can be developed. Assuming these relationships are maintained, the Statutory Board enables Waikato-Tainui to promote its values for the river to influential people on the regional council at critical times, such as the early stages of plan development. Within this forum there is also the potential to build better understandings of these values, and ultimately, more meaningful application of them through methods in plans.

The Waikato Regional Council is required to give effect to the vision, in accordance with the relevant provisions of the strategy, when preparing or changing its regional plans and policy statements. In reading this provision, one implication is immediately apparent – it gives a directive to the council to realise the vision through its policy documents. For this reason, it has the potential to be a very useful tool for achieving the tribe's goals.

The Agreement in Principle provides for Waikato-Tainui to have input into the allocation of water in the river. The settlement legislation will include a provision that prohibits *disposition* – the creation of a property right or interest in the river – that is inconsistent with the vision and without prior engagement between Waikato-Tainui and the Crown. In the Agreement, disposition includes the grant of an estate in fee simple or easement, a lease, or a licence.

Finally, the Agreement in Principle will include financial redress. This will provide for cultural and economic loss, the implementation of the settlement, education, a river clean-up fund, and initiatives to restore and protect the relationships of Waikato-Tainui with the river. A lack of financial resources is one of the major barriers to Māori participation in fresh water management and decision making (Bennett 2007). Therefore, the financial redress is essential to Waikato-Tainui promoting and ultimately achieving their aspirations for the river.

Settlement	Redress mechanisms
Te Arawa lakes	Statutory vesting of lakebeds
	Representation on Rotorua Lakes Strategy Group
	Management of non-commercial indigenous fisheries
	$400,000 to purchase fishing licences
	Financial redress of $10 million
Waikato River	Commitment to co-management
	Representation on Guardians Establishment Committee, Guardians of the Waikato River and Waikato River Statutory Board
	Waikato River vision and strategy
	Statutory provision to prohibit disposition of river
	Financial redress

Table 1: Summary of redress mechanisms

Conclusion

At a time when the future supply of clean, fresh water is a priority issue for Aotearoa New Zealand, it is critical that Māori have a voice in fresh water planning. In this realm, recent and proposed settlements, such as those that have been or are being negotiated between Te Arawa, Waikato-Tainui and the Crown, bring Māori closer to the decision-making table. They also create a focus for collaborative efforts to restore and protect water bodies that are not only significant to Māori, but to all New Zealanders. If other iwi negotiate such settlements then the future for our precious lakes and rivers seems brighter. And if the health of our water bodies is the ultimate priority, then everyone will benefit.

END NOTES

[1] See particularly Tipa and Teirney (2003), pp. 6-9, and the following reports of the Waitangi Tribunal: *Report of the Waitangi Tribunal on the Kaituna River Claim* (Wellington: Waitangi Tribunal, 1984), pp. 9–15; *Ngai Tahu Report 1991: Volume Three* (Wellington: Brooker and Friend, 1991), pp. 841–883; *Te Ika Whenua Rivers Report* (Wellington: GP Publications, 1998), pp. 12–16; and *The Whanganui River Report* (Wellington: Legislation Direct, 1999), pp. 55–79.

[2] Sustainable management is defined in the Resource Management Act 1991 as: 'managing the use, development and protection of natural resources in a way, or at a rate, which enables people and their communities to provide for their social, economic and cultural wellbeing and for their health and safety while (a) sustaining the potential of natural and physical resources (excluding minerals) to meet the reasonably foreseeable needs of future generations (b) safeguarding the life-supporting capacity of air, water, soil and ecosystems, and (c) avoiding, remedying or mitigating any adverse effects of activities on the environment'.

[3] These are lakes Rotorua, Rotoiti, Rotoehu, Rotomā, Ōkataina, Ōkareka, Tikitapu, Tarawera, Rotomahana, Rerewhakaaitu, Ōkaro (Ngākaro) Ngāhewa, Tuteinanga, and Ngāpouri (Ōpouri).

[4] Lakes Rotorua, Rotoehu, and Ōkaro have poor water quality Lake Rotoiti's water quality is deteriorating, and Lake Ōkareka is described as potentially vulnerable (ibid.).

[5] The loss of ownership of the Rotorua lakes is described in detail in White (1998). A brief summary, based on White's discussion, is provided here.

[6] The vision for the lakes of the Rotorua district, as encapsulated in the Strategy for the lakes of the Rotorua district (2000), is: 'The lakes of the Rotorua district and their catchments are preserved and protected for the use and enjoyment of present and future generations, while recognising and providing for the traditional relationship of Te Arawa with their ancestral lakes' (p. iii).

[7] The author understands that Waikato-Tainui refers to the Waikato descendants of the Tainui waka (canoe). The hapū (sub-tribes) who make up Waikato-Tainui are specified in the deed of settlement between Her Majesty the Queen in right of New Zealand and Waikato (1995) accessible, as at the time of writing, at http://nz01.terabyte.co.nz/ots/DocumentLibrary/WaikatoDeedOfSettlement.pdf.

[8] At the time of writing, the Waikato River claim has not been settled.

Ngā Pae o Rangitīkei – a model for collective hapū/iwi action?

Te Rina Warren

E rere te aroha i te ao e huri nei kimikimi kau ana te taunga horo pai,
Whakararo te tau, ko runga Aorangi, atea te titiro ki ngā ea e rere ana
ki tai,
Ka tau whakatau i a Rangitīkei, kohia ngā wai... (Wilson 2001)

This waiata, composed by Che Wilson (of Ngāti Rangi, Ngāti Tamakōpiri and Ngāti Whitikaupeka descent) reminds us as tangata whenua of our close affiliation to the land. It highlights the importance of one ancestral river, the Rangitīkei, as the confluence and mainstem of many rivers within Mōkai Pātea, Inland Pātea. In the new millennium, tangata whenua located around the Rangitīkei River have been reminded of how much our environment sustains us and ultimately of our responsibility as kaitiaki of Papatūānuku.

Over the past century hapū and iwi within the catchment area of the Rangitīkei River have been affected by many incidents that have had environmental impacts. There are generic effects on the land and rivers such as population growth and the development of infrastructure, as well as natural disaster effects such as severe flooding. During this time we were also reminded of some of our cultural strengths – the ability to work together for a common cause and mutual benefit without losing the rangatiratanga of each unit of the cooperative (Warren 2004). Effective and beneficial relationships have long been a tradition of Māori where relationships were historically formed to ensure strategic and common benefits (Warren 2007).

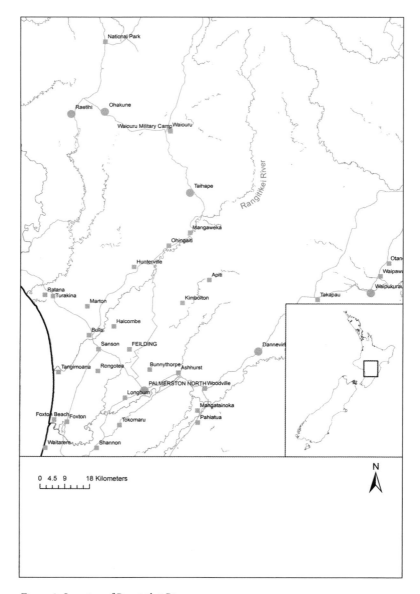

Figure 1. Location of Rangitīkei River.

In June 2003 at a series of hapū, iwi and marae hui it was decided that a unified hapū and iwi voice combined with collective action would better position hapū and iwi along the Rangitīkei River to address collective concerns.

This chapter examines the establishment of Ngā Pae o Rangitīkei: a unique collective of hapū and iwi which joined together to address environmental issues relevant for the Rangitīkei River. This chapter discusses how the group has evolved and some of the key challenges and lessons that have occurred during this process.

The location of the Rangitīkei River

The Rangitīkei River is located in the middle of the central North Island. The 241 kilometre river flows from the Kaimanawa Ranges situated to the north-east of Waiouru down through the central North Island past OTaihape, Mangaweka, Hunterville, Rata, Marton, Bulls and out to the Tasman Sea at Tangimoana on the South Taranaki Bight.

The main tributaries of the Rangitīkei River are the Moawhango Rahi River (which runs from the Kaimanawa Ranges to the west of the Rangitīkei) and the Hautapu River (which begins to the east of Waiouru). Both these rivers enter the Rangitīkei River near to Otoea (south of OTaihape) at a locally renowned swimming spot known locally as the Meeting of the Waters.

Hapū and iwi from marae within the Rangitīkei catchment area include (but are not limited to) Ngāti Tūwharetoa, Ngāti Rangi, Ngāti Tamakōpiri, Ngāti Whitikaupeka, Ngāti Hinemanu, Ngāti Paki, Ngāi Te Ūpokoiri, Ngāti Honomōkai, Ngāti Hauiti, Ngāti Pikiahu, Ngāti Waewae, Ngāti Matakore, Ngāti Rangatahi, Ngāti Manomano, Ngāti Parewahawaha, Ngāti Raukawa, Ngā Uri o Tuariki (Ngāti Apa), Ngāti Kauae, and Ngāti Tauira.

This highlights several of the characteristics of the Rangitīkei River. First, there are a number of hapū and iwi within the river catchment. Second, the hapū and iwi affiliate to at least four different waka. Importantly, there are a number of marae and home residences within the catchment that rely directly on the river and tributaries for water supply, which emphasises the importance of the general health of the Rangitīkei River as a source of drinking water.

Recent concerns along the river

Recent activities such as water extraction and water damming within the Rangitīkei catchment have affected both the water quality and quantity. Generally, water quantity is being affected by extraction for irrigation and diversion for power-generation. This affects water quality which impacts on the flora and fauna of the river. Water quality is adversely affected not only by extraction and diversion but also by pollutants and runoff from land-based activities. These affect the flora and fauna and water-drinking capability of the river for those who rely on it. Overall, these activities have impacted on the traditional uses of the rivers within the Rangitīkei. For example, practices such as tohi and mahinga kai have ceased as water quality and quantity has declined.

Previous consultation between Māori and those who had an interest in the environment was minimal and for the most part tokenistic. In the case of the 1965 damming of the Moawhango Rahi River, local accounts reveal that a few resident Māori were asked if they thought the dam might be a good idea at the time. The construction of the dam followed soon after. Similar instances of natural resource use in the Rangitīkei catchment have left hapū and iwi feeling disenfranchised by government processes. These processes and the ongoing concerns about the state of the Rangitīkei River and its environs led Ngāti Hauiti and Rauhuia Environmental Services to seek the support of affected hapū and iwi. The proposal that hapū and iwi collaborate resulted in what became Ngā Pae o Rangitīkei.

Rauhuia Environmental Services

Rauhuia Environmental Services was set up under Te Maru o Ruahine Trust. The Trust was set up by Ngāti Hauiti iwi members to provide advice to local iwi and in particular to Ngāti Hauiti. One function of Rauhuia has been to process resource consents on behalf of local iwi and to make recommendations to iwi regarding environmental issues and or impacts that a particular activity may have on iwi. In addition, the core function Rauhuia has is to provide consultation and administration support to Te Rūnanga o Ngāti Hauiti and, more recently, to Ngā Pae o Rangitīkei.

Rauhuia Environmental Services was formally established in 1998. It grew out of the need to address the resource consent requirements that are founded in the Resource Management Act 1991. Over time, Rauhuia realised there was an increasing number of consents for gravel extraction and water abstraction along the length and breadth of the Rangitīkei River. As issues and concerns were already being raised by the affected hapū and iwi, it seemed timely to convene hui to discuss those issues, especially the environmental issues that were common among hapū and iwi along the Rangitīkei River. However, a number of decisions needed to be made before this group would be established.

Establishing the group

Rauhuia Environmental Services led and administered the task of meeting with hapū and iwi. There were several challenges to establishing the collective. First, the relevant hapū, iwi and marae had to be identified. As Rauhuia has a track record of research about, for and with iwi within the Rangitīkei catchment they were advantaged by their knowledge of iwi history. In addition, both Rauhuia Environmental Services and Ngāti Hauiti engage readily with hapū, iwi and marae in the area. This facilitated the identification of relevant bodies but also meant that approaching and meeting with hapū, iwi and marae was a natural cultural practice. In essence, it was an extension of whanaungatanga to engage with neighbouring hapū and iwi. Hence in 2003, Rauhuia Environmental Services began extensive hui and communication with affected hapū and iwi groups to ascertain the level of interest in establishing a collective environment body for hapū and iwi.

Second was the challenge of being able to gather representative hapū, iwi and marae members to form a working party to establish a group. Coordinating a group of people from different geographical areas with diverse commitments required a large amount of energy. Again the collective was fortunate that this task could be undertaken by Rauhuia Environmental Services.

In June of that year hapū and iwi of the Rangitīkei River agreed that a working party be established to develop a formal agreement and collaborative direction with regard to the Rangitīkei River. This produced representatives from different (but not all) hapū and iwi as persons mandated by their marae and or Trust or Rūnanga to the working party.

Third, there was the need for the group to come to a common understanding of the purpose of the collective, its function, and the founding principles that would guide it. Several meetings occurred at different marae to confer and agree upon these aspects of the collective. The development of a charter for the group ensued, which was the beginning of Ngā Pae o Rangitīkei.

It could be argued that Ngā Pae o Rangitīkei is a new and perhaps revolutionary way to approach the contemporary issues that face Māori. However, the notion of alliance is not new for Māori. In establishing Ngā Pae o Rangitīkei traditional allegiances have in fact been re-activated to advance a common goal.

There is a diverse set of dynamics that occur with the creation of Māori collectives, which possibly pose a challenge in themselves. Historic relationships and engagements are sometimes called on for mutual benefit but in other circumstances negative historic memories need to be put aside to advance the common goal. Ultimately the success of a unified cooperative will lie in the desire and commitment to that common goal. In terms of Ngā Pae o Rangitīkei this goal is 'to preserve and enhance the mauri of the Rangitīkei River and its environs' (Rangitīkei River Inter-tribal Working Party 2004b:1). This clearly defined goal provides direction for Ngā Pae o Rangitīkei and ensures that relationships are formed with a common purpose in mind. This shared goal has been critical in ensuring that hapū and iwi politics contribute positive interventions to achieve a mutually desirable goal.

The discussion document

The Working Party produced a discussion document that outlined five specific areas for consideration. The mandated working party suggested that Ngā Pae o Rangitīkei would be a suitable name for the collective, given that the name represents all the pae maunga or ancestral mountains within the catchment. It also pays tribute to the many paepae or speaking mantles of the numerous marae within the catchment area. Essentially, it is a symbolic reference to the generations that have walked upon the marae of the Rangitīkei River and to all the ancestral mountains around the River, and it serves as a reminder of the common bond that all iwi within the catchment share.

The first point was that Ngā Pae o Rangitīkei would be a collective of hapū, iwi and marae that have mana whenua (Durie 1998) within the geographic boundaries of the entire Rangitīkei River catchment. The founding principle of the collective was to protect and enhance the mauri of the river. This principle superseded all political and social boundaries.

The collective would also include hapū and iwi who have mana whenua within the Rangitīkei River Catchment (Rangitīkei River Inter-tribal Working Party 2004a). The notion that Ngā Pae o Rangitīkei would be an inclusive group was to ensure all hapū, iwi and marae that have a vested interested in the Rangitīkei catchment would always have the opportunity to participate in the collective.

Second, the document highlighted that Ngā Pae o Rangitīkei was created to be a vehicle to advance tangata whenua rights by drawing on the rich and diverse history of the Rangitīkei catchment. It could also contribute by providing avenues for Māori advancement and the assertion of rangatiratanga with regards to the environment. A collective voice complemented by collaborative efforts allowed the potential for hapū, iwi and marae to protect the river catchment in perpetuity. The dominant concerns for hapū, iwi and marae at the formation of Ngā Pae o Rangitīkei included:

- Gravel extraction from the Rangitīkei and its tributaries
- The declining number of native fauna and flora
- Deforestation, erosion, pollution, diversion and other similar impacts, and
- Concern about commercial interests and impacts on the catchment area (Rangitīkei River Inter-tribal Working Party 2004a:3)

One of the concerns for Ngā Pae o Rangitīkei was that some of the more politically active hapū and iwi were consulted about resource consents that were outside their iwi boundaries. Local government agents and resource consent applicants were then advised of the appropriate hapū/iwi to consult. This highlighted the need for Māori to have a more collective approach to natural resources and developments. Moreover, it emphasised the need for Māori to be proactive in such matters instead of being reactive to external developments.

The third point examined the notion of a formal agreement. The Working Party for Ngā Pae o Rangitīkei required that all parties in the collective clearly understood the parameters and goals of Ngā Pae o Rangitīkei. A formal agreement could define the scope and objectives of the collective and also provide information to external organisations about how to engage with the concerned parties. This provided an avenue by which the hapū, iwi and marae of Ngā Pae o Rangitīkei could reposition themselves into being more proactive with regard to environmental concerns. The agreement would serve as a terms of reference for collective strategies and planning, identify the accountability of the group, and act as an information conduit to external bodies. Consultation processes with Māori have historically been a contentious issue for Māori. In this regard it was suggested that Ngā Pae o Rangitīkei could act as a vehicle to inform external agencies of the proper consultation processes that concerned the Rangitīkei River catchment.

Fourth, the supporting principles that would provide the parameters for Ngā Pae o Rangitīkei were considered. The document acknowledged that many of these principles were subject to interpretation (Rangitīkei River Inter-tribal Working Party 2004b), but the culture of the collective was paramount in terms of their interpretation in this context. They offered a foundation and starting point for Ngā Pae o Rangitīkei. The following values were agreed:

- Kaitiakitanga: that whānau, hapū and iwi govern their own particular areas and have a responsibility to the environment that encompasses many traditional notions such as rāhui or a sense of natural resource management
- Kōtahitanga: that unity creates strength where the collective group Ngā Pae o Rangitīkei can advocate tino rangatiratanga and kaitiakitanga for the mauri of the catchment
- Manaakitanga: that collaboration is key where support between hapū, iwi and marae can positively advance the aspirations of the collective
- Utu or reciprocity: acknowledges that relationships are mutual. This applies to people and the environment – just as the environment nourishes us, we must nourish the environment
- Tino rangatiratanga: is defined as hapū/iwi being the sovereign authorities with the right to manage the environment as guaranteed in Te Tiriti o Waitangi

- Atua: that we acknowledge our heritage, our ancestors, and our spiritual connections to the gods
- Mana: reinforces that hapū and iwi have a right to 'exercise power and control over natural resources' (Rangitīkei River Inter-tribal Working Party 2004a:5)
- Ahi kā: that individuals, whānau and hapū physically maintain a connection to the environment. This is a status for those who remain on their ancestral lands and
- "physically retain a connection to the lands that represent their hapu and iwi"

(Rangitīkei River Inter-tribal Working Party 2004a: 6).

Fifth, the future direction of Ngā Pae o Rangitīkei was considered. The intention of the working party for Ngā Pae o Rangitīkei was to "preserve and enhance the mauri of the Rangitikei River and its environs" (Rangitīkei River Inter-tribal Working Party 2004b: 1). This ensured that the collective could potentially gain political leverage, particularly with resource consent applications. In addition the group would also have the potential to:

- raise whānau awareness around issues
- advocate avenues and processes for protecting relevant sites
- facilitate various relationships including hapū, iwi and government agencies
- advise whānau and iwi of kaitiakitanga opportunities
- act as a supervisory body for activities within the catchment
- facilitate research and development
- develop national and international relationships
- develop plans for natural disasters.

(Rangitīkei River Inter-tribal Working Party 2004a:6).

The functions of Ngā Pae o Rangitīkei were not limited to these points, rather they were offered for discussion for a collective like Ngā Pae o Rangitīkei.

- Sixth, the document suggested that successful representation for Ngā Pae o Rangitīkei would involve:
- mandated representation from each of the participating hapū and iwi
- an appointed proxy
- consensus decision making.

(Rangitīkei River Inter-tribal Working Party 2004a: 7).

It was recommended that a charter for Ngā Pae o Rangitīkei could be developed as a formal agreement between hapū and iwi to establish the collective. The charter would formalise the hapū and iwi relationships and outline a mutually beneficial goal, complete with agreed principles for the collective.

In joining Ngā Pae o Rangitīkei, hapū and iwi agreed to place representatives on the group to deal with environmental issues that impacted on the collective. It was recommended that the charter be reviewed biannually to ensure progress was being made and to also reaffirm the commitment of hapū and iwi to the goals and objectives of the group.

Formalising a relationship: Charter for Ngā Pae o Rangitīkei

The Charter of Ngā Pae o Rangitīkei (The Working Party for Ngā Pae o Rangitīkei 2005) was signed at Rata marae in 2005 by a number of marae, hapū and iwi of the Rangitīkei River catchment. It was written in a similar vein to the discussion document and formalised a relationship between interested and affected hapū and iwi within the Rangitīkei River catchment. It provides parameters for development and activity with regard to the Rangitīkei River and ensures that mutual goals are clearly identified. The Charter is a simple document that outlines five areas to which hapū/iwi have agreed as a foundation for the collective hapū and iwi of Ngā Pae o Rangitīkei. The Statement of Intent frames the overriding intention of the collective, which is 'to preserve and enhance the mauri of the Rangitīkei River and its environs' (The Working Party for Ngā Pae o Rangitīkei 2005: 1). The Statement of Scope identifies the geographical area with which the collective is concerned; basically this is the Rangitīkei River and its catchment area from the source to the sea.

The Statement of Principles describes those principles that will guide the collective.

The Statement of Mutual Agreement expresses some further statements that provide the parameters of operation for the collective of Ngā Pae o Rangitīkei, which incorporate the Declaration of Independence (1835) and Te Tiriti o Waitangi as documents that 'affirm hapū and iwi self determination' (The Working Party for Ngā Pae o Rangitīkei 2005: 2). In addition, there is acknowledgement of those international laws, conventions and protocols that support indigenous rights and seek to protect the environment. Ngā Pae o Rangitīkei states its support for such international activities. 'Inclusiveness' is integrated in the Charter to provide an opportunity for those hapū and iwi that may not have signed the Charter or that may not as yet wish to join the collective to do so at any time.

The enhancement of mana is also mentioned in the charter and asks that all parties to Ngā Pae o Rangitīkei endeavour to enhance the mana of other parties. In this respect the charter asks that an environmental activity that may adversely affect another hapū or iwi of the collective is discussed within Ngā Pae o Rangitīkei to ensure others are not adversely affected by developments. Finally, the notions of cooperation and mutual respect are upheld to ensure all signatories are aware that 'working together for a common cause' (The Working Party for Ngā Pae o Rangitīkei 2005: 2) is fundamental to the collective.

The Statement of Declaration identifies the different hapū and iwi and their representative bodies. In many cases hapū and iwi have been represented by Trusts or Rūnanga. Where Trusts and Rūnanga are identified as representing hapū or iwi then communication with them as pre-mandated authorities has already been undertaken to ensure adequate and appropriate representation to Ngā Pae o Rangitīkei.

Some hapū and iwi do not have any pre-existing mandated bodies. In this case, communication with the relevant marae has taken place and their representatives to Ngā Pae o Rangitīkei have undertaken the appropriate processes to achieve representation on Ngā Pae o Rangitīkei.

Benefits for the collective

Discussing and formalising a cooperative that can protect and advance collective aspirations was only the beginning of the journey. Specific benefits for the collective include whanaungatanga, which has been strengthened through the collaboration of hapū and iwi to enhance the environs of the Rangitīkei River. Ngā Pae o Rangitīkei has also allowed hapū and iwi to advance and or develop strategic directions for the environment.

On a practical level hapū and iwi have been able to enhance the environment via relationships built through Ngā Pae o Rangitīkei, which have included:

- Ngāti Hauiti engaging in a project to protect a pā site overlooking the Rangitīkei River. Horizons Regional Council provided some sponsorship for fencing the whānau-owned land that contains earthworks and terracing.
- Proposals and discussions with Ngā Pae o Rangitīkei and local government about a recycling centre at a local school; and
- Initial planning stages are underway for restoration for Lake Oporoa, which flows into the Rangitīkei River. This project is currently being discussed with Horizons Regional Council and the Department of Conservation.

A profile for hapū and iwi has been developed in local, regional, national and international groups. In particular, relationships that have been formed with government agencies have led to:

- a raised profile and awareness of tangata whenua in local, regional and central government agencies, for example, Regional Council and the Department of Conservation
- hapū and iwi awareness of environmental activity at an early stage of the resource consent process
- some political ability to influence environmental decision making by actively contributing to Regional Council planning.

Ngā Pae o Rangitīkei has raised awareness of the appropriate processes for including and consulting tangata whenua, and these have been transferable to other hapū and iwi initiatives. In this sense there have also been some benefits for other groups. The formation of Ngā Pae o Rangitīkei has:

- provided local and central government with one clear contact point for the hapū and iwi of the collective
- provided points of reference for government agencies and other groups to engage with hapū and iwi of Ngā Pae o Rangitīkei
- provided an example of how agencies can engage actively and positively with hapū and iwi
- allowed groups to engage with hapū and iwi early in the resource consent process, thus allowing meaningful consultation
- encouraged groups to foster close working relationships and collaborations with hapū and iwi.

Challenges of the collective

Ngā Pae o Rangitīkei has faced and continues to face a number of challenges. The hapū and iwi representatives to Ngā Pae o Rangitīkei meet bi-monthly or when needed to discuss environmental activities that are taking place within the catchment and to discuss the opportunities for future developments. However, resource capacity is a challenge for the collective. Ngā Pae o Rangitīkei operates with limited human and financial resources. In this instance the group encounters challenges:

- To coordinate the representatives to meet, given the large geographical area. This requires considering travel and time commitments
- For hapū and iwi representatives to organise whānau, marae, hapū and iwi, employment, and other commitments
- To administer the group
- To implement the desired environmental projects of hapū and iwi.

These challenges have been mitigated to some extent through the support of Rauhuia Environmental Services, which has contributed to the administration of Ngā Pae o Rangitīkei. Relationships built with other agencies through the collective have allowed Ngā Pae o Rangitīkei and hapū and iwi to access some financial support. Ideally, Ngā Pae o Rangitīkei would employ a full-time administrator. In addition, hapū and iwi would also have the capacity to carry out their desired environmental projects.

One continual challenge for Ngā Pae o Rangitīkei is that there will always be groups and companies who want to fast track the resource consent process. In this case, Ngā Pae o Rangitīkei requires a good profile and strong relationships with local government to stay informed of pending resource consents. These are all issues that Ngā Pae o Rangitīkei continues to address.

The future of Ngā Pae o Rangitīkei

Undoubtedly others have established networks, methods and bodies to deal with their environmental concerns. However, for the hapū and iwi of the Rangitīkei this collective has provided a small but beneficial body to deal with distinctly local environment concerns and aspirations.

This chapter has outlined part of the journey for hapū and iwi of the Rangitīkei catchment in protecting and moving towards enhancing the environment. It has examined one example of collective action for advancing hapū and iwi environmental aspirations. There is still work to be carried out by Ngā Pae o Rangitīkei, and this will initially depend on the continued commitment of hapū and iwi. Increasing the capacity of the collective and of hapū and iwi is an important aspect of future developments. Full-time administrative staff and resources to implement and support environmental projects are also important for the future of Ngā Pae o Rangitīkei.

Other aspirations are to produce an environmental manuscript that profiles the relationship of hapū and iwi with the environment and an environmental conference. Ngā Pae o Rangitīkei also wants to further relationships with other groups and agencies. This includes seeking representation on groups and agencies that may assist hapū and iwi environmental aspirations and influencing environmental policy at all levels (local, regional, national, and international).

There are many steps left in our journey. Just as our tūpuna sought alliances to progress common causes (Warren 2007), Ngā Pae o Rangitīkei endeavours to align hapū and iwi with other concerned parties in order to protect and enhance the environment.

It is our responsibility as descendants of Ranginui and Papatūānuku to maintain, protect and enhance our environment for our own well-being and for the use of future generations. It is with this in mind that Ngā Pae o Rangitīkei continues to operate and to advance developments that support and nurture our environment for the benefit of our people today and tomorrow.

Mai i te matāpuna ki tai… e rere mai ko te awa Rangitīkei

Recovering our ancestral landscapes: A wetland's story

Margaret Forster

Drainage of wetlands has considerably transformed both the natural and cultural landscape. For example, the removal of natural waterways, plants and fish stock has severed the multitude of relationships that manawhenua have developed with the natural environment over time. As a result, many freshwater wetlands have simply disappeared and the remnants are fragmented and highly modified, with a diminished capacity to provide for the spiritual, cultural and physical needs of hapū and whānau.

This chapter traces the transformation of wetland ecosystems and provides a commentary of on social and cultural impacts of drainage, ecological degradation and loss of wetland biodiversity. The relationship between communities and wetland ecosystems and the contest between diverging Māori and European land use values and practices are discussed. Wetland-related events and experiences of the Ngai Te Ipu, Ngāti Hinepua and Ngāti Hine hapū in the Wairoa-Mahia region are used to illustrate these issues.

It is argued that despite extensive transformation, remnant wetlands remain highly valued ecosystems and, for local hapū, they continue to make a significant contribution to the spiritual well-being and identity of local hapū. As a consequence, such hapū continue to seek new ways to strengthen connections and develop new relationships with the transformed and highly modified ancestral landscape.

Restoration and enhancement initiatives in the Wairoa-Mahia region illustrate new opportunities to exercise kaitiakitanga responsibilities and obligations, to be active kaitiaki, and to ensure wetlands and lakes remain a central feature of hapū identity. Such initiatives are part of the wider politics of resistance; a recovery strategy, reclaiming those places and the associated knowledge and practices that are valued by hapū and promoting Māori interests in environmental management and protection. This chapter explores the cultural, social and political dimensions of the wetland story. A major focus is the relationship between the local accumulated intergenerational knowledge, experiences and cultural uses of wetlands by hapū and the recovery of control over and use of our ancestral landscapes.

The importance of ancestral places

Drainage of wetlands has considerably transformed both the natural and cultural landscape. Historically, wetlands were highly valued ecosystems, areas of immense importance to Māori communities (White 1998; Park 2001: 19–87) as these areas provided food and other useful resources but, more importantly, also sustained the community's spiritual well-being and shaped hapū identity.

In my grandparents' tribal rohe wetlands were a dominant feature of the natural landscape, with major coastal wetlands, lagoon systems and associated waterways that extended from Wairoa through to Mahia Peninsula. These included Whakaki Lake and the Whakamahi, Whakamahia, Ngamotu, Whakaki,[1] and Maungawhio lagoon systems and Whangawehi Estuary. There were also several freshwater wetlands among the dunes throughout Mahia Peninsula and many, such as the Opoutama wetlands[2], have been "highly modified by drainage, stock and weed invasion" (Whaley et al. 2001). Our communities settled in close proximity to these waterways and were dependent on the natural resources associated with these systems for sustenance, for day-to-day living, for the construction of settlements and waka, and for trade (Tomlins-Jahnke 1994). Very little of the original vegetation remains. Areas that were once forest vegetation have been cleared for agricultural activity, including sheep and cattle farming, cropping, orchards and housing settlements at Iwitea,

Whakaki, Nuhaka, Opoutama, Mahanga, Mahia Beach, Oraka Beach and Mahia (East).

Whakaki Lake has, both in the past and today, played a central role in the identity of the local hapū (Tomlins-Jahnke 1994: 19-20):

> *The tangata whenua of Whakaki desired a total way of life from this lagoon and its tributaries. Their ancestors are buried in several urupa around the perimeters of the lagoon. The spiritual connections are strongly bonded between the land, lagoon and people. The heritage bonds give the tangata whenua their pride, their mana and their spiritual culture (25 May 1992 from Huki Solomon to Parliamentary Commissioner for the Environment, Mrs Helen Hughes, cited in Parliamentary Commissioner for the Environment 1993a: 29).*

Hapū identity, while closely linked to key ancestors, is also shaped by relationships with the natural environment and associated resources. Tuna are a very important taonga to hapū from the Whakaki region (Tomlins-Jahnke 1994) and the local people are widely known as Kirituna (Huki Solomon, Joe Smith, Whakaki Lake Trust, pers. comms, cited in Parliamentary Commissioner for the Environment 1993b: 47). Literally meaning eel skin, the name Kirituna acknowledges the famed stocks of tuna at Whakaki, in the same way that Mahia was known for its kaimoana delicacies. In addition, Kirituna also acknowledges the extensive tuna knowledge base and associated practices developed by Whakaki hapū through a long association with this resource and the wetlands system.

Transforming landscapes and cultural loss

The reduction of the life-sustaining capacity of the wetland ecosystem, primarily through drainage and agricultural conversion, was accompanied by a corresponding decline in the manawhenua and spiritual well-being of hapū associated with those areas. Drainage of wetlands not only removed the water, the plants and the fish but also severed the multitude of relationships that manawhenua had developed with the natural landscape.

As settlers began to acquire large tracts of land, European interests, values and institutions of land use and management began to dominate the use and development of New Zealand natural resources. While Māori regarded wetlands and swamps as an important source of food and resources,[3] the European position differed considerably. Wetlands, from a European perspective, were areas of wildness and waste, of little value except after drainage when the rich soil was exposed, ready for conversion to pasture and cropland (Park 2002). Therefore, Māori preferential use and development of wetlands and associated natural resources were no longer a key, or even a passing, consideration in the new colonial land use and management regime.

Swamp drainage, for settlement and agricultural activities, and the introduction of new and sometimes invasive species, significantly altered the indigenous wetland ecology. This is not to say that Māori communities did not alter their local environment. Settlement and deforestation for horticultural purposes transformed the natural environment and, over time, some bird species disappeared as a direct result of Māori activity.[4] Māori also transformed wetland areas constructing for example pa tuna. As Māori communities became fixed to a geographical area and developed manawhenua relationships and obligations, a sustainable resource use ethic emerged, known today as kaitiakitanga.[5] Through the institution of kaitiakitanga, Māori have a long tradition of sustainable resource use, of maintaining the mauri or health of an ecosystem while balancing natural resource use and development. For example, wetland ecosystems were highly valued and essential mahinga kai sites and human activity was regulated to protect the integrity of the system. Indeed, despite a long association with the tribal area, the natural environment and associated resources were able to recover from the presence of Māori communities (Pond 1997a: 1, 9; Young 2004: 53–56). There was a wide range of indigenous biota and a considerable abundance of natural resources when Europeans began arriving and settling in New Zealand (Pond 1997a: 123–126; Young 2004: 53–56). However, European colonisation accelerated ecological transformation and native biodiversity loss (Pond, 1997a: 10–11, 123–126; Young 2004: 12, 58–78) as the natural environment was once again transformed; transformed by land-use values and developments introduced not only by Europeans but also by Māori. Māori have a long history of appropriation of European agricultural technology and knowledge and use of introduced animals and crops to provide provisions for the whalers, sealers and new arrivals, and later to participate in the new colonial economy.

Nevertheless, wetlands were still highly significant cultural areas to Māori and extensive drainage was not an option. However, extensive drainage became necessary if Māori wished to engage in the new settler economy, initially to participate in the flax trade and then in the early 1900s, as the demand for suitable land for agricultural purposes increased. In the Whakaki region flax export was a significant export earner from the 1860s through to 1925. Swamp areas were drained to facilitate commercial flax harvesting and the hill country cleared for pastoral farming and to fuel the steam boilers of the Tuhara flax mill.[6] By the 1920s the flax plantations were being replaced by pastures. Crown legislation and policy actively supported and accelerated the drainage and agricultural conversion programme. The 1876 Public Works Act, Counties Act 1886 (section 272) and the Swamp Drainage Act 1915 provided for large-scale drainage operations and the acquisition of "any land required for drainage purposes" (Park 2002: 163) including Māori-owned land. In addition, the establishment of Ratepayer boards under the Rivers Board Act 1884 and the Land Drainage Act 1893 enabled farmers' interests, especially drainage, to dominate the agenda. While drainage was in the main actively supported by the farming sector, there was evidence of support from some of the local Māori community. Records for 1946 indicate debate among Māori as to the most appropriate use of the lagoon – farming or fishing (Parliamentary Commissioner for the Environment 1993b: 16–17) – although "total drainage of the lagoon was never contemplated" (Parliamentary Commissioner for the Environment 1993b: 17).

Ecological degradation and biodiversity loss

It has been estimated that 85–90% (Taylor 1997: 64; Park 2001: 637) of New Zealand's freshwater wetlands have been lost, mainly as a result of drainage for agricultural purposes (Taylor 1997). This is a loss rate that ranks amongst the highest recorded in the world (Mitsch & Gosselink 2000). Although swamp drainage significantly reduced the number of wetlands, drainage was not the only cause of decline in wetland biodiversity. For example, the introduction of commercial fishing of eels and inanga,[7] and the introduction of new fish species significantly depleted native freshwater stocks (Pond 1997a: 3–5). Other significant factors include deforestation, deterioration in water quality, changes to waterway hydrology and riparian edge, vermin destruction campaigns,[8] overexploitation, and lack of knowledge (Pond 1997b).

The remnant wetlands, particularly those located on the lowland plains, are fragmented and highly modified. Wetland biota has been replaced by agri-industry products, significantly transforming the natural landscape, in some cases beyond recognition. Today, for example, there are few physical indications that the Hauraki plains were anything other than the farmlands, stop banks and miles of canals and drains that criss-cross the plains (Park 2002: 156). It was once a vast area of kahikatea swamp forests that contained several Māori river pā (Park 2002: 153–154); however, in 1911 after just three short years of drainage work 5200 acres of the plain had been drained and converted for settlement and agricultural use (Park 2001: 20).

Remnant wetlands are today highly valued ecosystems by Māori and several non-Māori groups such as bird watchers, recreational users, and environmentalists. The value associated with these ecosystems is in part related to the scarcity of these types of environments and the rich and diverse range of native flora and fauna that remain in these systems. Park points out that 'Had large-scale draining of swamps not de-watered and de-vegetated most of the nation's low-lying country, a great many species of New Zealand's indigenous flora and fauna from trees to birds and from orchids to insects would be far more common than they are today' (Park 2001: 27).

Wetlands[9] are the primary habitat for a fifth of New Zealand indigenous birds (Ministry for the Environment 1997: 24) and at least 8 of the 29 species of native freshwater fish (Ministry for the Environment 1997: 24, 85). In addition, wetlands have an important role in the regulation of the water table, particularly in their ability to act as drainage and filtration areas and aid flood prevention (Commission for the Environment 1986).

Transformation of surrounding catchment areas also had a substantial effect on the health and functioning of wetland systems. For example, deforestation of the hill country for settlement and agricultural activity accelerated erosion, increasing silt loads in waterways. This affected water quality and resulted in flooding events in the down stream wetland ecosystem due to increased water levels entering the systems from the upper catchment area during rainfall

Land-use activities including farming, horticulture, earthworks, and gravel extraction (Wairoa District Council 2004: 45) in the wider catchment area of the Wairoa district introduced several environmental challenges for Whakaki Lake and lagoon system. Siltation of waterways,[10] eutrophication,[11] reduced water levels and periodic flooding have been continuous issues in the Whakaki area as a direct result of transformation of the hill country and coastal forests. Reduced water levels and poor water quality affects irrigation, watering of stock and maintenance of fish stocks, and periodic flooding threatens neighbouring settlements and farming activities. Therefore, the fragmented and highly modified wetland system struggles to mitigate the effects of surrounding land-use activities and the health and functioning of the lake continues to depend on the regulation of upstream activities, a complex and politically contentious exercise.

The social costs of transforming wetland ecosystems

When conceptualising the impact of wetland drainage, degradation of wetland ecosystems and loss of associated biodiversity are immediately apparent. The New Zealand discourse on wetlands is, for the most part, focused on this ecological and biodiversity loss and the requirement for active protection (Commission for the Environment 1986; Taylor 1997; Department of Conservation & Ministry for the Environment 2000; Parliamentary Commissioner for the Environment 2001; Clarkson et al. 2003). This is a reflection of the global trend towards retention of biodiversity and sustainable use of natural resources. What is not so visible is the relationship between degraded natural landscapes and the hapū and whānau that once depended on these resources for physical spiritual and cultural sustenance. This aspect of swamp ecology is captured, to some extent, by research commissioned as part of the Waitangi Tribunal's native flora and fauna inquiry[12] and some of the evidence presented at the inquiry hearings. The discourse emerging from the native flora and fauna inquiry is centred primarily on demands for recognition of customary use and management rights based on customary environmental management practices and customary relationships between hapū, the local environment, and valued taonga species.

The transformation of wetland ecosystems, as a consequence of drainage and conversion, is a narrative of ecological loss and disconnection that has contributed to the fragmentation and modification of Māori communities. Wetlands once dominated the lowland plains; however, drainage has resulted in a significant decline, and the remnant wetlands have been isolated and disconnected from the surrounding waterways and environs, compromising the functioning of wetlands and their life-supporting capacity. Today, as a direct result of this fragmentation, these highly modified wetland systems and the native flora and fauna that remain, struggle to mitigate the ongoing effects of extensive agri-industry activity and, in particular, the environmental degradation that is a result of deforestation and sediment (siltation) and nutrient (eutrophication) overloads.

Another outcome of ecological decline and reduced biodiversity was a dramatic change in the relationship between hapū and the natural environment. A reduction in customary harvesting practices, related primarily to the loss and degradation of mahinga kai sites and associated natural resources, disconnected Māori communities from the local environment. Māori knowledge transmission is typically transferred through practice. Therefore disconnection from the whenua and a reduction in customary harvesting weakened and disrupted transmission of customary and local ecological knowledge of the area and associated customary harvesting practices related to native flora and fauna, further exacerbating the ability of hapū and whānau to assess the extent and impact of ecological changes. In addition, hydrological changes and the introduction of new flora and fauna required the development of new relationships and interactions with the rapidly changing natural environment.

Māori communities could no longer rely on customary harvesting and were becoming more dependent on the local settler economy and agri-industry. As early as the 1850s the ancestral landscape was being transformed into a foreign, unrecognisable environment to which Māori communities were struggling to relate. For example, Hine-i-Paketia, a Ngāti Kahungunu rangatira with manawhenua extending over Heretaunga, was reduced to selling the tribal estate as it was no longer able to provide for her people, "She was determined to sell her land because it was now useless. The birds and other game – the fruits of the land – had been destroyed by introduced predators" (Ballara 1990: 190–191). Great importance had been placed on the ability of the land to sustain the hapū, and the capacity to provide mahinga kai and other customary resources was to become seriously diminished as the Crown, first in 1876 in the Public Works Act, passed legislation supporting drainage and agricultural conversion. This conversion was accelerated in 1915 with the Swamp Drainage Act. These legislative provisions resulted in farming interests dominating land use and management decision-making and several large-scale drainage projects were established. Once- familiar landscapes of coastal forests,[13] dunelands,[14] freshwater wetlands.[15] and extensive lagoon and estuary systems were deforested first by Māori and then more extensively for agricultural activities and European settlement, culminating in the now familiar scene of open grassed spaces, cattle, sheep, and crops.

However, the greatest threat to hapū was the loss of manawhenua or authority that accompanied the inability to maintain a relationship with the ancestral landscape. Transformation of the ancestral landscape resulted in a reduced capacity of the whenua to sustain Māori communities, both physically and spiritually. Where this resulted in alienation the ability of the whenua to inform hapū identity and shape community values and practices was severely compromised. Hapū struggled to adequately exercise customary resource use and management practices and, as a consequence, to retain and develop associated environmental knowledge, history and harvesting practices. Today, hapū are still connected to a defined area, to a unique ancestral landscape, and while manawhenua may have diminished or in some cases been extinguished, the desire to retain a presence or re-establish a connection remains absolute.

Developing new relationships with the natural environment

For hapū, the transformation of the ancestral landscape to conform to European concepts of productive land use and European ideals of wilderness necessitated the adoption of new land-use practices and the development of new relationships with introduced species. Europeans introduced a wide range of new species that thrived in the New Zealand environment often displacing the native biota through competition for habitat (Young 2004: 12). Today, many of these species remain a threat to native biodiversity and to the integrity of the remnant wetlands systems.

Some introduced species, however, have become highly valued, for example, potatoes revolutionised Māori subsistence horticulture (Young 2004: 58) and, along with other introduced species such as pigs, barley, oats, peas, maize, and wheat, positioned Māori communities to engage actively in trade and export. Some introduced species, such as pork, potatoes and watercress, have become essential ingredients in what would be considered traditional Māori food, a boil up or hāngi.

Just as some introduced species have been appropriated into Māori cultural traditions so too have conventional European land-use practices such as agricultural activities. Agricultural activity was not a predominant feature of pre-contact Māori land use (Pond 1997a: 1, 33); nevertheless the agri-industry has become an important economic activity, to the extent that for many hapū farming is now considered a traditional Māori land-use practice.

However, the conversion of wetlands for farming and therefore the participation of Māori in agricultural industry was coerced – a direct response to Crown policy and practices. As land passed out of Māori ownership settler interests began to dominate resource use and development. Enactment of a series of public works and swamp drainage acts[16] established drainage districts and drainage boards that promoted land improvement schemes and the drainage of wetlands and conversion of what was considered by settlers as waste lands to productive agricultural areas. Settlement and agriculture began to emerge as the preferred land-use activities, and by the 1900s the demand for more land was high.

Criticism that remnant Māori freehold land was not contributing to the New Zealand economy, lying idle and going to waste, was the major argument for further alienation of Māori freehold land. Coincidently, this argument also supported the prevailing view and Crown policy[17] that productive agricultural use should dominate land use and development. Individualisation of title[18] also introduced much uncertainty in relation to occupation and land use rights. Multiple ownership proved to be a significant impediment to raising sufficient capital for land development (Loveridge 1996: 7–8). As a consequence, the capacity for Māori to participate in agricultural activity was low. Nevertheless, a desire to retain the remnant tribal estate in Māori ownership and intense political pressure towards productive agricultural land use saw agricultural activity adopted particularly in the Whakaki area, as the principle activity for Māori freehold land. Farming became an important and relatively common Māori land-use activity to prevent further alienation as a response to Crown policy that promoted the compulsory vesting of 'idle' land in Māori Land Boards (Loveridge 1996: 49).

The Māori incorporation system was a common option for Māori freehold land on the East Coast and several blocks in my grandfather's tribal area of Iwitea and Whakaki were incorporated resulting in the Whakaki 2N, Anewa and Te Whakaari incorporations.[19] Whaanga (2004) argued that, 'The foremost reason for establishing Māori land incorporations was to retain the land in Māori ownership. By farming their land, Māori hoped to prevent the government acquiring it for Pākehā farmers' (Whaanga 2004: 125). While incorporations may have been widespread on the East Coast, this system was not necessarily popular. When Whakaki 2N was first incorporated some hapū members dissented from the majority decision, concerned that incorporation would prevent occupation and use of natural resources including customary harvesting sites (Whaanga 2004: 136). Farming too, alienated hapū members from the ancestral landscape. While members were now shareholders and still owned the land, settlement and access were restricted and knowledge of, and connections to, cultural markers that resided on the ancestral landscape and their associated narratives diminished.

Māori farming activities were no different from European agricultural ventures in that agricultural activity made a significant contribution to ecological change and environmental degradation. Drainage and regulation of the water levels in Whakaki Lake was a regular and costly activity of Whakaki 2N incorporation (Whaanga 2004: 138). Although there is some evidence that incorporations did consider the social and cultural interests of the local hapū by providing beef for tangi and regular financial assistance to local marae, churches and some educational scholarships for the families of shareholders (Whaanga 2004: 138), in general, kaitiakitanga values were compromised, undermined by conventional agricultural practices, thus diminishing the ability of hapū to exercise manawhenua and therefore threatening the customary relationship with the ancestral landscape (Parliamentary Commissioner for the Environment 1993a: 30). Māori communities, despite being owners of the land, were prevented from maintaining an active relationship with the area as decisions made by drainage boards and district councils failed to reflect Māori interests (Coombes & Hill 2005: 3–5). In addition, Māori owned land, now managed on the owner's behalf by incorporations, promoted the agricultural agenda, restricting occupation or subsistence harvesting by hapū members. Drainage and the water-level regulations necessary to maximise agricultural productivity and maintain Iwitea village and the Whakaki 2N farm above water, threatened the life-supporting capacity of the wetland ecosystem by restricting the quantity of water in the system and destroying waterways and the spawning habitats of eel and fresh water fish and the bird breeding and feeding areas. However, despite substantial environmental degradation, loss of biodiversity and decline both in the integrity of the Lake and in the quality of the associated natural resources, hapū have remained active kaitiaki, particularly of the tuna resource, and customary harvesting has continued uninterrupted in the Whakaki wetland system.

Farming remains today a major use and main source of revenue of Māori freehold land. Attempts to align agricultural practice with kaitiaki values are, even by Māori owners, rare as the fundamental ethos of maximising productivity and generating profit dominates business practice. More sustainable farming practices to minimise environmental degradation are optional, although not popular ones when accompanied by decreased productivity and a compromised ability to compete with other businesses. Retiring areas of cultural significance from farming is another option. Although this has financial implications they are offset by cultural and spiritual gains that are accrued from becoming active kaitiaki and restoring the mauri of compromised ecosystems and the retention of native biodiversity. For example, in February 2000 624 hectares of Paparatu station,[20] including Lake Mangatahi and Te Houopuanga, was re-designated as a reserve under the Ngā Whenua Rāhui Kawenata[21] scheme. Both Lake Mangatahi and Te Houopuanga were named in Māori Land Court evidence to establish ahi kā of Ngai Tahu and Ngāti Ruapani hapū over this area (Tairawhiti Māori Land Court 1893: 214). Lake Mangatahi was an important resource for harvesting eel and the freshwater fish maehe and, according to a local narrative, is the site where Te Kooti[22] buried a diamond after a battle against European soldiers at Hurukino in 1868 (Tairawhiti Māori Land Court 1893: 205–220; Whaanga 2004: 185–186, 195–198). Te Houopuanga was an early Ngai Tahu and Ngāti Ruapani cultivation. The Ngā Whenua Rāhui Kawenata[23] is an agreement to retire this area from farming and develop an active protection and enhancement strategy. Provisions for the manawhenua relationship of local hapū and the practice of kaitiakitanga and cultural harvesting (Whaanga 2004: 199) are also part of the agreement.

Hapū based restoration

Recent efforts towards wetland restoration and the enhancement of Whakaki Lake is another strategy to protect the integrity of the remnant wetland ecosystems and is connected to the indigenous politics of resistance and cultural recovery. Hapū are seeking to recover their culture and their manawhenua by reconnecting with the ancestral landscape. An emphasis on sustainability and retention of biodiversity has emerged. Environmental enhancement and ecosystem restoration are new strategies for re-establishing connections with natural resources and for consolidation of existing knowledge and development of new knowledge. Such projects enable hapū to once again be active kaitiaki, to incorporate Māori interests in environmental management and protection and to exercise cultural obligations and responsibilities.

However, there are several difficulties in re-establishing a relationship with wetlands and associated natural resources. Many of these ecosystems have simply disappeared. In addition, remnant wetland ecosystems are often so highly modified or degraded that restoration becomes technically very complex and restoration to a pristine state almost impossible.

Whakaki

Activities related to the flax industry and agricultural development including drainage, diversion of waterways and clear-felling of the inland coastal forests, transformed the immediate area surrounding the Lake and the Whakaki Lagoon system itself. By the 1900s a large proportion of the wetlands area surrounding Whakaki Lake had been drained and converted to pasture (Coombes 2007). Drainage and agricultural conversion accelerated in the early 1900s and was facilitated by the 1908 Land Drainage Act, which established drainage boards whose membership was drawn from ratepayers. When the drainage boards were first established in the Whakaki area Māori land was still in customary title and some land was being leased to Pākehā farmers (Coombes 2007). Since these properties were not rated, Māori were excluded from participating in drainage decision-making

(Coombes 2007) as members of the drainage boards were mainly farmers and, not surprisingly, farming interests, as opposed to those of the local hapū or the wider community, dominated decision-making. Exclusion from the decision-making body did not prevent local hapū from voicing opposition to the large-scale drainage operations proposed by the drainage board. At least five petitions were submitted objecting to the composition of the drainage boards and to the ignoring of indigenous rights and interests in the decision-making process (Coombes 2007). In 1900 the Whakaki wetlands system was estimated to be 6000 hectares. By 1960 it had been reduced to 600 hectares (Coombes & Hill 2005: 19).

However, it was not until 1970s that the local hapū, lagoon recreational users and representatives of government agencies noticed major ecosystem changes (Parliamentary Commissioner for the Environment 1993a: 1). The changes were attributed to an artificial opening to release flood waters from Whakaki Lake through the sand dunes directly to the sea that began in 1956. This effectively reversed the natural drainage flow of the Rāhui Channel and allowed sea water to directly enter Whakaki Lake changing the lake's ecology at the new opening.

Ownership of the Whakaki Lake bed[24] resides with the Whakaki Lake Trust, which was established in 1969. The trust is responsible for the management and regulation of access and use of the Lake's natural resource albeit within the confines of Māori land and resource management legislation. The direct opening was vigorously protested and in 1973 the Whakaki Lake Trust began lobbying Government "to restore the Rāhui Channel and Paakaa outlet" (Parliamentary Commissioner for the Environment 1993a: 1). During the 1980s a joint proposal for restoration of the natural opening from the National Water and Social Conservation Authority, the Hawke's Bay Catchment Board and the Wildlife Service was developed but never eventuated. The opening issue was once again resurrected in 1990 by the Māori Standing Committee of the Hawke's Bay Regional Council. A Whakaki Lagoon Working Party was established and in December 1991 lobbied the Minister for the Environment for financial assistance, which was declined. In 1992 the Whakaki Lagoon Working Party approached the Parliamentary Commissioner for the Environment stating concerns over management of the lake. In August 1992 an investigation into the management of Whakaki Lagoon was initiated to clarify responsibility and the extent of the ecological decline of the Whakaki Lagoon system, and to identify potential strategies for enhancement of this wetlands ecosystem. The investigation, identifying both the direct role of Crown agencies in the ecological decline of Whakaki Lagoon and also the decline in hapū authority or manawhenua, recommended a significant contribution towards restoration. At the same time the Hawke's Bay Regional Council was developing a wetland enhancement and management programme and a decision was made to commit funds for major hydrological changes to the Rāhui Channel. Although the committed funds were insufficient and the Whakaki Lake Trust were required to raise another $85,000, the Trust was finally able to restore the Rāhui Channel and implement the Whakaki wetland restoration programme, and to begin the arduous task of restoring the mauri of this highly significant cultural resource.

The Whakaki Lake restoration programme was the first wetland restoration programme driven and led by hapū. During the restoration programme Whakaki Lake Trust has developed working relationships with Hawke's Bay Regional Council, the Department of Conservation, the Wairoa District Council, Eastern Fish & Game, and Whakaki 2N Incorporation. In 1996 restoration began with major changes to the lake hydrology. After fourteen months of excavation the Trust turned their efforts towards a large-scale replanting programme to protect and enhance the wetland and coastal ecosystems. Fencing and de-stocking, noxious plant and animal pest control, ecological monitoring and research related to customary harvesting, particularly of eels, are ongoing. Future plans also exist for the development of an environmental educational programme and a native coastal bird breeding programme.[25]

The Whakaki Lake Trust hapū-based restoration programme has received both international (Ramsar) and national (*"Well justified" awards for top conservation efforts,* 1 February 2001) recognition for its work to 'restore the natural hydrology and ecology of the Whakaki Lagoon and its associated large coastal wetland system' (*"Well justified" awards for top conservation efforts,* 1 February 2001).

Over the past century the local hapū have vigorously opposed those activities, particularly drainage, that have affected the integrity of Whakaki Lake and the surrounding wetland system. Also, the Whakaki Lake Trust has a long history of lobbying at the local, regional and national level

213

initially for restoration of the Rāhui Channel and then for enhancement of the lake itself. As global awareness and support for the conservation and sustainability agendas have grown, hapū and Crown interests have aligned and support and financial assistance for restoring the Whakaki wetland ecosystem have emerged. Since the 1990s the current political environment has become even more receptive, with several major wetland restoration projects supported through the Ngā Whenua Rāhui programme.

Hapū-based restoration programmes provide an opportunity to re-establish cultural connections with natural resources and exercise manawhenua rights and obligations. Consolidation of existing cultural knowledge and ways of knowing associated with wetlands and development of new knowledge provide an indication of the importance of the wetland resource to the community and informs cultural identity and well-being, kaitiaki practice, and social cohesion.

A narrative of ecological loss and disconnection

The transformation of wetland ecosystems as a consequence of drainage and conversion, is a narrative of ecological loss and disconnection that have contributed to the fragmentation and modification of Māori communities.

Remnant wetlands, like Māori communities, have been greatly influenced by Western European values and practices and have been highly modified as a consequence of contact with the West. Wetland ecosystems and Māori communities were expected to change to conform to European values and understandings in relation to appropriate land use and development and notions of modern society and progress. These views were implemented and enforced through legislation and through the normalisation of land-use practices, albeit based on European rather than Māori traditions of what counts as appropriate land use. The remnant wetlands are now interconnected and interdependent on the transformed environment, just as Māori communities became interconnected with, and interdependent on the new arrivals and later the wider New Zealand society.

Contestation has been an enduring feature of this interaction; contestation for authority and contestation to retain the integrity of wetland ecosystems and Māori communities. And regardless of the outcome this interaction has made a significant contribution to the shape and form of modern day wetland ecosystems and Māori society.

At worst, wetland ecosystems have disappeared, displaced by European styles of settlement and agriculture. At best, remnant wetland ecosystems have become fragmented and highly modified, competing with the transformed landscape and introduced species for survival and the maintenance of the integrity of the remnant system, in the same way that Māori communities are constantly responding and interacting with the wider New Zealand community.

Recent efforts at wetland restoration and enhancement are just one strategy for protecting the integrity of the remnant wetland ecosystems and are linked to the indigenous politics of resistance and cultural recovery. Hapū are seeking to recover their culture and their manawhenua by reconnecting with the ancestral landscape. An emphasis on sustainability and retention of biodiversity has emerged. Environmental enhancement and ecosystem restoration is a new strategy for re-establishing connections with natural resources and for consolidation of existing knowledge and development of new knowledge. Such projects enable hapū once again to be active kaitiaki, to incorporate Māori interests in environmental management and protection, and to exercise cultural obligations and responsibilities. Restoring the mauri of compromised wetland ecosystems and transforming the ancestral landscape are exercises in cultural recovery and the re-establishment of a cultural connection with wetlands.

Conclusion

The ancestral landscape is dynamic and constantly changing, a reflection of evolving community values and needs, a diversity in land use and ecological change. Since the arrival of Europeans the wetlands story has been dominated by settler understandings and aspirations. However, to find a more comprehensive picture and deeper understanding of the wetland story it is necessary to look beyond European values associated with wetlands, beyond the ecology, the science and the discourse of ecological health and ecosystem integrity. The wetland story is incomplete without reference to the extensive hapū relationships and the accumulated intergenerational knowledge, experiences and uses of wetland ecosystems and associated natural resources by hapū and whānau. Furthermore, despite a rejection in the dominant hegemony of Māori interests and values in the management of wetland ecosystems, that interest remains strong. Indeed, that voice has never been silent, as evidenced by a history of protests and dismay with the way wetlands have been used and managed to support agricultural interests. Contestation remains a consistent theme as hapū continue to assert Māori interests and aspirations to control and manage wetland resources, and challenge the dominant social and political discourse in an effort to recover control over and use of our ancestral landscapes.

Acknowledgements

This chapter was completed as part of a doctoral research project supported by a Ministry of Research, Science and Technology Te Tipu Pūtaiao Scholarship (MAUX0603).

END NOTES

[1]Ohuia, Wairau, Korito and Patangata Lagoon are part of the Whakaki Lagoon system.

[2]Opoutama wetland was estimated to be around 140 hectares in 1910 and was drained in 1966. Jacob's swamp, a 6.8 hectare wildlife management reserve, was once connected to the Opoutama wetlands (Coombes & Hill 2005: 771).

[3]For a comprehensive discussion of the importance of wetland ecosystems to Māori and the implications of drainage and agricultural conversion on native biodiversity refer to chapter 2 of *Effective Exclusion? An Exploratory Overview of Crown Actions and Māori Responses Concerning the Indigenous Flora and Fauna,* 1912–1983 (Park 2001).

[4]For a detailed discussion of the impact of Pre-European Māori on New Zealand biota and the natural environment refer to Anderson (2002, pp. 19-34) and Young (2004, pp. 37-56).

[5]For an overview of the concept of kaitiakitanga refer to papers written by the Nganeko Minhinnick (1989), Mere Roberts et al. (Roberts et al. 1995) and Māori Marsden (2003a, 2003b).

[6]The Tuhara flaxmill was built in 1881. There were also flaxmills at Tahaenui, Nuhaka and in the 1920s a modern electrical plant at the mouth of the Awatere Stream (Lambert 1977: 409, 745).

[7]Generic Māori term for the different varieties of whitebait.

[8]Indigenous fauna were killed to protect introduced game and game fish (Pond 1997a: 138–140).

[9]It is estimated that since British settlement 670,000 hectares of wetlands have been reduced to 100,000 hectares through transformation to farmlands (Park 2002).

[10]Siltation is the filling in of waterways.

[11]Eutrophication is the increase of nutrients in waterways often caused by the leaching of chemicals from the land due to farming and horticultural activities.

[12]Wai 262 research reports by James Feldman, Robin Hodge, Cathy Marr, Robert McClean, Geoff Park, Trecia Smith, Ben White and David Williams can be downloaded from the Waitangi Tribunal Website at http://www.waitangi-tribunal.govt.nz/resources/researchreports/wai262/. The *Effective Exclusion?* and *Mātauranga Māori and Taonga* reports have extensive sections on wetlands. The Rangahaua whānui national theme reports R *Inland waterways* by Ben White (http://www.waitangi-tribunal.govt.nz/resources/researchreports/rangahaua_whanui_reports/theme/whanui_themeq/themeq_white.asp) and theme U *The land with Al Woods and Water* by Wendy Pond (http://www.waitangi-tribunal.govt.nz/resources/researchreports/rangahaua_whanui_reports/theme/whanui_themeu.asp) also contain considerable material related to wetlands.

[13]Which in the Mahia region would have included "a mixed canopy of titoki, tawa, karaka, nikau, ngaio, pukatea and lemonwood. Kohekohe, wharangi, whau and mahoe dominated the sub-canopy" (Whaley et al. 2001: 29–30).

[14]Which would have been "dominated by populations of the sandbinders pingao, spinifex and sand tussock *(Austofestuca littoralis)*. The inner dunes had a sparse mix of sand pimelea, sand convolvulus, jointed wire rush, sand sedge, *Coprosma acerosa,* pohuehue (*Muehlenbeckia complexa*) and zoysia (Whaley et al. 2001: 30).

[15]Containing a "mosaic of raupo reedland, and sedge-rush-flaxland including *Baumea juncea, Isolepis prolifer,* jointed twigrush, sharp spiked-sedge, harakeke and lake clubrush. Other species included swamp kiokio, purei and Carex dissita. Manuka scrub, harakeke and cabbage trees occurred around the margins, and on hummocks and small low islands throughout" (Whaley et al. 2001: 30).

[16]Including the Highways and Watercourse Diversion Act 1858, Public Works Act 1876, Land Drainage Act 1893, Drainage Act 1908, Native Land Amendment and Native Land Claims Adjustment Act 1928, Swamp Drainage Act 1915 and a series of local swamp drainage acts for example the Hauraki Plains Act 1908 and the Southland Land Drainage Act 1914.

[17]Until the 1930s Government policy for Māori freehold land, emphasised productive agricultural use (Loveridge 1996: 153) and there were land conversion provisions for example in the Public Works Act and Māori Land Settlement Act 1905 that allowed the acquisition of any land required for drainage. Of the land acquired for drainage purposes a disproportionate percentage was Māori land (Park 2002: 156).

[18]The Native Lands Act 1865 transferred customary tenure to the British system of individual ownership in a direct attempt to destabilise Māori institutional arrangements and facilitate the alienation of Māori land into Crown and settler ownership.

[19]There are several hugely successful and large-scale Māori farming incorporations including Parininihi ki Waitōtara Incorporation in Taranaki, the Atihau-Whanganui Incorporation and the Morikaunui Incorporation located in Whanganui and the Wairarapa Moana Incorporation. Farming was also an early activity of the Wakatu Incorporation in Nelson although it has now significantly diversified its core business activities.

[20]Paparatu station is part of the Te Whakaari Incorporation located in the Wairoa, Hawke's Bay region. Hapū of Iwitea are major shareholders in this incorporation.

[21]A kawenata is a covenant an agreement between Māori land owners and the Department of Conservation towards a joint programme of conservation.

[22]Te Kooti constantly challenged the authority of the Crown and new settlers and was the founder of the Ringatu faith. Refer to Judith Binney's work for a more comprehensive account of life of Te Kooti and the Ringatu faith.

[23]Refer to the Department of Conservation website www.doc.govt.nz for information on the Ngā Whenua Rāhui fund and the Ngā Whenua Rāhui kawenata provision.

[24]Part Hereheretau B2L2, Block VIII, Clyde Survey District, Wairoa

[25]Information on the restoration work of the Whakaki Lake Trust can be found on the Ngā Whenua Rāhui website http://www.doc.govt.nz/getting-involved/landowners/nga-whenua-rahui/nga-whenua-rahui-fund/featured-projects/whakaki/.

HERITAGE AND PROTECTION

Environment as a marae locale

Merata Kawharu

From a Māori tribal worldview, the concept of 'the environment' has meaning in quite different ways from non-Māori perceptions. The environment and resources within have relevance not only in sustaining a group economically, but also politically and culturally. A whole cultural ethos and set of practices have developed in response to environmental challenges and opportunities. The environment is also seen as an ancestral landscape that encapsulates sites of significance. And from the perspective of tribal or sub-tribal identity, the environment provides markers or reference points that define one group from another. Central to this identity is the marae. Marae are the forums where tikanga or customs are performed, discussed or negotiated. Marae are the focal point where values of stewardship and management in relation to the environment and to people are grounded. Whare tupuna, or meeting houses, symbolise tribal heritage and celebrate noted ancestors whose deeds or actions, often in relation to protecting a group's interests in land or in relation to alliances that may have been formed through marriage, affirm descendants' ties to an environment and to a group. This chapter has three parts. It first explores values and principles that underpin marae as a way of conceptualising and understanding 'the environment'. It proposes an interpretation of the 'environment' as a 'marae locale'. It then considers the Māori Heritage Council's national Māori heritage statement 'Tapuwae' as it relates to 'marae locales'. Finally, it reflects on the Ngāti Whātua tribal community of Orakei in Auckland, as an example of their approach to dealing with environment in the terms encapsulated in Tapuwae.

Environment

Māori have a particular way of dealing with the present. There is a well known aphorism that says Māori walk backwards into the future, that is, they take the past with them in advancing into the unknown. Present and future circumstances are made sense of by referencing the past and therefore all contained within it – ancestors, gods and spiritual powers. Past, present and future are collapsed into one. Interpreting 'environment' then, is not simply about considering a place or landscape in the present, but also about taking into account times past or history, and all that it contains.

According to the Ngata dictionary, 'environment' is literally translated into Māori as 'taiao'. The Williams Māori dictionary translates taiao as 'world, country, district'.[1] Taiao translated in the way Williams suggests gives a sense of what is meant, but it is important to consider values of the kinship system to interpret taiao and to understand what is meant by 'environment' and associated terms 'world', 'country' and 'district'. 'Environment' has meaning not only in economic sustainability terms, where resources provide, for instance, the basic food and clothing necessities, but also in political and cultural/spiritual terms as well. All these elements are strongly intertwined. For instance, the bounties of the environment to sustain groups were linked to the way groups strove to protect – sometimes vigorously such as through battle or war – their access to those lands and resources. And the ability of groups to assert rights over a particular area was linked both to their identity and their political status, vis-à-vis neighbouring tribes and others. A group that wandered through, or utilised resources of, another's tribal territory did so carefully, lest their presence be interpreted as a threat. It was common practice to seek permission first, or to maintain close relationships, such as among neighbours, if temporary access to resources was to be sought. In other cases of course, groups deliberately avoided such courtesies and invaded for any number of reasons, generally because aspirations were to acquire control over lands and resources and thus enable the group to exercise a longer term or permanent rights in respect of them. In other words, at stake was mana whenua (or mana o te whenua), customary rights and authority of and over land.

As an orally based culture, Māori tribal groups have developed a range of sophisticated metaphors that symbolise and explain their economic, political and spiritual relationships with land. Although there is not the space to consider these layers in any detail, the following overview and examples may nevertheless illustrate some customary ways of interpreting 'environment'. A proverb from the Far North describes the relationship between people and their environment. The genre is common among many tribal groups throughout the country:

Ko Maungapiko te maunga,
Te Oneroa-a-Tōhē te moana,
Ko Kurahaupo te waka,
Te tangata o runga ko Pō,
Ko Te Aupōuri te iwi.
Maungapiko is the mountain,
Oneroa-a-Tōhē the sea,
Kurahaupō the canoe,
Pō the chief on board,
And Te Aupōuri the people.

Oneroa-a-Tōhē (90 Mile Beach) has sustained the lives of Te Aupōuri for generations since their ancestors arrived several hundreds of years ago. Te Aupōuri identify themselves in relation to Oneroa-a-Tōhē, their canoe origins and the wider landscape that they settled.[2] Another idiom of identity from the Far North highlights the importance of Maungapiko, referred to in the previous proverb. Maungapiko was a pā at Kapowairua.[3] The Waitānoni stream flows at its base and has been an important water resource for local people. Tōhē is a well-known ancestor from whom many of the Muriwhenua tribes descend. These elements of history and heritage are remembered in this way:

Ko Waitānoni te wairere,
Ko Kapowairua te kāinga,
Ko Tōhē te tupuna.
Waitānoni is the waterfall,
Kapowairua the home,
Tōhē the ancestor.[4]

The next proverb, well-known among Ngāpuhi, highlights the interrelationship between people and the environment and an identity that may be formed in respect of it:

> *Ka mimiti te puna i Taumārere,*
> *Ka toto te puna i Hokianga;*
> *Ka toto te puna i Taumārere,*
> *Ka mimiti te puna i Hokianga.*
> *When the fountain of Taumārere is empty,*
> *The fountain of Hokianga is full.*
> *When the fountain of Taumārere is full,*
> *The fountain of Hokianga is empty.*

In this example, the Taumārere and Hokianga water springs symbolise groups of people on the west and east coasts. It implies that the springs are linked, as people are. When one spring is empty, perhaps as when people on one coast are low in support or strength, the other spring fills up, like relatives on the other coast who come to the assistance of their kin.

The three dimensions of the environment – economic, political and cultural/spiritual – can be further briefly explained. The economic value of the environment is captured also in many proverbs such as:

Tāmaki-makau-rau.
Tāmaki of a hundred lovers.

Tāmaki kainga ika me ngā wheua katoa.
Tāmaki the place where fish, bones and all are consumed.

Tāmaki-herenga-waka.
Tāmaki where canoes are tied.

These sayings describe the popularity of the Auckland isthmus because of its fertile soil, plentiful fish supply, two harbours, lush forests and abundant birdlife. In the past the rich resources, as well as numerous volcanic cones on which to build strategic defence systems, were major attractions for many groups to settle in the region, hence the name 'Tāmaki of a hundred lovers'. Civilization generally established settlements because of life-sustaining opportunities provided by a surrounding environment. Similarly, among Māori, settlements and camps were strategically located near resources and waterways.

Politically, Māori traditionally referred to their surrounding environment as their rohe, or tribal territory. Many tribal sayings illustrate identity being intertwined with territory:[5] 'Mai Maketu ki Tongariro' 'From Maketu to Tongariro' – a Te Arawa marker of identity; 'Tamaki ki Maunganui',

'Tamaki to Maunganui' – a Ngāti Whātua marker of identity; and 'Te Rohe Potae' is the district of Ngāti Maniapoto in the King Country. Elder Tui Adams describes this territory in the following way:[6]

Nā mai i Aotea, te moana o Aotea, atu ki Horahora. Mai i Horahora, anā ki Wairākei, ki Ātiamuri. Atu i a Ātiamuri ki Taupō, piki tonu i ngā maunga teitei, ngā maunga huka, ki Ruapehu. Taka atu ki tērā taha, ki Waiōuru. Nā, ka huri atu ki Te Hauāuru, ki Whanganui. Nā hoki ake ana au noa ai i te Tai Hauāuru, nā tae noa mai anō hoki ki Aotea.

Commencing from Aotea Harbour, the boundary runs to Horahora. From Horahora, it travels to Wairākei and on to Ātiamuri. From Ātiamuri, it continues on to Taupō and then ascends those lofty and snowy mountains, on to Ruapehu. It then drops down to Waiōuru on the other side there and then turns westwards to Whanganui. It then returns along the west coast, finally returning to Aotea.

The spiritual dimension of the environment is succinctly described by northern leader Māori Marsden. He offers a worldview of the wider 'universe', but the values apply to 'environment' as well:[7]

...Māori perceived the universe as a 'Process'. [They postulated] ...a world comprised of a series of interconnected realms separated by aeons of time from which there eventually emerged the natural world. This cosmic process is unified and bound together by spirit.

Within the natural world, patterns of behaviour developed in response to opportunities and constraints provided by the environment. The doings of ancestors provide examples to descendants in respect of what to do or not to do. The 'trial and error' experimentation and subsequent development of environmental management techniques are often recorded in myths. Myths may provide 'models', imperatives and messages that validate and legitimise contemporary norms and practices. The ancestral/mythological realm then, has very real meaning and purpose for present action. We are reminded of the importance of times past and of the examples set by ancestors' exploits in the words of Sir James Henare:

E kore e mōnehunehu te pūmahara ki ngā momo rangātira o neherā, nā rātou nei i toro te nukuroa o Te Moananui-a-Kiwa me Papatūānuku. Ko ngā tohu o ō rātou tapuwae i kākahutia ki runga i te mata o te whenua – he taonga, he tapu.

> *Time will not dim the memory of the special class of rangātira of the past who braved the wide expanse of the ocean and land. Their sacred footprints are scattered over the surface of the land, treasured and sacred.*

A traditional worldview of the environment may be illustrated in the following way:

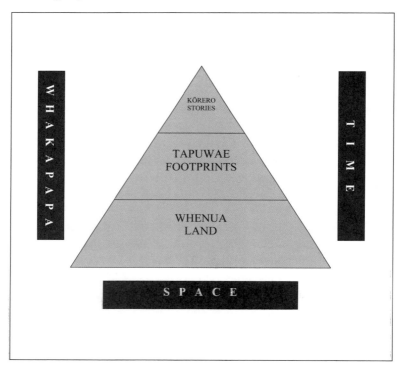

Figure 1 A customary worldview of the environment.

This diagram emphasises the enduring aspect and life-sustaining qualities of land (whenua), which in turn has enabled Māori to explore, exploit and manage its many resources. Reference to tapuwae, the sacred footprints of ancestors, highlights the importance of their experiences, which have been preserved in oral traditions or stories (kōrero), and passed down through generations (whakapapa) over time.

Values and practices – kaitiakitanga

The values briefly outlined thus far, i.e. economic, political and cultural/spiritual, underpin the practice of kaitiakitanga or trusteeship. Kaitiakitanga pervades not only the environmental realm but also the social. Implementing kaitiakitanga is as much about managing resources of the environment as it is about managing people. It applies to people, particularly between kin group leaders and the wider kin group. An important reason for exercising kaitiakitanga is to promote and enhance socio-political status. Accountability, reciprocity, guardianship and trusteeship equally apply to leaders and their people as they apply to the relationship between people and their environment. The performative application of marae principles, of kaitiakitanga, is seen in, for instance, the rituals of encounter between tangata whenua (hosts) and manuhiri (guests). Key to those rituals is the manaaki or hospitality offered to guests, who in turn recognise the authority or mana of their hosts to provide hospitality. Manaaki was applied in the same way in relation to resources. They were looked after and managed. The purpose was threefold: to cement the association of the hapū with lands and resources and therefore its status. Second, to be able to receive something in return (for instance, food provided by Tane and Papatūānuku), and not least of all, to maintain an economic and political resource base for future generations.

Kaitiakitanga is not simply an 'environmental ethic' then, but rather a socio-environmental ethic. It is about relationships between humans and the environment, humans and their gods and between each other.[8] And as I have argued elsewhere, kaitiakitanga continues to find centrality in Māori kin-based communities because it weaves together ancestral, environmental and social threads of identity, purpose and practice.[9]

Marae

The forum where history, ancestral connections and reference to land and resources have particular significance is the marae. The marae is the focus of a wider ancestral landscape and the central focus of kin group identity. It embodies the relationships between people and their environment and between people and their forebears. The environment may be considered as an extension of all that marae symbolises, and vice versa, marae are an extension of a wider environment. This collapsing of space from a tribal perspective is reflected in the following explanation by Tapsell:[10]

> *...marae represents the core, the very essence of their genealogical identity to the surrounding lands, which they interpret as* mana o te whenua. *[Elders] see their home marae as both a tangible (physical) and intangible (spiritual) space to which they belong* – turangawaewae – *which metaphysically embodies the 'now' within their 'ancestral past'.*

Environment, then, may be considered as a marae locale. All within it – rivers, lakes, mountains, forests, sites of significance – are an ancestral landscape that has particular meaning to a group of people, a hapū or iwi.

Meaning may of course be ascribed to a mountain or site of significance by groups who formerly lived in close proximity, but whose tribal territory has moved elsewhere. Traditions remain particularly strong, however, to groups where mountains, rivers or significant sites are oriented from a focal and local marae perspective. Often, these geographic markers are in close proximity, if not also clearly visible, from marae.

The emphasis of ancestral connections to landscapes is captured in another of Sir James Henare's kōrero: 'When I look at these landscapes I see my ancestors walking back to me.'[11] Sir James' philosophical approach to the environment is further demonstrated in a marae forum as symbolised in the whare tupuna or ancestral house. In describing the symbolism of the meeting house, renowned carver Pakariki Harrison states succinctly:

> *The meeting house (whare whakairo) is conceptualised metaphorically as a human body, usually representing the eponymous ancestor of a tribe. At the apex of the gable, attached to the tāhuhu or ridgepole is the kōruru (head). The maihi (bargeboards) are the arms, outstretched to welcome guests. The tāhuhu is the backbone and the heke (rafters) are ribs.*
> *People in the house are protected in the bosom of their ancestor ...* [12]

These houses, whether elaborately carved or halls, are narratives or symbolic expressions of the continued exercise of mana or authority over lands, waterways and oceans. The exercise of authority is, however, tempered by the extent of hospitality – manaaki – offered to guests, and marae act as the primary socio-cultural place where mana and manaaki are performed. While these values and traditions can be observed on marae and in the carvings of meeting houses, they can also be observed in oral forms, notably whaikōrero or formal speech making, or in proverbial sayings such as those noted above.

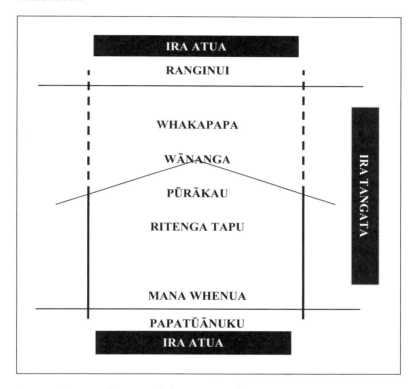

Figure 2. Diagram showing symbolic connections between marae and wider environment, extending between Ranginui and Papatūānuku, and the values that are activated in encounters with manuhiri/visitors.

The above diagram illustrates how a meeting house is a metaphor for an ancestral landscape or environment. The poupou or upright posts represent at one level ancestral actors on the landscape. At another level, the poupou extend from the floor or papa of the house, through to the sky or rangi and are symbolic of Tane (God of the Forests) separating his parents, Ranginui and Papatūānuku, so that the 'human principle' or ira tangata, may exist between the 'divine principle' or ira atua, as represented by Ranginui and

Papatūānuku. The house, therefore, symbolically connects both ira atua and ira tangata. The environment is also the meeting point of these two realms. The relationships between atua, tūpuna (ancestors) and uri (descendants), whether performed on an ancestral landscape or in a marae context, are further reinforced in the concept mana whenua, which as described, is customary authority of a kin group over lands. The marae and meeting house are the ultimate expression of mana whenua.

In sum, the environment, as a marae locale, contains a series of cultural reference points. It embodies links between humans and the wider cosmos and is, therefore, taonga, or a treasure.[13] For purposes of relating the concept to the present discussion, a brief overview is that it is a system of ordering the wider universe, and the many events and people who have lived within a marae locale over many generations. As an organising principle, it emphasises events being associated with people where, for example, reference to an event may be made in these terms: 'In the time of Tane, great fires occurred' rather than 'In the year..., great fires occurred'. In post-contact times, it is more common for date references, but emphasis on the doings of ancestors and a mapping of the universe according to whakapapa or layers continues to be important. And in some cases, the relationship between ancestors and their environment may be compared with other periods when descendants lived and whose physical environment has changed, for example, due to pollution, species depletion, erosion or some other harmful environmental pattern. In these cases where comparison between generations is made, reference to earlier periods may be to highlight a particular model of an appropriate environmental management process (or inappropriate practice, whatever the case may be). By all accounts, reference to a whakapapa worldview or paradigm enables patterns of relationships between humans and their physical environment to be established, as they occurred at different points in time.

Tapuwae

In attempting to capture the values and principles underpinning terms such as Māori heritage and environment, the Māori Heritage Council of the New Zealand Historic Places Trust has recently completed a document that aims to guide the Trust in its work associated with Māori heritage, and convey to a wider audience matters of importance to iwi in dealing with heritage protection, conservation and promotion. Known as 'Tapuwae', in reference to Sir James Henare's proverbial saying and the messages contained within it, it is the first of its kind that, in effect, presents a national-level statement on Māori heritage.

As background to understanding Tapuwae, the following are the main motivations for creating a statement on heritage:[14]

- Māori heritage remains undervalued at national level and in non-Māori communities. It is often seen as of value to Māori only;
- The contribution of heritage to a healthy and vibrant economy and society is not well understood. If appropriately managed, the potential contribution of Māori heritage to social, cultural, economic and environmental goals is immense;
- Iwi/Māori communities need assistance with understanding and protecting their heritage and how it can contribute to their health and well-being in years to come;
- The relationship between Māori heritage and the 'future' of iwi/Māori communities is not well understood;
- Many property developers have a poor understanding of heritage generally and Māori heritage specifically.

Tapuwae has an aspirational function: 'to assist in the interpretation and protection of cultural heritage, landscapes and knowledge of tangata whenua that embodies our marae.' It emphasises the importance of the following:[15]

1. Māori heritage places (environment) as taonga;
2. The past;
3. Kaitiaki practices;
4. Kōrero or stories;
5. Markers of mana.

Each of these points is briefly discussed. A starting point for Tapuwae is that Māori heritage places (as found within the physical environment), are taonga. In other words, this includes a kin group's estate, which contains material and non-material elements, and which in turn shape a group's identity and status.[16]

Tapuwae is modelled on the idea of the past informing present and future practice. It recognises that the past encapsulates stories of cultural existence that has shaped, and been shaped by, a changing environment.[17]

Māori land-based and built heritage has undergone significant change, particularly since European contact, and in more recent times with the expansion of towns and cities, roads and highways, further encroachment into wāhi whakahirahira (important places) has occurred. Urban expansion and rural development have seriously undermined physical and cultural environments.

Kaitiaki values and practices noted above remain critical if the environment and associated cultural traditions and heritage are to be protected. A further aspect of kaitiakitanga as it is interpreted in Tapuwae is its creative potential. In exercising kaitiakitanga, or resource management and trusteeship, it not only protects heritage, but also enables new opportunities to make the environment and heritage vital, alive and available to succeeding generations and the wider community.[18] The idea of creation is underpinned by age-old practices of Māori adaptation to new challenges and innovation. For example, challenges of ancient times required new and great navigational feats to cross the Pacific from Ra'iatea to Aotearoa; there were challenges and opportunities brought by European settlers that saw new tools, materials, knowledge and systems of trade enter kin-group society; and there are contemporary challenges faced by communities today to preserve and develop sustainably, ancestral landscapes and associated knowledge. Earlier and pre-contact challenges facing kin groups were concerned with economic, political and cultural survival. Today those challenges are possibly less concerned with economic survival (although groups such as Ngāti Porou and Te Whānau a Apanui could argue the opposite, having just successfully negotiated a deal that protects their interests in the foreshore and recognises their rights to continue fish harvesting), but certainly cultural and political survival. The creative potential of the wider marae locale is broad. Even if economic incentives today differ from traditional times, there are nevertheless new opportunities to engage marae locales, stories and descendants to create, for instance, cultural tourism ventures, educational programmes and other initiatives.

The story telling aspect of creativity is crucial. It is the stories, as reflected in waiata, pepeha, whakapapa and whaikōrero, that cloak marae locales. Oral narratives weave together ancestral connections with landscapes, describe life crises, and contextualise relationships between people that have been forged or broken. There is also a present dimension to story telling: the narrator reaffirms his or her place in a wider genealogical world by referencing ancestral actors on landscapes.

Kōrero/story telling has a further pragmatic function. Narratives not only help explain the heritage 'value' of a place, but also indicate what may be appropriate in terms of sustainable development, protection and management. In reflecting on these ideas in interpreting the meaning of 'heritage', Tapuwae makes the following comments and describes the relevance of kōrero or stories to heritage:[19]

> *Māori communities are concerned to protect and further their heritage for it is a source of identity, culture and mana that has sustained iwi and hapū communities over many generations. Māori heritage is considered in an holistic way – it is not merely the physical places held in high esteem by their communities (as important as these are), but also the knowledge and stories about those places and the experiences that one can have at those places and more. Most particularly Māori heritage is the kind of experience and consciousness that is created and maintained through interactions with places of Māori heritage.*

Ōrākei

In interpreting and applying the principles so far outlined, this chapter now turns to the Ngāti Whātua o Ōrākei tribal community in Auckland. Their interpretation of 'marae locale', of 'environment', hinges on understanding the events and actions not only of Ngāti Whātua ancestors, but also of those with whom they dealt, from Captain Hobson to provincial and Crown representatives and city council officers, who contributed to the almost entire loss of their tribal estate. As explained, the loss of title to their ancestral lands where their marae once stood was a final blow to an already demoralised community. Those experiences have shaped who Ngāti Whātua o Ōrākei are today, and drive them in articulating a vision for their present and future development.

For the Ngāti Whātua tribal community at Ōrākei, their growth and outlook had been constrained in no small measure by government policies that by 1951 resulted in all but three and ¼ acres of their ancestral lands, which formerly covered in excess of 3,500 acres, being taken. By the end of 1951, their meeting house had been torched and a ¼-acre cemetery remained. The rapidly growing city of Auckland enveloped them and left the community isolated and forgotten, not least because they had no marae. They were now deprived of a cultural and economic base. Their plight for the first five decades of the 1900s has been described in the following way:[20]

> Sometimes, hopes were made buoyant. The attitude of the Native Land Court, and even some of the findings of the Kennedy Commission, for example, encouraged the community to plan for a revival.....They were much heartened also by Waikato support and by the mana of Te Puea Herangi. But at other times hope was turned into despair by the uncompromising stance of successive governments and city councils. Finally, terse reference to them by a prime minister as 'a blot on the landscape' dispelled any illusion. The Crown ... was bent on their removal. Their ancestral village was an untidy anachronism, certainly no adornment to the now prestigious Tamaki Drive....By 1951, the community had reached a state of turmoil and bitterness. While they were unified in fighting out the last stages of the losing battle for the marae, their unity was undermined by the covert rivalry among family groups for the homes being dangled before them. Finally,...the Crown took the last acres of the village (except, for no stated reason, the chapel and cemetery).

Elders pleaded, in vain, that their remaining lands not be taken:[21]

> We the owners assembled here today representing the majority of owners in the block desire to inform the Minister that we do not wish to sell this land for the reason that it is ancestral land for which we do not think we should accept money. We would, however, be prepared to make this land a Māori Reserve under the Māori Land Act 1931, controlled by trustees representing ourselves as owners. We think that the reserve should be inalienable but that the trustees should have power to exchange with Crown land to square up the boundaries.

Once the last of the lands were taken, a community representative stated, 'Hard for me to realise that Crown has taken this. I point out if at all possible we would like this land returned to us.'[22]

Some forty years passed before title to lands was restored to the community in 1991 and when another meeting house (that had been built almost twenty years earlier on lands above the former site of the village in the Ōkahu Bay) and marae could finally be said to belong to Ngāti Whātua. 1991 was a pivotal time in their rehabilitation as a kin group.

A whole generation had grown up without a marae, and without all that marae provides, in guiding the kin group in terms of protocols, and in terms of being able to properly fulfil duties as tangata whenua in exercising manaakitanga to visitors. Title to a wider estate, their wider marae locale that they have called their 'whenua rangatira' was also recognised. Notably, the principle of a trust estate, of representatives overseeing the management of their whenua rangatira, as elders had attempted to argue in 1951, was also established.

Some present challenges

What the Ngāti Whātua community endured is unique but their experiences are well known throughout New Zealand. Other tribal groups also suffered from the loss of lands if not marae as well. Challenges today for Ōrākei, like elsewhere, are not simply about protecting physical places, but equally importantly reviving a knowledge base and interpreting it in ways that are meaningful. These challenges, which I call 'the challenge of the marae', I have summarised as including:

- Re-establishing mana whenua and a cultural footprint in a multi-cultural society;
- Re-affirming credible tribal leadership;
- Re-learning traditional knowledge and values and applying them (such as through the arts of formal speech-making, carving and tukutuku);
- Reviving traditional knowledge among rangatahi/tai tamariki/youth.

For many Ngāti Whātua o Ōrākei descendants, their marae is familiar but marae knowledge is still limited or unknown. A small fraction of the wider descendant community, perhaps some 5%, actually lives in the Orakei community near the marae. Many of those and many others of the wider descendant community have actually very little to do with the marae. The marae may stimulate interest, but it is in fact culturally obscure. Disconnection is not only with marae, but also the wider marae locale, or ancestral landscape that are now the farms, Crown lands, reserves, parks, and Auckland city. These were the pa, kainga, harbours, and forests that gave sustenance to forebears' economic, cultural and political needs; in essence, their heritage and identity.

Given the extent of disconnection, rejuvenating the marae, including associated value systems among Ngāti Whātua, is, therefore, essential, now more than ever. This includes finding ways that re-centralise the marae in the lives of the descendant community. This revival process also includes an educative process in transmitting traditions about the wider marae locale. Narratives associated with, for instance, important pā sites and villages scattered throughout the isthmus on the northern Manukau Harbour shores, Waitemata Harbour shores, and places in between, and narratives about tribal leaders of times past, are important markers of the identity of Ngāti Whātua. They also provide clues for what is important in shaping associated heritage management plans.

A strengthened knowledge base among tribal members and a strategic process for transferring this knowledge among the wider civic community will also contribute to a strengthened cultural footprint in the region. And in an ideal world, the rejuvenation of heritage that is shaped by knowledge, history, people and places will do much to build not only marae communities, but also a strong and inclusive society generally. Marae locales may play a far greater role in cross-cultural situations and in terms of informing national identity.

Concluding comments

Layers of history that describe people's relationships with lands and resources, the trials and tribulations they faced in confronting challenges to their survival, are part and parcel of interpreting environment today. The immediate physical environment is one part of a wider cultural environment that extends to other places and to other times.

Marae embody the relationships between people, between people and their wider ancestral landscape, and between people and those who have gone before them. To understand marae is to understand the environment and its associated heritage. Taking into account the ancestral values of and relationships with surrounding lands and resources, from a tribal perspective, the concept 'environment' may be considered a 'marae locale'. Marae are the manifest symbol of a group's identity and symbolise a kotahitanga or unity between the human, material and non-material worlds. Tapuwae, the Māori Heritage Council's statement on Māori heritage, is an important step in contributing to understanding the breadth of heritage protection and preservation issues facing tribal groups. The particular challenges Ngāti Whātua face, as noted in this chapter, demonstrate the importance of considering their marae locale and heritage as taonga, of better understanding historical narratives about their territory, and interpreting this to their present and future descendants, if a secure identity and place in wider society is to be assured.

END NOTES

[1]Ngata at http://www.learningmedia.co.nz/ngata/; Williams 1985:362.

[2]McRae 1987:43. Te Aupōuri identify with other canoes as well. Waitangi Tribunal 1997:C19:11.

[3]McRae 1987.

[4]James Henare Māori Research Centre 1996:185-186.

[5]Kawharu 2000.

[6]Adams in http://www.teara.govt.nz/NewZealanders/MāoriNewZealanders/NgatiManiapoto/4/ENZ-Resources/Standard/3/en.

[7]Marsden in Kawharu 1998:16.

[8]Kawharu 1998:18-19.

[9]Kawharu 2000:350-351.

[10]Tapsell 1998:54.

[11]http://www.historic.org.nz/publications/gfx/Heritage%20Landscapes%20report.PDF

[12]Harrison, P., n.d. 'Tanenuiarangi'. P.1.

[13]See Tapsell 1998 for detailed analysis on taonga.

[14]New Zealand Māori Heritage Council 2008:6.

[15]New Zealand Māori Heritage Council 2008.

[16]Tapsell 1998.

[17]New Zealand Māori Heritage Council 2008:5.

[18]New Zealand Māori Heritage Council 2008:12-13.

[19]New Zealand Māori Heritage Council 2008:9.

[20]I.H. Kawharu 1975:10-11.

[21]I.H. Kawharu 1975:12.

[22]I.H. Kawharu 1975:12.

Outstanding universal value: how relevant is indigeneity?

Mason Durie

Introduction

Within the concept of indigeneity it is possible to recognise distinctive criteria that can be used to assess the value of heritage and valuable sites. Essentially those criteria are based on the nature of relationships between entities in a linked-up environment. Relationships between people and the natural environment, between tangible and intangible dimensions, between organic and inorganic material, and between past and future constitute the foundations upon which indigenous populations understand the world. An energy flow that spirals outwards connects the multiple threads so that even very small objects become part of a wider context that gives them shape and meaning. Arising from indigenous understandings of relationships it is possible to identify key principles that have potential application to the way in which sites and objects can be valued.

The workshop

This chapter is based on an address to the World Heritage Committee's Pacific Workshop, held at Turangi, New Zealand, in February 2007. At the Workshop Pacific views on assessing 'outstanding universal value' as criteria for defining world heritage sites were discussed.

The Pacific Workshop provided an opportunity to reflect on the broad issues relating to heritage, universality, and how peoples in the Pacific value precious sites. Immediately before the Workshop there had been newspaper comment about cultural values as a basis for environmental planning. It concerned the Tongaririo National Park, a World Heritage site, close to the venue of the Workshop and referred in particular to Mount Ruapehu. Though for most of the year the mountain is dormant, there was an ever-present potential for volcanic eruption and the widespread deposition of ash, stone, larva and toxic fumes. But the more immediate threat would apparently come from a build up of water in the crater lake at the top of the mountain resulting in a lahar that could flood the low lying land below. At least that was the alarming news published in a column in the *Dominion Post* in January 2007 (Long 2007). Because there had been a lahar disaster in 1953, with loss of life, the article claimed little had been done to avoid a repetition and the Department of Conservation was accused of being negligent in not taking more active cost-effective measures. Cutting an outflow channel into the mountain, the article claimed, would be the best and quickest solution. In addition, because Māori had been against carving out a channel and favoured an approach that would leave the mountain's face intact, the article also dismissed cultural views about the mountain's integrity as if they were of mystical significance only. The Department was accused of 'political correctness' for taking indigenous views into account.

The Director-General of the Conservation Department was quick to respond with a detailed rebuttal of the article's claims concluding that they had been 'alarmist, unhelpful and untrue' and dismissing cheap but short term options (cutting a channel) as risk laden in the longer term (Morrison 2007). The Director-General also took exception to the way in which Māori cultural perspectives about the environment had been trivialised and reaffirmed the Department's position that 'In the real world of decision-making, culture and technical arguments must sit alongside each other, not in opposition.'

Cultural Views

Clearly, however, there was some reluctance to accept perspectives and philosophies that sat outside the world views of some commentators. Debate about the relevance of cultural perspectives alongside scientific and technical evidence is not new. A problem, if there is one, arises when the criteria adopted by one system of knowledge, such as science, are used to decide on the validity of another system that subscribes to different criteria (Waldram, Herring, & Young 1995: 214–218). Trying to understand religious faith for example, as if it should obey the rules of science, leads nowhere. That does not mean religious faith has no validity. Similarly because cultural views are not cast in scientific or technological jargon, it does not negate their relevance, although for someone not versed in the culture, there might be difficulties in understanding. While 'cultural perspectives' tend to refer to the views of ethnic minorities, in effect, the total appreciation of the environment and its meaning is determined by the cultural views held by populations and communities. In much of the developed world, science and technology constitute the dominant cultures to the point that other approaches to understanding are not always well tolerated – as the article in the *Dominion Post* demonstrated.

Indigenous views of the world

Indigenous peoples have cultural values that shape the way they view the world and determine attitudes to the land, human creativity, and the relationships between animate and inanimate objects. While there are significant differences between indigenous peoples in their historic and recent experiences, there are also remarkably similar ways of understanding nature and their part in it. A common starting point is a sense of unity with the environment (Kame'eleihiwa 1992: 23–25). The tribe of Ngati Tūwharetoa, for example, has an expression that links them closely to their environment: "Ko Tongariro te maunga, ko Tūwharetoa te iwi." "Tongariro is the mountain and Tūwharetoa are the people" and implicit in the statement is the notion that mountain and tribe are bound together by both time and place. A bond with the land and the natural environment is the fundamental feature of indigeneity (Walker, 1990: 11–15). The land is an extension of tribal and personal identity, and the relationship is reflected in song, custom, hunting, approaches to healing, and the utilization of physical resources.

Arising from that environmental relationship it is possible to identify five secondary characteristics of indigeneity. The first reflects the dimension of time and a relationship with the environment that has endured over centuries; the second, also derived from the environmental relationship, is about human identity, creativity, and social order. The third characteristic is a system of knowledge – indigenous knowledge – that integrates indigenous world views, values, and experience, and generates a framework for understanding the human condition. Application of that perspective to natural resources and human endeavour provides a basis for the fourth characteristic, environmental sustainability for the benefit of future generations. Finally, indigeneity is also characterised by a language so strongly influenced by the environment that it is not spoken as a first language in other parts of the world (Durie, 2004).

Ahiowhio Wharite: A Spiral of Ecological Synergy

Underlying the world views of indigenous peoples and at the heart of indigeneity, it is possible to identify an 'ecological synergy spiral'. The spiral is basically about relationships and especially relationships that are complementary and mutually reinforcing. The spiral moves from the small to the large, from individuals to groups, and from people, plants, fish and animals to the earth and the sky. It is based on an outward flow of energy, away from microscopic minutia, and towards a sense of union with greater entities in an ever-expanding environment (Salmond 1978: 166–167). Moreover, as it progresses, the spiral brings together life in all its forms including inert materials. Relationships between objects are established. Ultimately the spiral moves towards the cosmos so that all objects, species, planets and stars can be incorporated in an interacting system that gives meaning and insight to existence. Within the spiral, knowledge comes from locating matter and phenomena within wider ecological contexts rather than attempting to understand and value objects and systems solely according to their intrinsic component parts. The energy flow is centrifugal rather than centripetal (Durie 1999: 351–366).

There are three reasons for introducing the spiral of ecological synergy into the discussion. First, in this world view, human identity is grounded (Royal, 2002). People cannot be fully understood without taking into account the natural environment which has nurtured their ancestors through childhood and into adult life. The phrase tangata whenua captures some of the duality – people and the land – and recognises that in every region some people have longstanding bonds with the land that sets them apart from others who do not share those bonds (Kawharu, 1977: 60–62.). The point is further emphasised by the concept of tūrangawaewae, a term linking individuals with a site or location that underpins their identity, as well as the identity of their relatives. Even after two or more generations of urban living, the link to that site remains an important component of personal distinctiveness. Moreover, the human-land relationship is synergistic; if the land is despoiled, human integrity is similarly harmed.

Second, just as people take on qualities derived from the natural environment, inanimate material objects possess their own form of life, a mauri, which both distinguishes them (from other objects) and also unites them within a wider network of entities. Stone, for instance, whether in a natural state or used for construction cannot be fully understood without recognising the wider environment within which it lies. The great pyramids of Egypt are remarkable feats of construction and masonry. Yet their full value cannot be judged only in terms of architectural and engineering perfection. Instead, the relationship of the pyramids to the desert, the arid climate and the not too distant River Nile creates a more dynamic appreciation of their significance. The nature of the mauri – the vitality – of the pyramids depends not only on the structure and form but also on the relationship of the construction to the wider environment. In an indigenous world objects that appear to be inanimate are not regarded as lifeless or static since they also possess an identity of their own and are part of a wider network. Belonging to that network creates a vibrant relationship that is at odds with the view that motionless objects lack life. In the language of global warming and climate change, so-called inert objects may well have carbon credits that ultimately add to the world's equilibrium. There are energy chains within, and dynamic relationships beyond.

Third, the spiral of ecological synergy is built around the dimension of time. Human endurance, and to an even greater extent, environmental endurance, is a product of a finely tuned process measured over millennia rather than decades or even centuries. Survival over time does not depend on dominant species or population growth but on the dynamic interaction between systems and participants caught up in the spiral. Enough is now known about global warming to add weight to time-tested indigenous views that rampant destruction of forests, plundering of oceans, and intentional unbundling of carbon chains locked into fossils, do little to guarantee future equilibrium. To that end indigeneity is about people and their natural environments growing older together. Relationships in time are as important as spatial relationships and the ecological perspective, which underlines indigenous world views, places emphasis on both past and future relationships. The spiral gains momentum from a distant past and travels out to a future, well beyond human comprehension.

Universal Value

It may not be immediately obvious how ecological synergy is relevant to 'outstanding universal value'. However, in considering the meaning of outstanding universal value, which is the overarching consideration for nominating world heritage sites, it is important to recognise that indigenous understandings are not necessarily the same as the views of other populations.

The criteria that are used to define outstanding universal value have been extensively debated by the World Heritage Committee (United Nations Educational Cultural and Scientific Organisation 1994), and were further examined in Kazan in 2004 at a meeting of the International Council On Monuments and Sites (ICOMOS – a non-government organisation of heritage professionals engaged in conservation of places of cultural heritage and value). There appeared to be agreement that the criteria for outstanding human value, established in the 1972 Convention, were still appropriate:

1. a masterpiece of human genius
2. unique or at least exceptional testimony
3. outstanding example
4. outstanding universal significance, i.e. transcends national boundaries and of common importance for humanity.

There has also been clarification of the dimensions of the criteria and the relevance of the tests of authenticity and integrity. In addition, in the Nara Document (1994) the immaterial/intangible values of cultural heritage are recognised: '... sources of information may include: form and design, materials and substance, use and function, traditions and techniques, location and setting, spirit and feeling, and other internal and external factors'.

While a wide interpretation of outstanding universal value seems possible, uncertainty has been expressed by some indigenous peoples, especially in the Pacific, that the various instruments used by the World Heritage Committee do not adequately recognise the significance of indigeneity as a criterion for measuring 'outstanding' or 'value', or more simply as a significant indicator for valuing heritage. Although the Nara document introduced the possibility that 'spirit and feeling' could be used as evidence of value; and although sites can represent aspects of the landscape that hold cultural significance from the historical, aesthetic, ethnological or anthropological points of view, there is some concern that indigenous world views could sit awkwardly within frameworks that have been primarily designed from other perspectives.

A Pacific Approach to Valuing Heritage

Taking into account the values identified in the 'spiral of ecological synergy' and assuming that they have some meaning for Pacific peoples and other indigenous groups in the Southern Hemisphere, indigenous Pacific views are likely to differ from the Nara and Kazan conclusions in three important respects.

Tangible and Intangible Fusion

First the distinctions between tangible and intangible qualities become blurred when viewed through an indigenous lens. Insofar as inert and inanimate objects have a mauri, a life of their own, and do not exist in isolation but are part of a network of interacting entities, it is difficult to conceive any creation as a purely physical structure which has no connection with an external world. The two dimensions – tangible and intangible – are brought together by an interaction of energy and a mutual connection along a spiral that accommodates people and their material cultures. Heritage is seldom divorced from culture, people, and humanity. There is a fusion between material and immaterial, tangible and intangible qualities.

Continuity in Time

Second, heritage has a temporal dimension that moves simultaneously in two directions. In indigenous worlds not only is a connection with the past highly valued but when an object or site can at the same time demonstrate a link to the future it is even more highly prized. Whenever the future is reflected in the past, and future generations can relate to ancient treasures as if they were contemporary wonders, endurance is seen to have a timeless quality. Rather than seeking 'historical authentication' and confining heritage to a distant past, indigenous peoples are more inclined to link authenticity to uninterrupted human engagement and intergenerational commitment. In this respect an ongoing relationship with successive generations, rather than simply the passage of time, provides authentication. People are not distant bystanders marvelling at a bygone wonder, but remain active participants providing the connection to modern times and through their children to the future.

Ecological Harmony

The third point is not dissimilar to the first; but rather than emphasising a link between tangible and intangible values, the focus is on a link between valued sites, the surrounding terrain and the wider natural environment. Value comes from the nature of that link and the way in which interaction continues over time. As part of a unique landscape that provides not only material resources but also sustenance, access, and distinctiveness, heritage is especially valued when it is in harmony with the environment and part of the ecological backdrop. *Blending* with the natural environment confers value but *being part* of the natural environment adds a sense of harmony and integration that is important to indigenous world views.

Universality

A requirement for universal appeal is one criterion for recognition as a World Heritage site. In any worldwide context, universality is an important consideration, the more so as global engagement increases and inter-state collaboration develops. But there is some way to go before there is universal agreement about what is valuable and how it should be valued. Valuing objects because of their human and ecological connections, a central theme in this paper, would not necessarily be seen as the most important consideration by all peoples and cultures. At the same time value based entirely on engineering triumphs or architectural wonders could be seen by some cultures as failing the important ecological test. Moreover, if an indigenous criterion for outstanding value is based on integration into a unique environment, then distinctiveness rather than universality becomes the more important consideration. While the Tongariro National Park has an appeal that goes well beyond New Zealand, and is therefore rightly considered as a site worthy of world-wide recognition, the Park's uniqueness is not entirely locked into its scientific and aesthetic properties, but is also a product of local relationships and local narratives.

The bridge between the two parameters – universal and local – may well be captured in the notion of 'representative of the best', which leaves room for other representations to give expression to their local values. Nonetheless the concept of universality does have some significance for indigenous peoples, if only because the world views underlying indigenous culture, environmental management, and ecological synergy can be found in indigenous populations throughout the world. In that respect, a case can be made for indigeneity, with its cultural, ecological, and temporal dimensions, to be listed as an important criterion in determining outstanding universal value.

Outstanding Universal Value

The purpose of this paper has been to examine indigenous values and world views and their relationship to the criteria used to determine outstanding universal value. Four propositions have been introduced:

1 The characteristics of indigeneity, a primary characteristic – a close and enduring relationship with the environment – and five secondary characteristics:

- Time, measured over centuries
- Human identity
- A system of knowledge
- Environmental sustainability
- A unique language

2 A spiral of ecological synergy built on extended networks, interacting relationships, an outward flow of energy that shapes:

- a grounded human identity
- the relationships between animate and inanimate objects
- the dimension of time

3 A Pacific approach to valuing heritage that gives emphasis to:

- the fusion of tangible and intangible qualities
- a two-directional time frame (past and future)
- ecological harmony.

4 The interface between universality and distinctiveness.

Principles

On the basis of these propositions it is possible to make some preliminary comments on indigeneity and outstanding universal value by identifying a set of principles that might be applied to the process of valuing heritage sites: connectedness, mauri, continuity, contextual significance, and reciprocity. The principles are essentially derived from the nature of relationships and reflect indigenous philosophies and world views.

Connectedness, for example, is a principle that sees value in cohesion and accord between objects, between people and their surroundings, and between elements within the wider environment. It has both tangible and intangible dimensions and places importance on human relationships with sites. The *mauri* principle proposes that all matter, organic and non-organic, has an intrinsic dynamic core that confers an element of uniqueness, but within a network of interacting entities. The tangible-intangible divide becomes irrelevant since objects are seen as having a life-force that contradicts any notion of inertness. A third principle, *continuity*, has both a past and a future; by linking different periods of time it also links one generation with another and provides a sense of coherence that extends over centuries. Heritage is as much about protecting the future as commemorating the past. The principle of *ecological significance* stresses the importance of external relationships as evidence of worth; it contrasts with estimates of worth that are based on intrinsic qualities alone and locates sites within a natural environment. And the *reciprocity* principle expects that heritage sites will not only be afforded value by neighbouring communities but will also contribute to indigenous endeavours. The contribution may take the form of incubating threatened species of plants or animals, or providing an alternate economic resource, or maintaining a cultural link that will contribute to the cultural security of future generations.

Because indigeneity is often portrayed as a function of spirituality there is a tendency to assume that it cannot be measured by quantitative methods. But indigeneity is more a function of measurable relationships than nebulous associations. The principle of connectedness for example can be assessed by the quantity of meaningful relationships over time using oral history methodologies, written histories, land-court records, references in songs and narratives, and linguistic markers. The quality of those relationships can also be assessed by constructing a multi-dimensional instrument to measure intensity, duration, character, and reciprocity.

The mauri principle can also be quantified; a chemical analysis, for example, will reveal the composition of an object and its relationship to other elements within the environment while qualitative accounts will be able to determine how the object is perceived by others. Continuity is similarly measurable by scientific and historic means as well as through family and community narratives. Among other methods, contextual significance can be determined by environmental impact studies that focus on the relationships of sites with the natural environment, while reciprocity can be quantified by economic, educational, and biological sustainability measures.

The primary purpose of this paper, however, has not been to quantify indigeneity but to explore the ways in which indigeneity might be relevant to determining 'outstanding universal value'. On the basis of evidence to date, it would appear that the values, philosophies, and principles that are part of indigenous world views can add further understandings to the depth and breadth of 'outstanding universal value'. Essentially value is a function of relationships – between people and the natural environment, between tangible and intangible dimensions, between organic and inorganic material, and between past and future. Relationships constitute the foundations upon which indigenous populations understand the world. In deciding the criteria for world heritage sites, the World Heritage Committee might therefore consider the prospect that indigeneity is a sufficiently important marker of heritage to warrant explicit recognition.

There's a rumble in the jungle – 1080 poisoning our forests or a necessary tool?

Shaun C. Ogilvie, Aroha Miller and James M. Ataria

A central theme for Māori and the environment is the protection of taonga species from the ravages of introduced animal pests such as possums, mustelids, and rodents. Sodium fluoroacetate (known also as Compound 1080 or simply '1080') is used in Aotearoa-New Zealand for the control of introduced animal pests, including possums. Methods of 1080 use include aerial application (by fixed-wing aircraft or helicopter) using cereal or diced-carrot baits. While this method can be effective for reducing pest populations (Livingstone 1994; Eason 2002), dropping 1080 from aircraft, which we explore in this chapter, is a highly controversial practice for Māori.

What is 1080?

The name '1080' was assigned to sodium fluoroacetate when it was being assessed as a rodenticide in the USA in the 1940s (Eason 2002). It was the one-thousand-and-eightieth compound to have been assessed at the time. In pure form, 1080 is a fine white powder that is water soluble. Manufactured 1080 is identical to 1080 found naturally in poisonous plants in Brazil, Africa, and Australia. Presumably these plants have 1080 content as a means of defence against browsing animals. The highest concentration of 1080 observed in nature is in the seeds of a plant from South Africa (Meyer 1994), and is about five times the concentration used in possum baits in New Zealand. Compound 1080 has also been measured in very low concentration in tea leaves. As 1080 dissolves easily in water, it will leach from baits and has been shown to be broken down by microscopic organisms in soil (King et al. 1994). Compound 1080 is a broad-spectrum poison; it is toxic to a broad range of animals, though there are marked differences between different species. Dogs and other carnivores are the most sensitive; herbivores (animals that eat plants) are less sensitive; and birds, reptiles and fish are less sensitive again. At high concentrations 1080 has been shown to kill insects, with one article published in the 1950s showing that 1080 applied to soil under plants will be taken up by the plants and in turn kill aphids feeding on the plants (David 1950).

Advantages and disadvantages of 1080

The main advantages of 1080 are that it is highly effective for reducing possum and rabbit numbers, it is cheap compared with other poisons, and it breaks down in the environment. The main disadvantages are that 1080 applied from aircraft is highly controversial; dogs can be poisoned by eating carcasses of pest animals that have eaten 1080, and there is no antidote available.

Māori perceptions of 1080

For Māori there is a wide range of opinion on 1080, from strong support to strong opposition. The Environmental Risk Management Authority (ERMA) recently undertook a reassessment of 1080 use in New Zealand. Part of the reassessment process included invitations to the public for submissions on 1080 use. At least 28 written submissions were received from individuals or groups identifying as Māori, from all over New Zealand. To gain a better understanding of Māori perceptions of 1080 we reviewed those twenty eight submissions.

A summary of the issues that most frequently arose in the submissions is given in Table 1. The most commonly raised issue (in over half of the submissions) was that not enough consultation takes place with iwi in areas where 1080 use is planned.

Issue	% of submissions raising the issue
A need for clear communication, consultation, or collaboration with iwi in areas where 1080 is used	57%
Continued research into the effects of 1080 on the environment, flora and fauna, especially taonga species	39%
General opposition to toxins in the environment	32%
Need for continued investigation into suitable alternatives to 1080	32%
Effective and appropriate monitoring pre- and post-1080 controls	32%
Iwi would like to be involved in the design, planning and implementation of pest management plans	25%
Aerial application of toxins affects the mauri, kaitiakitanga, wairua, and tikanga of the controlled area	21%
High non-target species fatalities	21%
Use of locally appropriate approaches to 1080	14%
Overspill of toxins to waterways and crossing property boundaries	14%
A feeling of reduced ability to carry out customary practices, i.e. collection of kai or rongoā in control areas	14%
Preference for ground baiting rather than aerial application	11%

Table 1. Issues submitted by Māori on aerial application of 1080, during the 1080 reassessment process.

There is often concern at the lack of investigative research into the effects of 1080 on the environment and a belief that Māori should be more directly involved in such research. At present, much existing research is not trusted as it is carried out or funded by the parties that use 1080. Involving Māori in research would improve the relationships between involved parties, clear the path for better communication and consultation, and increase confidence in research outcomes.

About a third of the submissions mentioned that in general, Māori are opposed to the use of toxins in the environment, regardless of the benefits to be had through the control of pests. Although many submitters recognised that the use of 1080 was essential to control pests, with the positives outweighing the negatives, there is still a strong feeling that this is pollution of the environment. By the same token, an equal number of submissions stated they would like to see continued investigation into suitable alternatives to 1080. Future research could realistically lead to a more environmentally and culturally acceptable alternative to 1080, potentially eliminating many of the concerns held by Māori regarding the polluting effect of 1080 in the environment.

Almost a third of submissions stated they would like to see effective and appropriate pre- and post-control monitoring, with some advocating that iwi should be employed in this process, as well as involving iwi in the design, planning and implementation of control plans. Implementation of these plans will, without doubt, increase Māori ownership of a management plan that in turn will encourage Māori participation and responsibility for pest control, fulfilling kaitiakitanga responsibilities and leading to stronger bonds with the environment and its health.

Nearly a quarter of submissions perceived that the aerial application of 1080 negatively impacts on important cultural values, especially the mauri and wairua of people, animals, rivers, trees, mountains, forests, land, and seas. This is particularly important in wāhi tapu and mahinga kai areas, which often contain much cultural and historical significance for iwi (Barlow 1991). The death of non-target, and often taonga, species was also mentioned in a fifth of the submissions. This links directly to the previous issue, in which the death of non-target species from the aerial application of 1080 negatively impacts on the mauri and wairua not only of those individuals suffering mortality, but also on the wider ecosystem including prey, predators, habitat, and environment. All these factors are interlinked, their wairua and mauri are connected, and therefore the balance of the whole community is affected.

Other concerns were also voiced in the submission process. The use of locally appropriate processes in the application of 1080 should be encouraged. What is often the most economical method of pest control – the aerial application of 1080 – may not be the most appropriate for a particular area. Preference is for the use of other more expensive but more suitable methods, such as ground baiting. This allows greater control over the use of 1080 in the environment, helping to alleviate concerns about the way this toxin is used. The overspill of 1080 to waterways and adjoining properties raised the issue of the perceived indiscriminate use of 1080 across the control area. While the use of GPS systems have markedly improved the precision of aerial drops, there is still concern that where the baits land is somewhat arbitrary, leading to toxic baits entering waterways, properties bordering the control area, and wāhi tapu sites.

All the issues raised above contributed to a feeling of reduced ability to carry out customary practices, which was mentioned in 14% of submissions. One potential solution to these issues was raised in a small number of submissions, in which a preference was expressed for ground baiting rather than aerial control. As already mentioned, ground baiting allows for greater control over the use of 1080, and this could support Māori calls for more targeted methods of application. This would decrease the impact on the mauri in the control area, allow Māori to retain kaitiakitanga over the environment, comfortably and safely carrying out customary practices, while at the same time reducing vertebrate pests.

Research example: 1080 uptake in plants of importance to Māori

Aside from appropriate consultation, the carrying out by Māori of research into 1080 that specifically addresses issues of importance to Māori, was viewed by the submitters as very important. There have been a number of concerns regarding 1080 residues in the environment (Para 1999). The risk of humans being poisoned by plants used for food or medicinal purposes has been identified as a key research issue. Support among Māori for aerial application of 1080 is minimal, particularly in culturally significant areas such as sites where food and water are gathered or historical sites. During aerial application of 1080 baits, it is possible that 1080 residues that have leached into soil may be absorbed by plants (Atzert 1971; Rammel & Fleming 1978). Depending on the period of time that 1080 persists in plant tissues, plants could remain toxic after the risk of primary poisoning has gone (i.e. after baits have degraded and become non-toxic). Ogilvie et al. (1998) showed that 1080 can be taken up by broadleaf and ryegrass, and persists for at least 38 days. In this research example, the aim was to investigate the risk of human 1080 poisoning through plant species used by Māori as food and medicine.[1]

Culturally important plant species were identified through discussion. It was agreed that the focus of this research should be on pikopiko (*Asplenium Bulbiferum*, also known as hen and chicken fern) and karamuramu (*Coprosma Robusta*). Pikopiko shoots, which are used as a food source, emerge in August, at a time when 1080 application operations are commonly undertaken throughout New Zealand. Karamuramu is used throughout the year as a medicine, applied both externally and internally for a number of ailments, including being taken as a tea for urinary complaints.

A field study was undertaken in State Forest Block 100, south of Lake Waikaremoana, grid reference E 2861485, N 6252803. Ten wild-growing individuals of each plant species were selected. A single Wanganui No. 7 cereal 1080 bait[2] was placed in a smaller wire cage (10 mm mesh size) at the base of seven of the plants of each species (within 40 mm distance of each plant). The other three plants of each species were experimental controls, and as such an empty cage was placed at the base of these plants. The cages were deployed around baits to prevent them from being eaten by wild animals during the course of the experiment. Five-gram samples of shoot (pikopiko) or leaves (karamuramu) were collected at various time points out to 56 days after the baits were deployed. Samples were then analysed for 1080 content at Landcare Research, Lincoln.

No 1080 was detected in any of the control plant samples, suggesting that 1080 is not a natural component of the two study plant species. No 1080 was detected in any of the experimental pikopiko samples. In one of the experimental karamuramu plants 1080 was detected 7 and 14 days after bait placement (Figure 1). The maximum concentration measured was 5 parts per billion (ppb) on day 7, while 2.5 ppb was measured after 14 days. The 1080 maximum of 5 ppb is an extremely small proportion, about 0.0004% of the 1080 originally present in a single bait. At and after 28 days there was no 1080 detected in any of the karamuramu plants.

In summary, we were able to find no evidence of 1080 uptake in pikopiko. Karamuramu, however, did take up 1080, though the maximum concentration seen was a tiny fraction (0.0004%) of the original 1080 in the bait and this 1080 did not persist in karamuramu – it was completely gone after 28 days. To assess the toxicity risk to humans, at the maximum 1080 concentration of 5 ppb, a person weighing 70 kg would need to consume 28 tonnes of this karamuramu to have a 50% chance of dying of 1080 poisoning (full calculations are in Ogilvie et al. 2006). We therefore concluded there is negligible risk of people being poisoned by consuming plants that have taken up 1080 during aerial control operations.

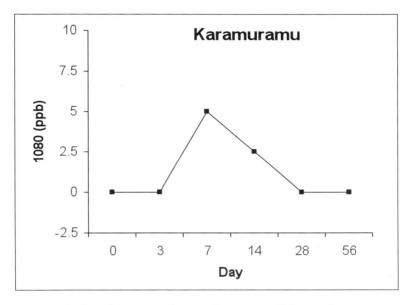

Figure 1. Uptake and persistence of 1080 in karamuramu. Values are the maximum measured in any plant at each time point.

Making 1080 scientific information readily available for Māori communities

Following the completion of the plant research described above, our Māori community collaborators conveyed their unease that the research only addressed a small fraction of their concerns about the environmental fate of 1080. They consequently posed the question "how can Māori communities more easily access existing scientific information on the impacts of 1080 on non-target species of cultural importance?" We therefore created a tool whereby published scientific literature on 1080 could be made readily available to Māori communities.

A total of 143 scientific literature items on the impacts of 1080 on non-target species were sourced and reviewed. The information was converted into an interactive foodweb database (Figure 2) allowing it to be presented in a holistic and pictorial fashion.

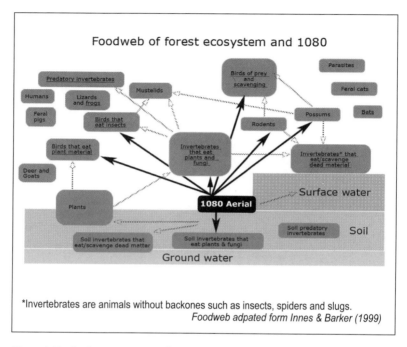

Figure 2 Foodweb representation of aerially-applied 1080 in a forest ecosystem.
This foodweb forms the conceptual starting point of the database of 1080 non-target
information, by allowing users to click on hyperlinks within ecosystem compartments to
access information.[3]

The database is designed to arrange the information in a series of interconnected layers through which the user can navigate to source information that includes research and risk summaries for each species and copies of the original scientific papers where they have been able to be included. Information for a total of 19 native bird species, two native frog species, two native bat species, six plant species, 1080 in surface water, and 17 types of insects, spiders and slugs is available.

This database is now publicly available. It is a new tool that has been readily adopted by Māori communities and it allows a new way for them to access information and therefore make their own risk assessments on the use of 1080.

The future of 1080 use – where to from here?

While our analysis of Māori submissions on 1080 showed that more consultation with Māori by 1080 users needs to be undertaken, in instances where genuine attempts to embrace and promote the Treaty of Waitangi principles have occurred, many Māori concerns have been satisfactorily addressed resulting in robust outcomes that are supported by all parties. A particularly pertinent example is that of the Lake Taupo and Lake Rotoaira Forest Trusts. These trusts manage about 50,000 hectares of Māori-owned land, much of which is planted in forestry. The Trustees are responsible for ensuring the performance of the plantations and protecting native and exotic flora and fauna. A key aspect of this responsibility is mitigating the damage of possums, ferrets, stoats and rats, which threaten the future of the forests and birdlife. The Trusts have created working partnerships with the region's principal pest control operator, Epro Ltd, and with Environment Waikato, the Regional Council acting for the Animal Health Board. Through these partnerships, protocols have been created that ensure meaningful and timely consultation, and that those proposing to use 1080 on trust lands enter into any consultation in good faith. The Trustees have, through the partnerships and the resultant protocols, been able to make amendments to the pest control activities that resulted in allaying many of the Māori landowner concerns about the risks of 1080. Perhaps future development of such partnerships could mean that Māori have a stronger voice in expressing means to mitigate risks and even enhance the benefits of 1080 use.

New and emerging technologies – A future without 1080?

There are a number of initiatives focussed on alternatives to 1080, at differing stages of development, completion, and availability for general use. In recent years there has been a focus on enhancing the tools available for ground control of possums, hence supporting communities in the quest to be self-reliant. One recently available tool that has been adopted by Māori communities is Feratox®, cyanide encapsulated into small-pea-sized capsules. In the field the capsules are deployed with non-toxic 'teaser' bait in bags stapled to trees, which possums break open to access the non-toxic baits. When bitten, the Feratox capsules will release the cyanide content and the possum will usually succumb quickly. Advantages of this method are that possum carcasses will usually be found near the site where the Feratox was placed, so the numbers of animals removed from the control area can be counted and income can be gained from gathering possum fur. Feratox is also considered to be one of the most humane toxins available, as compared with the use of other toxins, possums die quickly.

Much work has recently done on the development of humane kill-traps for possums. Kill-traps, as with Feratox, have the advantage that possum carcasses can be counted and fur collected. There are a number of different possum kill-traps now available on the market.

Looking more to the future, Landcare Research is working on the development of biological control agents for possums. Immuno-contraception is one technology being explored. With this technology, the immune system of the possum is exploited in such a way that it inhibits reproduction, hence potentially rendering the possum infertile (e.g., Duckworth et al. 1998, 2007; Polkinghorne et al. 2005). With such technology, if a significant number of individuals can be rendered infertile there will be huge advantages for possum control, significantly reducing reliance on poisons such as 1080. However, technology such as immunocontraception is very much at the high-tech end of the spectrum, and it may be quite some time before it becomes commercially available.

1080 – A necessary tool or poisoning our forests?

ERMA (Environmental Risk Management Authority, New Zealand) released their decision on 1080 use in August 2007. While the decision-making committee decided to allow the continued use of 1080, it also decided to place additional controls on aerial application of 1080 and put the users of 1080 on notice that a tighter management regime is required for aerial drops of 1080. There were four key parts to this tighter management regime: 1) the establishment of a watch list, requiring reports on aerial 1080 operations to be provided to ERMA to enable active monitoring of all future 1080 aerial operations; 2) the strengthening of existing controls to further mitigate risks involved in 1080 aerial drops; 3) the promotion of best practice in relation to pre-operation planning, consultation and notification, and management of 1080 aerial operations; 4) recognition that further research should be undertaken, both on alternatives to 1080, and on the effects of 1080 in specific topic areas where there remains a lack of knowledge and a degree of public concern.

While the decision could be considered a 'green light' for the continued use of 1080, it might be better described as a 'blinking amber light' – 1080 can still be used, but additional controls indicate caution. A significant component of the caution sits within Māori-specific issues. If the new controls and management regime and recommendations achieve the intentions of the ERMA decision-making committee, then in future Māori will have a more effective role in the appropriate and effective use and management of 1080.

Looking again at the question posed in the title of this chapter, the outcome of ERMA's decision on the continued use of 1080 suggests that 1080 is a necessary tool. However, with the new and emerging technologies described above, foundations are being set in place to build a future without the need for 1080. Tying together the key themes of this chapter, it is important that Māori are involved in the development and assessment of alternatives to 1080 to ensure that these alternatives are not only effective for controlling animal pests, but most importantly are also culturally acceptable.

END NOTES

[1] The people of Tuhoe were partners in this research and we would particularly like to acknowledge James Waiwai and Jim Doherty.

[2] Animal Control Products, Private Bag 3018 Whanganui, New Zealand, approximately 6 g in weight, (0.15% 1080 by weight).

3Available at www.lincoln.ac.nz/1080

Toxic environments: Māori Vietnam veterans and Agent Orange

Cherryl Smith

From 1964 to 1972 New Zealand troops fought in the Vietnam War. Māori men who served in Vietnam made up an estimated 67% of the New Zealand Armed Forces. In 2007 I was part of a small team who volunteered to film the testimonies of over 50 Māori Vietnam veterans.

Men in Vietnam were not only exposed to the trauma of war, they were also exposed to Agent Orange, a powerful herbicide that combined chemicals 24 D and 245 T with TCDD, a toxic dioxin compound. Agent Orange was used as a defoliant to clear forest to provide troops from the United States of America and their allies with increased visibility of the enemy and to enable easier access. Between 1961 and 1971, United States aircraft sprayed an estimated 72 million litres of toxic chemicals over provinces in Vietnam, including 44 million litres of Agent Orange, containing 170 kg of dioxin. The aerial spraying programme, called Operation Ranch Hand, covered approximately 9% of the land area. Dioxin is an extremely poisonous chemical that can cause cancer, immune system deficiency and birth defects. In the first decade after the war, it is estimated that over 50,000 children in Vietnam were born with deformities to parents who had been affected by toxin exposure.

My cousin served in Vietnam. He and his closest friends incurred a huge cost on their health as a result of their service. Although it could not be proven, they felt the health problems of themselves, their children and grandchildren were related to exposure to Agent Orange. As a result of our early discussions with Whanganui veterans, we began to gather and film the testimonies of Māori veterans. We began to gather filmed testimonies for two reasons. Most important, film testimony enables future generations of a veteran to be able to hear their war experiences first hand and this was particularly important because of the health impacts on children and grandchildren. The second reason was more broadly educational – to create an archive of the veterans health during and after the war.

The interviews were conducted in Kaitaia, Kaikohe, Auckland, Whakatāne, Tauranga, New Plymouth, Palmerston North, and Whanganui. Some common experiences began to emerge as the veterans described their experiences. We were deeply affected by the stories of men and families who have been left to suffer. Their stories made us realise how much their involvement in Vietnam had affected not only their whānau but all of us as a people. We not only lost Māori men in battle, we also lost the health of the men who returned and we will live with the intergenerational health impacts of the whānau who are still affected.

Going to war

Most of the Māori men who went to Vietnam were from rural Māori communities and most were confident of knowing their tūrangawaewae. Most were born in the 1940s when the birth rate for Māori was at its highest, women having an average of six children. Large families were common and many of the veterans were raised knowing how to hunt, fish, and survive in the bush. They were often key food providers for whānau, able to kill sheep, lambs, rabbits, and able to fish and dive to gather seafood. They were also knowledgeable hunters, able to hunt wild pigs, deer and possum. Many Māori families during the 1950s and 1960s were still able to be largely self-sufficient when it came to food. Whanaungatanga was strong, which meant that collective efforts were valued.

About half those interviewed were fluent speakers of Māori. They had grown up with te reo Māori as the language in their homes and they were steeped in tikanga. They were from a generation whose parents had often been disciplined for speaking Māori in schools. Some had learnt Māori later at Māori boarding schools they had attended. When the veterans described their fitness and sporting achievements it was clear that they were some of the fittest, strongest young Māori men in their hapu and iwi. They were men who would have held key leadership roles if they had returned to their communities and were healthy.

A number of the veterans had joined the Regular Force cadets in school at the age of 15. As cadets they were familiar with army training and army life. Māori Affairs had careers advisors who advised Māori students about potential career paths. Former Māori Battalion veteran Colonel Pita Awatere was at one time a Māori Affairs Officer. Schools in the 1950s and 1960s were very focussed on a manual curriculum for Māori boys, particularly if they were regarded as non-academic. Not many Māori boys left school with School Certificate or having gained University Entrance; they were guided either towards the army or trade training. In the army many were able to get trade certificates as electricians, carpenters, mechanics, panel beaters, etc. There was also an army school for further education based at Waiouru.

Enlisting in the army

All the veterans had uncles or relations who had served in previous wars. Vietnam veterans were a generation raised in the shadow of the exploits of the Māori Battalion, which had fought in the Second World War. They had heard of the heroic and brave exploits of their fathers, uncles and grandfathers, who had served in the Battalion. Some noted that Māori war veterans returning from the Second World War were supposed to be given land blocks but many of these were either uneconomic, or were in difficult terrain, or required money to be able to turn them into economic blocks.

The majority of those who joined the army were eager to enlist. For some it was a way to get further education through a trade; for others it was a job and an income. The army could provide a career path. When the Vietnam war started very few said they knew anything about Vietnam or what the people of Vietnam were fighting about. But many stated that they wanted to go to war because it was an adventure.

It was common to be told that in the 1960s when some of the men enlisted they were below the legal age of 21. A number lied about their age or forged a signature. Not all their whānau were happy when they enlisted. Many told stories of opposition to their enlistment and how mothers, fathers or grandparents had tried to stop them. Other whānau supported them joining.

Fighting in Vietnam

A number of the veterans described how karakia and other ceremonies were carried out for them before leaving to go to battle. Traditionally, Māori warriors underwent ceremonies that dedicated them to the protection of Tūmatauenga. Karakia were recited that placed them in a realm to be able to deal with the rigours of warfare, and when they returned they were brought back to te ao marama, the world of light. Warfare was considered a world where strict rules were to be observed, rules regarding tapu. Some whānau held karakia and ceremonies for those who went to war and for when they returned.

Conditions in Vietnam were harsh. Jungle and guerrilla warfare was waged in hot humid conditions. Jungle warfare involved being in terrain that could hide the enemy effectively, both on and under the ground. Traps that maimed rather than killed were intentional tools of guerrilla fighters. As one person commented, if you injured someone it took three men out of the picture, if you killed them, it was only one. It was a demoralising and psychological war. Some of the Māori men said they felt at home in the forests, they were familiar with the realm of Tāne Mahuta. The forest provided cover and protection. This did not mean that the men were immune from the horrors of war – it was still kill or be killed.

Many of the men believed that Māori were 'natural warriors', that being sons of Tūmatauenga meant there was a natural ability inherent within them to be superior fighters. The Māori Battalion felt it had proved the prowess of Māori men in battle. In Vietnam, jungle warfare put them into a situation that advantaged men who had knowledge of the forests back home. They moved more easily in the terrain. Some recounted stories told by the enemy of the battle prowess of Māori. Many of the men believed their tupuna were with them, protecting and helping them.

A number of men mentioned that it was mainly Māori men who were lead scouts and tail scouts, which required longer and more intense periods of hyper-vigilance. They reported higher rates of combat exposure and longer periods of combat duty. Despite their high numbers in the service few Māori made it to be officers. Only a small number of Māori attended Officer's School.

In Vietnam the enemy did not necessarily wear a uniform, which meant they could be any Vietnamese person. This meant that men had to be in a state of preparedness for attack for longer periods of time. Some of the men talked about the horrors of war and how as Māori there were things done that they were unable to put to rest properly when they came home. If there was removal of items from dead bodies as 'mementos' such as photos or papers, it meant that Māori men sometimes felt they carried kehua when they came home. Some have returned to Vietnam in order to put those kehua to rest. Some talked about utu and how they believed that it was important to reciprocate against the enemy troops. They talked about how fear drove them to kill people who 'may' have been innocent, and how those kehua came also home with them. Māori men we spoke to stressed that they were trained professionals who did not fall apart in a theatre of war in the same way the raw recruits of the United States had done at My Lai. But they did come across dead women and children and some of them too became kehua.

As Vietnam was the first televised war, the local news was filled nightly with horrific images of the reality of war. It was shocking for people to see burning villages, images of children screaming in pain, corpses heaped in ditches and the dehumanising that occurs in war time. The anti-war movement grew stronger at home as the war progressed, but the New Zealand government stood by its ally, the United States. It was not until the My Lai massacre, where 500 unarmed villagers were killed by American troops, that the tide turned and public opinion caused the American government to begin the withdrawal of troops.

Conscription was used in the 1960s in Australia and the United States – those men whose birth dates were selected in the ballot were conscripted into the army unless they could obtain an exemption. This meant that many of the men were forced to go into the army rather than choosing to go. New Zealand troops were not conscripted but came from volunteers among the Regular Forces. The men commented on how much of a difference this made in combat. Professional soldiers with lengthy training were placed with conscripts who had only weeks of training. The New Zealand men felt they were professional soldiers not able to rely on men alongside them in combat. Some felt that this was also reflected in the high United States and Australian casualties.

While the Vietnam War movies and some written sources have talked about the drug use among American soldiers, Māori veterans spoke about the drug use as more of an American problem than among their own troops. One veteran commented that if anyone in their unit had been drunk or smoked marijuana he would have shot them himself as it meant that they were unable to be alert enough in the field and would put the whole unit at risk. They were, however, issued with free cigarettes and most did develop smoking habits. They also felt that smoking helped with stress release.

Whanaungatanga in war

The bonds built between men during war are often lifetime bonds. In the war strong bonds and comradeship were built with other men, Māori and Pākehā, who served in Vietnam. Stories were told of how some of the men looked out for their relations from home, from the same hapu and iwi. Many of the veterans believed that because they had been through the war together and seen what they had seen, only other Vietnam veterans could understand them. Officers still retained respect even after the war and often carried on the role of pastoral care of other men when they returned home. Stories of officers still taking care of their men by making sure they and their families were cared for, were not uncommon, and these relationships are still extremely strong today. Māori veterans told us that they travelled all over the country to attend other veterans' funerals and to pay respects to families. As one veteran expressed it, they had to know each others' weaknesses and strengths; that was a critical factor for forming close bonds. Mistakes are costly in combat and they needed to be able to trust each other completely.

Vietnam was like anywhere else that Māori are, when overseas; they found out where everyone came from and looked out for others who came from the same hapu and iwi.

Agent Orange – The struggle to be believed

Most of the veterans described the spraying of Agent Orange while they were in Vietnam. They all mentioned how it made little impression at the time when they observed the planes flying overhead. At most they were told it was an insect repellent or a defoliant. Some washed in the rain because it was cool in the humid conditions. They observed it covering them and their equipment and going into waterways. Some noted that they must have drunk it because it was on everything. If told anything, they were told that the defoliant was safe, even though it killed all living plants that it touched.

Agent Orange was used to clear forest as a way of opening up such areas for tanks and helicopters. Two-hundred-metre lanes were created by the spraying. A number of the men described seeing the bulldozers coming in to clear the land after the trees were dead. Both Whiskey and Victor Companies, where many of the men we interviewed were, were involved in the work of protecting the land clearance teams. This meant they were exposed to the residue through the dust in the hot season and the mud in the wet season.

It was not until after the war that many of the veterans became aware that they might have been affected by toxins. The realisation happened by degrees, such as when they were talking to veterans about the health problems they were experiencing. Wives having miscarriages or children born with unusual symptoms added pieces to the puzzle. Talking to other veterans about their children also provided clues. Reports did come from overseas of Vietnam veterans sharing similar health impacts. The awareness took many years but with the advent of the internet, access to overseas veterans and to research became much easier.

When veterans did begin to suspect possible illnesses were caused by toxins, they faced a bigger battle. Medical research did not clearly prove the veterans' claims. Veterans had to face the disbelief of medical investigations that did not have the research to 'prove' toxic causes.

Political barriers have also caused delays in the hearing of the veterans' concerns. The Reeves Inquiry, a government-commissioned report into the effects of Agent Orange on the children of Vietnam veterans, negated veterans' concerns by stating there was no established link between the health problems of children and their fathers' exposure to Agent Orange. It also stated there was only one recorded occasion of troops being in or near an area being sprayed by herbicide. This error was repeated in 2001 in the McLeod Report. In response, John Masters, a commanding officer in Vietnam, produced a Defence Forces classified map that showed that Phuoc Tuy Province had been sprayed. Following this a Health Select Committee on Agent Orange was set up that was able to review New Zealand Army files that detailed the spraying and the placement of troops in Vietnam. It was clear New Zealand troops had been exposed. As a result of the Health Select Committee report, the government finally moved towards an acknowledgement of some health impacts, an apology and some compensation for Vietnam veterans in 2008.

Coming home

The sharp difference between the Second World War and the Vietnam War was that the veterans from Vietnam were social outcasts when they returned home. Vietnam was a socially and politically unpopular war. In the 1970s the war was televised and for the first time images of death, burning villages, napalm, and screaming women and children were beamed into living rooms. Anti-war activism was high and massive protests were held against the war. Protesters carried banners proclaiming the soldiers to be 'baby killers'. High profile incidents such as the murder of women and children by American soldiers at My Lai was assumed to be the behaviour of all soldiers in Vietnam. Images from My Lai of women and children lying in ditches were carried in protest marches.

Unlike the Second World War, the Vietnam War was never won. Once troops were withdrawn, successive governments swept the War under the carpet. When the veterans returned, under what they described as a 'cloak of shame', they were shunned and felt as if they were abandoned by a country they had fought for. Some of the veterans talked of being flown home in secrecy and how in some cases whānau did not know they were coming. Some outlined how they arrived at Whenuapai airbase and were told to change into civilian clothes and were then supposed to return home.

When the Māori Battalion returned from overseas after the Second World War, thousands of people had lined the docks and travelled to Wellington to greet them and to mourn those who had died. They travelled from iwi to iwi, where tributes were paid to them and where once again the loss of those who had died in battle was recognised. They returned as heroes and remain honoured today among Māori communities.

Not only was there public rejection and government rejection, veterans also spoke of being rejected in Returned Servicemen's Association Clubs (RSA). Initially they were refused full entry to the RSA and instructed not to wear their medals of service. Other veterans claimed that Vietnam was 'not a real war'. It wasn't until 31 May 2008 that a public apology was made by the government to the veterans. A whakanoa (spiritual cleansing) ceremony was also held bringing together tohunga from around the country.

Post-Traumatic Stress Disorder and the impact on whānau

Post-Traumatic Stress Disorder (PTSD) is a mental illness that results from being subjected to trauma, particularly life-threatening trauma. PTSD sufferers commonly re-experience the trauma through recurrent flashbacks and dreams. They become very sensitive to people, places and things that may trigger reminders of the event. PTSD has only been formally recognised as an illness since the 1980s, but has gone under other names such as shell shock and combat or battle fatigue. Unrecognised and untreated, veterans who have PTSD can become suicidal and depressed, can have long-term anxiety and panic attacks, and are at higher risk of becoming addicted to alcohol and drugs through self-medicating.

PTSD is common among war veterans generally, but according to one study of 756 Vietnam war veterans, Māori suffered higher rates of PTSD. According to the research, the higher rates can be explained by the fact that Māori had higher rates of combat exposure, were more likely to be in lower ranks and were more likely to be in high exposure roles.

The higher exposure of Māori soldiers to high risk roles was confirmed by the Māori veterans themselves. As already stated, roles in the army such as lead and tail scouts in the jungle were predominantly undertaken by Māori. In 2007 Māori veterans and whānau are still suffering severe symptoms of a debilitating illness. Only a few of the Māori veterans to whom we spoke had been formally diagnosed with PTSD, but the majority described PTSD type symptoms and had not had adequate support to help them and their whānau. We became aware also of a number of veterans who were socially removing themselves from everyone; a number had committed suicide. Since the 1980s enough has been known about PTSD for treatment to be successful or to enable improvements in the life of the veterans and their whānau, but Māori veterans are generally not getting help.

While the men may be suffering PTSD symptoms, there was another major health factor in Vietnam and that was Agent Orange. The connections between the impact of toxins and impacts on the mental health of those who have been exposed to toxins is not yet fully understood. The line between mental health causes as a result of toxins or as a result of PTSD is not clear. However, it is not uncommon for people exposed to toxins to report mental health impacts such as increased anxiety and depression.[1]

Many of the veterans spoke openly about their mental states during their interviews and freely admitted to anxiety, depression, aggressive and violent behaviour, as well as battles with alcoholism. A few talked of the need to be constantly on alert in war, to be in a continuous state of hyper-alertness, which they were unable to switch off when they returned home. Many of the memories remain present and they were extremely careful about what questions would be asked, as the interviews could have triggered a panic attack or high levels of anxiety. Despite the passing of decades, many still have recurring nightmares where events are still very real.

Consequences for whānau

A number of veterans referred to the fact that after the war they did not feel comfortable with whānau. They felt most comfortable and safe with their friends who had been through the war. Very few of the veterans we spoke to lived within their own rohe, most lived outside the rohe even though whānau wanted them to return. Most said they did not want to share the horrors of what they saw with whānau and there were many reasons for their reluctance to do so. They did not want whānau members to carry the images with them. They felt that there could be no true understanding of what they had experienced. For many it was still too painful to talk about particular incidents because these triggered flashbacks, panic attacks and uncontrollable breakdowns. Sometimes these memory flashbacks could happen anywhere, without warning. They talked about nightmares, reliving events as if the events were still happening to them today rather than 40 years ago.

It was common for veterans to have relationship and marriage breakdowns. When relationships do survive the toll on women and children was high. Many veterans openly declared their inability to control their anger and their problems with alcohol. They also talked about the illnesses their children carried. Partners had miscarriages and still-born children. Some veterans described children's and grandchildren's illnesses such as cleft palate, tumours, unusual rashes, infertility, disability, stroke-type illnesses, cancers, anxiety and depression. Some of the greatest suffering was expressed by veterans over the fact that they may have passed on to children illnesses and disabilities that can result in intergenerational problems. Some of their children discussed the possibility of not having children because they might pass on their own health problems.

Conclusion

Despite the recent moves by government to recompense Vietnam veterans, this package will fall short. The most urgent need among the veterans and whānau was access to integrated health and veteran services support that is able to work with whānau. Access to financial support through Veterans Affairs tends to be a protracted, complex process. It is also a flawed process because it relies on proving disabilities and for men who fought for their country it is demeaning to have to prove illness or disability to access help. Many men have been reluctant to access that help.

During the filming of the testimonies of the veterans, not one interview went by without tears either by the veteran, their whānau, or us, the listeners. Their stories say much for the ability of the human spirit to endure despite the hardships of their lives. One of the most difficult things for the veterans has been being believed about the impacts and consequences of Agent Orange. What stands out in the stories of Vietnam veterans, repeated across select committees, in public inquiries, in the media, in reports on veterans and children of veterans, are consistent stories of poor and at times extremely poor health outcomes for children and grandchildren. One day scientific evidence may just agree with what the veterans are saying, but by then they may all be dead.

END NOTES

[1]People Poisoned Daily Tour. Testimonies of people exposed to toxins.

Biocolonialism and resisting the commodification of biodiversity in Aotearoa

Jessica Hutchings and Angeline Greensill

To maintain growth and higher profits in the new global economy, governments, science and businesses are increasingly adopting unsustainable practices, exploiting so called 'new and undiscovered' territories and knowledge that have been managed collectively and shared by indigenous communities for many generations. This exploitation of environmental resources is merely a continuation of the paternalistic colonial mindset of 'we know what is best'.

These attitudes and behaviours towards the environment and indigenous peoples are representative of the new right and free trade agenda that was legitimised and fuelled by the global project of regulatory reform of the early 1980s. These reforms essentially rolled back environmental protection laws, health and safety protections, and workers and citizen rights. This new right and free trade agenda is commonly referred to as 'neoliberalism' and promoted by global corporates and western governments as the development paradigm of the new century. However, as global profits of unaccountable corporations increase, the general effect is the exploitation of working and poor peoples, indigenous communities, and the environment. The neoliberal agenda is socially and environmentally exploitative and is tipping the carrying capacity of Papatūānuku. While this exploitation sits alongside the trade advantages of corporate led globalisation and significant innovation in unaccountable new technologies the results can be measured in the *true* costs of production where there is an increase in the exploitation of people and the environment. The consumption patterns of the neoliberal paradigm are moving further away from conserving the interrelated and holistic patterns in nature so strongly valued by Māori and other indigenous communities.

The environment and her resources that have been sustainably managed for generations, and used for customary and cultural purposes by the worlds indigenous communities, are now seen by the global economy, western governments, science and business as the 'new pot of gold' (Howard 2001). Industrialisation, the green revolution and monocultures (Howard 2001; Shiva 2000) have destroyed most of the biodiversity in the 'first' world and all eyes are on the resources that lie within the untapped states and tribal areas of indigenous peoples, including Māori within Aotearoa.

The exploitation of indigenous knowledges and resources provide the fuel for the unethical neoliberal agenda of 'free' trade. This agenda seeks unfettered access to the world's natural resources for the purpose of commodification and profit, which in turn fuels the mechanisms of the capitalist economy. However, this right to consume or use anything from anywhere under this redefined version of neoliberal 'freedom', is based on the theft of indigenous and traditional ecological knowledge and environmental resources. This theft impacts on the freedom of millions of indigenous and third-world peoples and species to survive with integrity, dignity and wellbeing (Shiva 1998).

This chapter documents two neoliberal policies proposed by the Labour-led Government in the years 2006 and 2007 that specifically relate to biodiversity and Māori. The first is the proposed framework for bioprospecting in Aotearoa/New Zealand, and the second is a proposed bilateral (free-trade) agreement on the regulation of natural medicines referred to as the proposed Australian and New Zealand Therapeutics Authority (ANZTPA).

We have specifically chosen to focus on these two neoliberal policies as we have been actively involved with many others in resisting the commodification of traditional ecological and indigenous knowledge and life forms. We are Māori women activists, mothers, growers, academics, and are members of Te Waka Kai Ora (the Māori Organics Network) and Nga Wāhine Tiaki o Te Ao, a collective of Māori women that strongly resists the development and use of genetic engineering in Aotearoa/New Zealand. It seems appropriate to take advantage of this chapter to draw critical and urgent attention to these issues that threaten our future cultural survival as indigenous peoples.

Bioprospecting: Harnessing benefits for New Zealand

On 9 July 2007, the New Zealand Government released a policy framework discussion document entitled, 'Bioprospecting: Harnessing Benefits for New Zealand' (Ministry of Economic Development (MED) 2007). This discussion document was the subject of formal consultation processes between the Crown and iwi for a seven-week period with formal submissions closing on 12 October 2007. Although the status of this document is for discussion purposes only it clearly signals the Crown's position with regard to the future management of biodiversity and bioprospecting in Aotearoa/New Zealand. Furthermore, this paper raises serious concerns regarding the Government's failure to recognise permanent sovereignty over traditional knowledge and natural resources as outlined in Te Tiriti o Waitangi, as well as for the life giving, regenerative and diverse capacity of nature.

We raise two issues in this chapter regarding the proposed bioprospecting framework; the first is the continued valuing of the global economic neoliberal agenda to guide the use of biodiversity on a domestic level in Aotearoa/New Zealand, which amounts to nothing less than biopiracy; and the second issue is the relationship between this proposed policy framework and the WAI262 claim.[1] Both these issues highlight the lack of rights Māori have to protect and value the life-sustaining capacity of biodiversity on which Māori cultural well-being is founded. They further illustrate how the narrow rules of neoliberal commerce are commodifying biodiversity through western property rights systems and creating monopolies of ownership and control over the planet's biological wealth for the benefit of unaccountable corporations and global markets that are commonly known among third-world and indigenous communities as biopiracy.

Bioprospecting - Biocolonialism and biopiracy

Biodiversity is a wide concept and refers to the 'variety of landscapes, ecosystems, species and genes including their different functional processes' (Toledo 2007).

Māori communities often talk about biodiversity in terms of Ranginui raua ko Papatūānuku me ona tamariki. According to The Indigenous Peoples Council on Biocolonialism, 90% of the world's biodiversity is situated in the lands of indigenous peoples (Howard 2001). Hence this overlap of the remaining pockets of the world's biodiversity and indigenous territories makes indigenous peoples vulnerable to the theft of biodiversity, known as bioprospecting within their regions. There is a direct correlation between cultural diversity of peoples and biodiversity and it is well documented that the cultural and physical survival of indigenous peoples is directly related to the conservation of the remaining pockets of biodiversity (Howard 2001; Hutchings 2001; Shiva 1998). A key feature of biodiversity use is the associated knowledge that is held collectively within indigenous communities about different uses of biodiversity. This knowledge is seen as just as important to hunters of biodiversity known as bioprospecters. Hence the knowledge of indigenous peoples is often seen and described by the neoliberal paradigm[2] as the key to 'unlocking' or 'releasing' the properties of biodiversity potential that could lead to the development of a commercial product and ultimately profit. Both the biodiversity itself and the associated traditional ecological and indigenous knowledge, are seen as a potential mine ready for stripping bare.

In Aotearoa/New Zealand there has been very little protection from bioprospecting, although the Crown has implemented a Biodiversity strategy. The domestic biodiversity strategy was a result of ratifying the International Convention on Biological Diversity that emerged from the Rio Earth Summit of 1992, which makes references to the protection of indigenous biodiversity and the protection of mātauranga Māori. However, as with most Crown policies claiming to 'protect' Māori interests, the options presented are always 'soft' options that fail to truly protect Māori from the exploitation of hungry global corporates awaiting the raw materials of indigenous knowledge and biodiversity to feed even more monopoly-driven profit.

The fact is the Crown plays a key role in facilitating biopiracy through its own Department of Conservation (DOC) that manages eight million hectares of native forests, tussock lands, alpine areas, wetlands, dunelands estuaries, lakes and many islands, which amounts to about 30% of New Zealand's land area. DOC is the agency that also manages permits to collect or research plants, animals or geological samples as well as the taking, holding or releasing of protected species. Despite the fact that Māori have approximately 1.6 million hectares of land left to protect from exploitation, the law allows DOC to give out permits for biopirates to rape, pillage, and destroy biodiversity in the interests of 'research'. For many decades the Tuhoe people from Te Urewera have experienced their biodiversity being claimed and its use being controlled by DOC.

The Government's proposed framework for bioprospecting, 'Bioprospecting: Harnessing Benefits for New Zealand', was taken around the country to provide Māori communities with an opportunity to comment. The sales job of the very well-paid Māori consultants delivering the Crown's message was that there is currently no protection for Māori from bioprospecting activities and it is in Māori interests to agree to some type of framework. However, all frameworks presented by the Crown fail to uphold Te Tiriti o Waitangi rights or protect biodiversity and Māori knowledge from theft and commodification. The remainder of this section looks at some of the key issues to emerge from the crown's bioprospecting policies.

Bioprospecting has been defined by the Crown as:

...the collection of biological material and the analysis of its
material properties, or its molecular, biochemical or genetic
context, for the purposes of developing a commercial product.
(Ministry of Economic Development 2007: 32).

This neoliberal definition fails to account for the impact on life forms and indigenous livelihoods that is a direct result of bioprospecting. Hence third world communities, Non-Government Organisations and indigenous communities have redefined bioprospecting as biopiracy and biocolonialism. The ETC (Erosion, Technology and Concentration) group define biopiracy and biocolonialism as: 'the appropriation of the knowledges and genetic resources of farming and indigenous communities by individuals or institutions who seek exclusive monopoly control (patents or intellectual property) over these resources and knowledge'.[3]

In many situations, seed companies have claimed to be the inventors or originators of crops that have not been modified but rather have been pirated from other communities. According to the Indigenous Peoples Council on Biocolonialism, these companies may use:

some genetic screening to get a genetics based description of the agricultural or medicinal plant. And simply use the language of genetics to pretend novelty and invention over something that has been common knowledge over centuries, even millennia…[furthermore] biopirate companies are analyzing the genetic makeup of exotic plants with large product markets. Their aim is to be able to create synthetic versions of the products that can be manufactured anywhere in the world (Howard 2001: 13).

The vital input to this practice is biodiversity, which in the neoliberal worldview is no longer seen as the key to a sustainable existence but rather as the raw materials for unaccountable technological development resulting in global monopoly driven corporate profits.

Language, biocolonialism and the exploitation of the feminine

Language and meaning is an important indicator of relationships and power dynamics and often provides a key for us to read in between the lines to understand further the value set and morality behind what is being said. The use of language by the Crown in their bioprospecting consultation document reveals a framework and relationship with nature that is representative of colonial, masculinist, hegemonic ideologies[4] based on domination of ecosystems and nature. Examples of this are the numerous references to bioprospecting being able to 'optimise possible benefit capture [of biodiversity]' (MED 2007: 3). The benefit capture refers to monopoly-driven profit and protections for global corporates through intellectual property right regimes. It is clear that there is no reverence for the life-giving regenerative capacity of nature and biodiversity, but rather it is valued as a commodity, an input, and a raw material.

The title of the document, 'Bioprospecting: Harnessing Benefits for New Zealand' also raises concern. Nature, and her diverse ecosystems, landscapes, regions and territories, are to be harnessed as though she is some wild untamed beast that needs to be reined in. For decades ecofeminists (e.g. Baker 1993; Plumwood 1986; and Hutchings 1997) have highlighted issues concerning the mechanistic understanding of nature that has in turn allowed for the development of an instrumental value to be placed on nature, wherein the value of nature was measured in the value it derived for others. Plumwood (1986: 120) notes that, 'This enabled man to justify the merciless exploitation of the natural world and ultimately to seek to control and dominate that world. Viewed as closer to nature than men, women in this context were also treated instrumentally'. Ecofeminism also argues that the relationship science and dominant society has with nature stems from the Enlightenment, which feminised nature, hence providing the legitimacy to move in and exploit the feminised body of nature herself, therefore arguing a direct correlation between the exploitation of women and the exploitation of the environment (Hutchings 2003). This type of critical analysis is pertinent by making visible another layer of what is happening with regard to the commodification of nature and knowledge through bioprospecting/ biocolonialism.

WAI 262 and Government's plans for biopiracy

The WAI 262 claim directly raises issues on bioprospecting, ownership of biological resources, and mātauranga Māori. The claim was heard from 1998 to 2007 and seeks:

> *recognition and protection for mātauranga Māori and rights in*
> *respect of indigenous flora and fauna and called into question*
> *not just the protections given by the intellectual property regime,*
> *the Protected Objects regime, aspects of the education system, the*
> *environmental decision-making regime and those parts of the health*
> *system that involve rongoa, but also the wider decision-making process*
> *including the way in which the Crown negotiates international*
> *instruments on behalf of New Zealand (Ngati Kahungunu 2007).*

Specifically the claim addresses the following issues:
- The nature of the Māori interest in indigenous flora and fauna and Mātauranga Māori
- Intellectual property protection for taonga works
- Biological and genetic resources of indigenous and /or taonga species
- Tikanga Māori and Mātauranga Māori
- Te Reo Māori
- Relationship of kaitiaki with the environment
- Taonga species
- Rongoa (Ngāti Kahungunu, 2007).

Since the claim was brought against the Crown in 1991, many of the original claimants have passed on, as have some of those who have given evidence throughout the nine-year hearings process. During that time the Crown has moved ahead on policy developments that directly relate to the claim, and those on which the claimants are seeking resolution, with the Crown possibly negating the Tribunal process and potential findings. An example of this was the establishment in 2001 of the Royal Commission of Genetic Modification (RCGM) by the Government who made the strategic 'fence sitting' recommendation of 'preserving opportunities' regarding the future use of genetic modification in Aotearoa/New Zealand. The Crown has subsequently clearly set its science policy direction and regulatory framework with regard to GM, biotechnologies and other new technologies based on the RCGM findings and recommendations, thereby negating any finding by the Waitangi Tribunal regarding WAI262 and genetic modification (GM).

Similarly, the same situation applies to findings of the WAI262 claim and bioprospecting policies of the Crown. When Tribunal hearings on WAI 262 ended in June 2007, the Crown did not advise claimants that the current consultation on bioprospecting was being contemplated; rather it earnestly sought the Tribunal's guidance on these issues. Of issue is the considerable amount of work that was undertaken on the discussion document 'Bioprospecting: Harnessing Benefits for New Zealand' that appears to have had no input from Māori. A briefing paper prepared for iwi by Ngati Kahungunu Incorporated made the following statement with regard to the Crown's bioprospecting discussion document:

> *Although the Wai 262 claim is mentioned in different parts of the Crown discussion document, no information is given on the issues raised by the claimants before the Tribunal. Specifically although there is some discussion about the need to protect mātauranga Māori, the Crown discussion document does not seek submissions on the key issue of Māori interests in the indigenous species themselves and implies that the bioprospecting framework is intended to be created within the context of the existing legal framework and in particular the historical vesting of species in the Crown, the Crown's ownership of the Department of Conservation (DOC) estate, and the Crown's ownership of the foreshore and seabed, even though these are all matters to be considered by iwi to be a breach of the Treaty. (Ngāti Kahungunu 2007)*

The behaviour of the Crown in releasing the discussion document four weeks after the end of nine years of hearings for the Wai 262 claim is evidence again that the Crown has failed to act in good faith, with reasonable cooperation and consideration for the Treaty partner. Furthermore, the discussion document sets out a series of soft options for bioprospecting that represents the interests of the Crown to plunder biodiversity for science and profit but fails to protect life forms, traditional knowledge and Māori communities. For example, the Crown suggests that options for protecting matauranga Māori could include a voluntary register, a code of best practice for bioprospectors, and an advisory council to a Competent National Authority (MED 2007: 41). None of these soft options place power in the hands of Māori communities to control biopropsecting activities but rather relegate Māori to advisory and consultative positions outside Crown processes where Māori participation is Crown controlled, limited and facilitated to provide commentary with little ability affect policy outcomes. Furthermore none of the options presented value the diversity and self-regenerating capacity of life forms that is essential to indigenous and Māori worldviews of the environment.

Proposed neoliberal regulation of rongoa through a bilateral agreement with Australia

In 2006, Ngā Wāhine Tikai o te Ao worked with Te Waka Kai Ora (the Māori Organics movement) to give evidence in the WAI 262 claim over the fast tracking of a proposed bill to establish a joint regulatory authority with Australia to regulate natural remedies, known as the Australia and New Zealand Therapeutics Products Authority (ANZTPA). The Authority would have been established under a bilateral agreement between Australia and New Zealand. This proposed bilateral authority would govern and regulate medicines that included natural remedies, complementary and alternative medicines, as well as rongoa. This proposed bilateral agreement again contained all the impacts that neoliberal polices have on indigenous peoples, some of which have been described in this chapter with regard to bioprospecting/biocolonialism. The need to resist yet another neoliberal affront motivated our participation to resist the establishment of the ANZTPA.

The consultation process for the Crown on the proposed bill and regulations for ANZTPA failed to account for the impact the bilateral agreement would have on rongoa, with initial consultation documents being released with no mention of the impacts this would have on Māori. In fact, further down the track the Crown decided to tell Māori that rongoa was exempt from the regulations and the impact on rongoa would be negligible. It was at this point that Te Waka Kai Ora took issue.

First, for the Crown to tell Māori that rongoa was exempt required the Crown to define what rongoa was in order to provide them with a clear understanding of just how it was exempt. To begin with it is clearly inappropriate for the Crown to define a mātauranga-based tikanga and practice such as rongoa from their neoliberal western colonial perspective. Besides, it was clear to us that rongoa was not exempt and was in fact captured in the broad definitions of natural medicines and therapies that opened it up to commercialisation and commodification. Some of the other key issues Te Waka Kai Ora (2006) raised at the Tribunal hearing were as follows:

- Rongoa is a taonga and not for commodification or theft;
- Lack of recognition of the right of Māori to permanent sovereignty over natural resources as outlined in Te Tiriti o Waitangi;
- Lack of protection under current intellectual property right regimes to protect rongoa from theft through patents, intellectual property rights regimes and profit-driven corporates;
- Failure on behalf of the Crown to act in good faith and involve Māori in a Treaty-based dialogue on this issue;
- Implications of a neoliberal, free-trade paradigm and the implications for indigenous knowledge and the life-supporting capacity of nature;
- Lack of due process to address the constitutional issues that would arise between the Crown and iwi/hapu/whanau and Māori as a result of globalisation;
- To view and treat Māori knowledge through a western knowledge lens allows for the standardisation of Māori knowledge and further perpetuates colonisation;

- Total disregard of already existing centuries-old Māori frameworks, kawa and tikanga to regulate the use of rongoa;
- The sharing of sovereignty with Australia to establish control and regulate rongoa through a bilateral authority, and
- The failure of the Crown to accord due process and await the findings of Wai 262 to provide direction on the regulation of rongoa.

Following the presentation of evidence by Te Waka Kai Ora in December 2006 on the above issues, Nga Wahine Tiaki o te Ao requested the Waitangi Tribunal recommend an injunction on the proposed bill that was to establish the ANZTPA. This was not upheld and the Tribunal directed us back to consultation with the Crown over the matter. In July 2007 the bill to establish the joint ANZTPA failed to gain support in Parliament, which was a great win for all those involved in its resistance. The impact on rongoa, rongoa practitioners, and mātauranga Māori should ANZTPA have been established, would have been devastating, as the end result would have been nothing less than the privatisation and regulation of rongoa that would eventually have made way for the full commodification of this taonga.

Although this matter is not over, and domestic producers and rongoa practitioners will be subject to new regulations not currently present but in all likelihood milder than the trans-Tasman regime, Māori must be ever vigilant about the regulations and protections these regimes fail to provide for rongoa, practitioners, and growers. The failure of ANZTPA and all its neoliberal aims is a great win for democracy and the life-supporting capacity of nature. However, neoliberalism is a well-oiled machine that we know will rear its ugly head in the future, so we watch and wait ready to resist and strike back when further attempts are made to steal, thieve, and commodify our taonga.

Summary

The speed and rate at which the global economy and governments are stealing natural resources and knowledge from indigenous communities to further neoliberal aims are alarming. This neoliberal attack is relentless, as can be seen in the proposed Crown frameworks for bioprospecting and the failed ANZTPA, with all aspects of Papatūānuku me ōna tamariki being affronted by property rights regimes and regulations. These regimes and regulations expand monocultures and create monopolies of ownership and control over the planet's biological wealth while depriving the poor of basic resources and eroding the cultural livelihoods of millions of indigenous peoples (Shiva 2000). This global economic agenda of neoliberalism continues to create unsustainable monocultures and abides by the narrow rules of commerce to commodify biodiversity and indigenous knowledge, both of which are antithetical to the diverse Te Ao Māori relationships with the natural world.

The two neoliberal policies reviewed in this chapter significantly impact on the permanent sovereignty of iwi/hapu/whanau and Māori to protect the life-sustaining capacity of Papatūānuku. Although both these policies have not been passed into legislation, they are clear evidence of the Crown's neoliberal-driven agenda in dealing with Māori knowledge and nature. Furthermore, the legislative framework is amended time and time again to make the easing in of these neoliberal policies that impact on our indigenous rights part of a normalised development paradigm in Aoteaora/ New Zealand, commonly referred to as the knowledge economy. To be seen to be anti this type of neoliberal paradigm, is to be seen as anti-progress, anti-development, and threatening to the growth of New Zealand's knowledge economy. This was clearly evident in the anti-terrorism raids of 15–19 October 2007 where Tūhoe communities and activists who actively engaged in raising community awareness of such issues were the target of police brutality and human rights breaches.

Neoliberalism and free trade cannot set the rules for our relationships with nature and her life-sustaining ability. Neoliberalism must make way to allow for relationships where biodiversity and people are valued over profit. Life and nature must be valued for its diversity and life-giving, self-regenerating capacity, not for profit or the advancement of the neoliberal agenda of monopoly-driven corporates and western governments. As neoliberalism becomes the 'normalised' development paradigm of the 21st century, it is vital that our children and grandchildren learn to resist this violent and unsustainable form of development. We must teach the future generations to return constantly to valuing the natural rhythms and wisdom of our regenerating earth. Māori communities do not value biodiversity for its potential to harness, unlock or unleash profit or to transform our economy and build economic prosperity; rather it is valued as being integral to who we are. Biological diversity is a critical factor in the survival of our cultural diversity and well-being as indigenous peoples.

END NOTES

[1]This claim was brought by Ngati Kuri, Te Rarawa, Ngati Wai, Ngati Porou, Ngati Kahungunu and Ngati Koata and was heard by the Tribunal between 1998 and 2007. The claim sought recognition and protection for matauranga Māori and rights in respect of indigenous flora and fauna.

[2]Neoliberal paradigm refers to western governments, profit-driven global monopolies and corporates.

[3]www.etcgroup.org accessed 5/1/08.

[4]When discussing hegemonic, colonial, masculinist ideologies I am referring to the pursuit of particular interests to maintain domination, systems of thought that maintain the capacity of the dominant group to exercise control. This is not achieved through visible regulation or the deployment of force, but rather through a lived system of meanings and values whereby Māori accept their subordinate status as a colonised race and accept the cultural, social, and political practices of the colonial dominant elite (Johnston et al. 2000).

Type II Diabetes and the long-finned tuna

Marie Nixon-Benton

Background

Traditionally New Zealand Māori meticulously observed and recorded all aspects of life (through both oral and visual means). Specialised practitioners used karakia, waiata, whakairo, whatu, raranga, tukutuku and moko to document and transmit information crucial to the overall wellbeing of tangata whenua. While chronic diseases such as Type II diabetes mellitus, heart disease, and cancer manifest very specific symptoms, indications of these symptoms are not present in the oral and visual histories of Māori from the period of first arrival in Aotearoa through to the beginning of colonisation and thereafter. Contemporaneously, reference was made to diabetes mellitus with its very distinctive symptoms in European societies.

Pyke (1999) reports that in the fourth century AD Indian scholars described the clinical features of diabetes and noted that ants clustered around the urine of diabetics. Similar observations about sweet urine were made in China in the seventh century AD by Chen Chuan and later by Avicenna, an Arab physician of the eleventh century. An English physician, Thomas Willis, rediscovered the sweetness of diabetic urine in 1674 and was the first to use the Latin word mellitus (honeyed). A hundred years later another English doctor, Mathew Dobson, also identified sugar in the urine of diabetics but he made the crucial observation of an excess of sugar in the blood.

Diabetes was rampant during the fifteenth, sixteenth and seventeenth centuries in the middle classes of the northern European countries where diets consisted of many courses of roast meats dripping with fat, rich sugary pastries and plenty of butter and cream. Their meals also lacked coarse red or green leafy vegetables. Two schools of thought then emerged: one believed in replacing the sugar lost in the urine and the other thought it best to restrict the intake of carbohydrates. None of the physicians of those times knew what they were treating and they believed diabetes was a disease of the blood, kidney, liver or stomach or a combination of these. Eating as little as possible seems to have been the most effective therapy, with the French physician Bouchardat noting that the limited availability of food in Paris during the Franco-Prussian War of 1870–71 resulted in a reduction in sugar in the urine of his diabetic patients. Medical scientists slowly homed in on what might be causing diabetes. The liver remained the chief suspect, then in the nineteenth century, French scientist and medico, Claude Bernard, discovered that the liver stored glycogen and secreted a sugary substance into the blood. He assumed an excess of this secretion caused diabetes (Pyke 1999: 14).

The chronic non-communicable diseases currently afflicting many contemporary Māori such as Type II diabetes, cancers, heart disease, mental illness, allergies, and asthma did not exist in Māori before the urbanisation of the 1950s. The staple traditional diet for the rurally based hapū provided all the essential nutrients required to prevent the manifestation of the non-communicable diseases such as Type II diabetes, cancers, and heart disease.

Medical research findings tend to indicate that these chronic diseases develop as a direct result of lifestyle choices, particularly from intake of high saturated fat, high sugar and high salt foods all present in many of the food choices consumed today. This modern diet contrasts sharply with the staple diet of Māori before the 1950s, a diet rich in the unsaturated fatty acid omega-3 derived primarily from the staple long-finned eel or tuna. Indeed modern medical science suggests that a diet rich in finfish with omega-3, protein, and unsaturated fat in preference to saturated fats such as meat and carbohydrates and the drinking of plenty of water are to be recommended. In other words, what tūpuna Māori were eating and the lifestyle choices they were making within a holistic environment acted as a health intervention to promote well-being; thereby preventing the development of any chronic diseases. Therefore the accumulated customary knowledge from tūpuna is worth exploring and using in a contemporary setting to address contemporary issues such as the current Type II diabetes prevalent in Māori.

The Public Health Commission of New Zealand (1991) claims their statistics indicate Māori health has declined considerably since colonisation and urbanisation, with the development of chronic non-communicable diseases developing that were previously non-existent. Since the 1960s diabetes mellitus Type II has become four times more common in Māori than in European New Zealanders. However, other lifestyle risk factors that contribute to Type II diabetes cannot be ignored, such as:

- smoking
- lack of exercise
- obesity (and food intake abuse)
- socio-economic factors (resulting in) inappropriate housing, inadequate education, high unemployment and a high rate of accidents
- excessive alcohol and food intake and/or drug abuse (Public Health Commission 1991: 23).

The traditional Māori diet

It appears that at the time of Captain Cook's arrival in New Zealand in 1769 Māori enjoyed good health, a fact well documented by Cook in his diary. Extracts from Cook's diary confirm that at the time of his arrival Māori were healthy and no mention is made of any chronic diseases being observed or recorded. Wright St Clair (1986) claims that in 1770, Joseph Banks, Cook's companion explorer and an accomplished and gifted scientist and naturalist, objectively observed the diet and the status of Māori health, providing a very detailed account. He recorded that Māori apparently had skin and eye problems caused by the smoke used for cooking and heating. Cook spent six months on the New Zealand coast in 1769 circumnavigating the islands and going ashore at numerous places. His diary states 'that the Māori diet consisted of dogs, birds, (especially sea fowls) fish and eel, sweet potatoes, yams, coccos, wild plants such as sowthistle and palm cabbage and a type of bread made from the roots of the local fern. Their food was simple in their cookery, a few stones heated hot and laid in a hole, their meat laid upon them and covered with hay, seems to be the most difficult part of it. Fish and birds they generally broil or rather toast, spitting them upon a long skewer' (Wright St Clair 1986: 21). Cook also noted 'that the local Māori he met were all very healthy, with no excess fat on them, very fit and very good natured; and that he did not see any skin eruptions or sores (Ibid: 21).

Typical Māori daily diet up until the 1950s

The typical customary daily diet of the traditional Māori was derived from the abundant resources readily available in the local environment either adjacent to or within easy access of sea water or fresh water. The daily diet did not change dramatically with the arrival of the European in the late eighteenth century when domestic sheep and dairy animals farmed for food as an economic commodity were introduced. The meat was not preferred over the traditional staple foods such as the freshwater long-finned eel, the saltwater conger (not a staple but a supplement), local fish, shark (a seasonal supplement) seafood, bird and available seasonal vegetables such as water cress, pūhā, local fruits, and berries. A typical daily diet at the time of European arrival included:

- fresh water consumed in the morning but quite separate from food
- two protein-rich meals that included a daily intake of unsaturated fatty acids rich in omega-3 from eel, fish, shark, seafood, bird at midday and late in the afternoon depending on the day's activities
- local seasonal vegetables and fruits that grew abundantly that were consumed daily, notably kūmara with pūhā and water cress to purify and cleanse the body.

In summary, the traditional Māori diet at the time of arrival of the first European was similar to what global health experts recommend for good health today, that is: daily water, protein and finfish foods that contain the fatty acid omega-3, and five or more vegetables and fruit. Until the Māori urbanisation of the 1950s (and thereafter) the staple diet was principally the daily consumption of the long-finned eel/tuna that contained the unsaturated fatty acid omega-3. Recent medical and scientific research and clinical trials prove that the omega-3 derived from finfish prevents chronic non-communicable diseases such as Type II diabetes, heart disease and mental illness – none of which existed before the Māori urbanisation of the

1950s. It was in the 1960s and thereafter that Type II diabetes symptoms manifested in Māori. Type II diabetes has now become a significant health issue for Māori, reaching epidemic proportions resulting in premature death and loss of quality of life.

The *New Zealand Herald* (March 1 2006) reported and headlined the research findings 'Traditional Māori kai help in fight against cancer'. Professor Kevin Gould (2005) from Otago University's Botany department (in conjunction with Auckland University Research) found that traditional Māori food plants rival some European wonder foods for goodness. The commonly eaten pūhā was found to have more than three times the antioxidant level of blueberries, and some less frequently eaten items, such the fruit of the swamp maire (maire tawake), had up to 18 times more. Blueberries are notably one of the most antioxidant-rich foods in the Western diet. Higher intakes of certain antioxidants lower the incidence of some cancers, which may help to explain why pre-European Māori appear to have low levels of such non-infectious diseases.

Nixon's 2007 doctoral thesis 'Credibility and Validation through Syntheses of Customary and Contemporary Knowledge' explores in detail the staple long-finned eel diet containing the essential fatty acid omega-3. This was presented as a metaphor for 'Hauora' – optimal Māori health and well-being. Type II diabetes mellitus was offered as a story, given its occurrence in Māori subsequent to urban migration and thereafter. A ten-year study of Waikato hapū supported the thesis that regular consumption of the long-finned eel and holistic practice through established lifestyle choices are associated with the prevention of Type II diabetes mellitus.

Agri*Quality* Laboratory, Auckland, confirmed the presence of omega-3 through assay testing completed in 2003. First, various parts of the fresh and smoked long finned eel were analysed, then the eel samples were tested for deterioration over a 24- and then a 48-hour time-frame. The quality of omega-3 from the long-finned eel did not alter over time, exposure to light or handling but the quantity did slightly diminish through smoking.

The long-finned eel known as tuna

The fresh water long-finned eel was very important to traditional hapū Māori because of its availability as a food supply and the mana attached to the ownership of an eel weir. Both the eel and the weir were classified in

Māori culture as a taonga and have been important for hui, tangihanga and other social activities, including gift and economic exchange. Discussions with Tainui kuia and kaumātua as the customary knowledge carriers confirm that the long-finned eel was preferred because the short-finned eel had too many bones. The species are not only different in structure and taste but also in habitat and breeding habits.

Moriaty (1978: 54) claims eels prefer still waters such as lakes, dams and swamps but are also found abundantly in rivers or streams and in areas where the water velocity is low. They have been known to travel on and over land for up to several kilometres to connect with water or mud. Eels are mainly carnivorous feeders.

Tesch's scientific analysis of the nutrients in the freshwater long-finned eel found:

- 86.5% total fatty acid content
- 66.2% unsaturated fat
- 20.3% saturated fatty acids
- 11.4% glycerine
- 2.8% lecithin fat binding agent to cleanse fat (Tesch 1977: 367).

Cairns (1941) recorded that New Zealand hosts five types of eel but only two species are dominant – *Anguilla dieffenbachii* and *Anguilla australis schmidtii*. The following comparison demonstrates the differences:

Anguilla dieffenbachii long-finned eel	Anguilla australis schmidtii short-finned eel
1. dorsal fin longer than ventral fin	1. dorsal fin equal length to ventral fin
2. teeth in a narrow band	2. teeth in club shaped formation
3. eye above and forward of jaw angle	3. eye directly above jaw angle
4. thick lips	4. thin lips
5. broad head	5. narrow head
6. prominent nasal organs	6. Small nasal organs
7. wide mouth gap	7. narrow mouth gap
8. strong jaws	8. small jaws
9. broad tail	9. narrow tail
10. over 180 cm long	10. seldom grows over 90 cm long
11. weight up to 18 kg	11. weight 1.8 kg
12. skin is a dark grey colour	12. skin is a very dark olive green colour. (Cairns 1941: 53B)

Table 1. The difference between Anguilla dieffenbachii and Anguilla australis schmidtii.

Careful research and analysis of the short- and long-finned eel, has discovered that the breeding differences do have similarities but the actual breeding locations are very different. Both species have inhabited the same waterways for over 160 million years and the off-spring always return to the exact rivers, streams and tributaries through a genetic need or desire. Both species undergo unique metamorphic changes, from a salt-water to a fresh-water species. However, the breeding ground for the short-finned eel is local, whereas the breeding ground for the long-finned eel is in the Sargasso Sea in the North Atlantic Ocean.

Cairns' (1941: 143) early research hypothesised that the short-finned eel larvae came down the Australian East Coast into the Tasman Sea by the ocean currents, ocean depths and salinity measurements and that either the deep water off the Australian Great Barrier, and or near the Equator, were the most likely breeding-grounds for New Zealand short-finned eel (Jones 2005: 13B).

Cairns (1941: 143) notes that eels metamorphose into the normal tubular eel shape although devoid of any pigment and so are known as glass eels. He comments:

> *when the glass eels begin to migrate into fresh water they may be anywhere from one to three years old. Whilst in the estuarine waters the glass eels quickly develop into fully pigment elvers and adjust to fresh water. Subsequent migrations from the estuaries into fresh water involve both elvers and glass eels and may happen after, during or before the main migration from the sea. These migrations are known as eel fares from which the term elver is derived.*

Generally these occur at night and may involve as many as four different age classes. The upstream migration continues well into the upper reaches of river systems and elvers and glass eels (and adults) can overcome even large obstructions such as waterfalls and natural dams by the simple expedient of travelling overland in damp conditions, with a motion much like snakes. Eels can live for a long time. Males may live for 25 years, and females reach the age of 36 years before feeling the urge to begin the cycle all over again; however, females as young as ten and males as young as six may begin the downstream migration to breed (Cairns 1941: 143).

Recent research has determined that the native short-finned and long-finned eel are different species with very different habits and metamorphoses. The long-finned eel does not develop into a glass eel until it is a short distance from the waterway tributary to which it belongs. When entering the migratory waterway it changes into what is known as an elver. Indeed it is this metamorphic adaptation from a salt water environment to a freshwater habitat that enables the long-finned eel to proceed to whatever waterway its predecessors inhabited. This process has been happening for over 200 million years.

In contrast, the long-finned eel lives much longer, with the female breeding at aged 100 years, and it is believed they travel to the Sargasso Sea located in the North Atlantic Ocean. The Sargasso Sea, named after the seaweed that lazily floats over its entire expanse, rotates itself slightly and changes position as its surrounding currents change with the weather and temperature patterns during different seasons. Global research on the habitat of various types of long-finned eel is ongoing. Nixon's 2007 research has confirmed the significant presence of the fatty acid omega-3 in the native New Zealand long-finned eel.

Possible link between omega-3 derived from eel and type II diabetes

There appears to be a link between the long-finned eel as the staple Māori diet and the lack of to Type II diabetes. For most hapū the long-finned eel was eaten daily, either what they caught in nearby lakes, streams and rivers or what they traded. This provided a regular source of the essential fatty acid omega-3. Modern scientific testing has confirmed that the oily component of the eel is in fact unsaturated fatty acid omega-3, and medical research has indicated that a regular dietary intake of omega-3 derived from finfish prevents Type II diabetes (and other chronic non-communicable diseases). Tūpuna were aware that regular consumption of the long-finned eel ensured good health.

Omega-3 is a particular type of polyunsaturated fat used by the body to make various hormone-like substances that control many body processes. Because the body cannot manufacture essential fatty acids, they must be consumed in our food to ensure good health. The colour varies from a pale, light yellow to orange, with a characteristic odour ranging from bland to fish-like. Also of scientific interest is that the omega-3 from the long-finned eel is very stable and does not deteriorate with handling, time or exposure to light.

Fatty acid	Source	Total fatty acid %
a-Linolenic acid	Freshwater fish	1–6
	Marine fish	1
	Linseed	45–60
	Green leaves	56
	Grapeseed	10–11
Eicosapentaenoic acid	Freshwater fish	5–13
	Codfish	9
	Pacific anchory	18
	Mackerel	8
	Herring	3–5
	Sardine	3
Docosahexaenoic acid	Sardine	9–13
	Pacific anchory	11
	Mackerel	8
	Codfish	3
	Herring	2–3
	Freshwater fish	1–5

Table 2. Shreeve (1992). Common food sources for omega-3 fatty acid (p. 87).

Dyerberg and Bang first reported a lower incidence of coronary heart disease in Greenland Eskimos, a finding that was attributed to their diet, which was rich in fat from whale, fish and seals. Further analysis revealed that the Eskimo had lower levels of plasma cholesterol and triglyceride and high plasma concentrations of certain polyunsaturated fatty omega-3. Contemporary medical research verifies that populations that included seafood as a major part of their dietary intake had lower rates of cardiovascular disease than those populations that did not. This initiated numerous studies and claims (some of which are not scientifically proven) and research into long chain omega-3 and chronic non-communicable diseases such as:

- coronary heart disease (CHD)
- arthritis (and inflammation)
- immunological conditions

- diabetes mellitus Type II
- kidney diseases
- skin disorders
- cancers, and
- brain development (Dyerberg and Bang 1979: 443).

Omega-3 development

The Australian Government Fisheries Research and Development Corporation (2004) issued advice about the importance of the essential fatty acid omega-3 in disease prevention but emphasised that it should not be considered in isolation. It has a premium place in a healthy diet for most people with the Mediterranean diet recommended as the ultimate diet for good health and disease prevention. The Mediterranean diet, when directly compared with the typical Western diet consists of more bread, more vegetables and legumes, more seafood, less meat (beef, lamb and pork, which can be replaced by poultry), no day without fruit, no butter or cream rather olive oil or other mono-saturated oil sources such as canola, sunflower, soybean or palm. Nutritionists increasingly advocate the Mediterranean diet, which contains seafood, as a healthy diet for people at risk or suffering from coronary heart disease. Omega-3 seafood fats have a positive effect on risk factors for heart disease such as platelet aggregation, which is responsible for blood viscosity (stickiness of the blood), high blood pressure, and the metabolism of plasma lipoproteins (blood fats). People with diabetes need to exercise caution when supplementing their diet with omega-3 fish oil capsules (where one gram of fish oil is about 30% omega-3 fatty acids) because dosages of between four and ten grams per day (equivalent to or more than one to three serves of seafood per day) may result in increased levels of blood sugar (glucose). Lower doses (2.5 grams per day), however, have been shown not to affect glycaemic control, although they still provide useful effects on heart disease risk factors. Generally, eating seafood does not create a problem and is actually an advantage. Omega-3 intake can reduce insulin resistance in skeletal muscle. A high dietary proportion of omega-3 fats have been implicated in increased insulin resistance; hence an increase in dietary omega-3 fats from seafood may address this (Australian Government Research & Development Corporation 2004: 13).

Why Type II diabetes has now become an epidemic

Why did Type II diabetes mellitus abruptly manifest symptoms following the urban Māori migration of the 1950/60s and later? The sudden occurrence of Type II diabetes is primarily due to the abrupt change in the staple diet and the holistic rural lifestyle. Other chronic diseases and their symptoms such as cancers, heart disease, and mental illnesses also manifested abruptly from the 1960s. Urban migration brought instant change from a hierarchical social structure with historically established boundaries to people living as they pleased without the restrictions of the traditional hapū and whānau. Māori could obtain money and assets for themselves in their own names, including cars and modern conveniences, and they could also readily obtain alcohol. While many had greater freedom and money to spend on what they preferred, many of the long-established values, especially dietary habits, were abandoned with consequences such as the development of many chronic non-communicable diseases, for example, heart disease and mental illness; incarceration through increased criminal activities; death and injury through accidents; alcohol and drug intoxication; suicides; poverty; and unemployment. The unavailability of the eel as the staple Māori diet is reflected in the poor health and lack of well-being in Māori, especially in the high incidence of diabetes Type II and the periphery diseases caused by it. The decline of the traditional fresh water long-finned eel for Māori has been as a result of:

- the introduction of recreational trout and carp in the 1880s
- pastoral farming effluent dumped into waterways from the 1880s
- industrial waste dumped into waterways from the 1880s
- the development of over 600 hydro-electric generating power stations that reduced the number of long-finned elvers available to develop because from the 1930s they were destroyed during migration by the hydro-electric turbines.

Since the establishment of New Zealand's pastoral farming from the 1880s, the development of hydroelectricity generating stations from 1945, and forestry and its associated industries, the rivers of New Zealand and their tributaries have been utilised for the disposal of effluent, animal carcasses, and toxic and chemical waste. Local government and their predecessors, Town and County Councils, had only moderate by-laws to enforce and have usually allowed farmers and industry to unnecessarily pollute waterways. As a consequence, these waterways have become heavily polluted and unless stringent by-laws are introduced and enforced immediately the effects of pollution will be irreversible within twenty years. Today hapū and iwi tribal members believe the polluted streams and over-fished lakes can no longer sustain the practice of discharging pollution to waterways. The pollution is contributing to the ill health of Māori. Pollution has substantially altered the taste of the long-finned eel, forcing many Māori to stop eating the traditional eel food source.

Health intervention based on the diet and holistic lifestyle

The adage 'you are what you eat' is now regarded as definitive from a contemporary global perspective. Research in the last decade has seen an abundance of data on nutrition and nutritional supplementation. The results continue to demonstrate that the type of food eaten does determine health, wellness and longevity and that some foods offer medicinal qualities. Tūpuna had an innate understanding that the food they ate, especially the staple eel diet, was directly related to health, wellness, and longevity. In fact all aspects of food were revered through the process of tapu to ensure survival, disease prevention, good health, well-being and longevity. The result was that no chronic diseases manifested and that people were healthy.

As modern medical research and clinical trials continue, the evidence is overwhelming that a diet rich in omega-3 derived primarily from finfish, daily consumption of water and a variety of vegetables, fruits, nuts and berries, together with a holistic lifestyle that includes regular exercise will prevent the chronic non-communicable diseases. In other words the advice and direction offered today by medical and health professionals is similar to the choices made by tūpuna before the urbanisation of the 1950s. It was at this time that chronic diseases such as Type II diabetes suddenly appeared and quickly reached epidemic proportions. Modern science recommends the following lifestyle choices, reflecting tūpuna choices:

- drinking plenty of water to hydrate the body and brain
- eating a variety of fresh seasonal vegetables and fruits
- including a regular consumption of finfish with the omega-3 benefits

- reducing the amount of saturated fats and increasing unsaturated fats
- getting regular exercise.

In summary, the customary knowledge inherited from tūpuna reflects what modern medical science suggests for the prevention of chronic non-communicable diseases such as Type II diabetes, cancers and heart disease. The dietary and lifestyle choices made by tangata whenua before urbanisation prevented the chronic diseases currently afflicting Māori and now described by the health professionals as epidemics.

Ka whakahokia e hau te taonga nei ki te take o ngā maunga takoto atu.
Ka toimaha koe, tīkina atu.
I shall return this gift to the base of the mountains to remain there.
In time of need, fetch it.

Mā te whakaaro, mā te kotahitanga, ka whai oranga Te Taiao

Huhana Smith

Almost all the environmental laws in New Zealand include both natural and historic significance in their definitions. Despite provisions for protecting historic places within landscape, these laws have proved weak compared with other countries. In particular, Māori cultural and spiritual values in landscape have often been over-ridden, with incentives for protection almost entirely lacking (New Zealand Historic Places Trust 2003: 19).[1] While iwi and hapū representatives in tribal areas may be connected to ancestral lands with close links to the landscapes and resources around them, their memories and associations within such areas are in danger of evaporating as the population ages, and as stories, memories and associations are not passed on.

Māori have become disassociated from cultural significance within landscapes for a variety of reasons – the legacy of colonial regimes, alienation of lands, migrations, reinterpreted histories, or disturbances that occur when ancestral landscapes are appropriated for development. Conversely, archaeology consultancies operating on behalf of developers may contribute to site destruction. Territorial authorities' inaction in dealing with issues (New Zealand Historic Places Trust 2003: 5) facing iwi and hapū adds to the difficulties for contemporary kaitiaki in protecting cultural significance in landscape. Kaitiaki navigate considerable complexity in the resource management process to maintain and restore cultural and spiritual values in landscape, but only where these attributes are recognized, reconciled with, and respected can they be protected.

This chapter has two purposes. First, it overviews some attempts within the last fifteen years to set out structures or policies for protecting Māori cultural heritage within natural and cultural landscapes. These include the Parliamentary Commissioner for the Environment's Historic and Cultural Heritage Management in New Zealand Report 1996, the Historic Heritage Management Review 1998, the Taonga Māori Review 1998, and the Historic Heritage Think Tank 2003. While these attempts at heritage protection appear to cover a complexity of needs, they have failed to embed protective policies and laws with more effective outcomes. Second, this chapter finishes with a localised iwi and hapū-led case study.

In the Ngāti Tūkorehe tribal region of Kuku, a south western coastal area of Horowhenua, Te Ika a Maui (North Island), the hapū of the area have envisaged, catalysed, and collaborated with others, to realise the challenges of ecosystem restoration within ancestral landscape. With the implementation of a Geographical Information System (GIS) project called Ahi Kā Roa Cultural Landscape Assessment, they have taken practical action, created pilot projects, and used place-based learning processes to realise change within the intricate dynamic that constitutes Māori natural resource and cultural landscape management in Aotearoa today. Global Positioning Systems (GPS) and mapping technologies have allowed them to rearticulate 'archaeological' assessments for wāhi tapu and other important Māori cultural and spiritual values within significant landscapes; and to activate protective strategies to maintain their ahi kā or Ahi Kā Roa – the principle of keeping the home fires burning on lands, and a potent metaphor that symbolises long-term occupation and care of the environment.

An overview of historic and cultural heritage management in New Zealand

In 1996 the Parliamentary Commissioner for the Environment's report (The PCE Report) on historic and cultural heritage management in Aotearoa emerged from various concerns raised by individuals, iwi and hapū, and community groups over the ongoing modification of wāhi tapu and significant Māori archaeological sites in several areas of the North Island.

The PCE Report evaluated heritage management under the Resource Management Act 1991 (RMA) and the New Zealand Historic Places Trust Act 1993 (HPA). The review critiqued the protection mechanisms within these laws, revealing deficiencies in meaningful protection over iwi and hapū land and water-based wāhi tapu, their cemeteries, battle sites, or other sacred grounds. The review highlighted the lack of coordination between agencies involved in the management of historic and cultural heritage.

At that time, the New Zealand Historic Places Trust/He Pouhere Taonga (HPT), Department of Conservation/Te Papa Atawhai (DOC) and other local authorities all tended to talk past each other. They often worked apart or ignored the needs and concerns of Māori organisations. This lack of liaison was (and still is), matched by a lack of resources to better assist iwi and hapū in protecting their cultural areas through planning and assessment, or by accessing HPT information systems.[2] The HPA has proved inadequate in dealing with Māori values associated with archaeological sites within cultural landscape, a shortfall not helped by the Māori Heritage Council having limited decision-making or binding powers. With these gaps, local authorities (as outlined in their policies and plans) (Parliamentary Commissioner for the Environment. 1996: 67–68) fail to provide protection for cultural sites within the areas deemed important to iwi and hapū.[3]

Historic Heritage Management Review 1998

When the Historic Heritage Review eventuated from the PCE report, it also found poor commitment to Māori land and water-based heritage. Based on these identified shortfalls, in February to April 1998, HPT and DOC convened a series of hui to review historic heritage management in Aotearoa.[4] This review of the government's obligations for the conservation of Māori cultural landscape under the Treaty of Waitangi revealed a prolonged lack of national direction and local control. Cemeteries, battle sites and other areas of spiritual significance became test cases in assessing the effectiveness of the heritage management system in Aotearoa.

Many concerns were heard at the heritage meetings held around the country and at the centralised national hui in Turangi in June 1998. The collective voices were very clear. Iwi, hapū or whānau were entitled to manage their own affairs as expressions of tino rangatiratanga, kaitiakitanga and maintenance of ahi kā in their respective regions. Action, responsibility, and guardianship of valued resources or cultural landscapes, should be shifted to iwi and hapū in their own regions – whether systems were devised to actively protect and manage areas as possible partnerships, or projects were co-managed with other government entities. The Historic Heritage Review revealed that short of providing resources, legislative and policy support, central government had no relevant role to play in local heritage management. The people on the ground, linked by whakapapa to each other, could define heritage areas within their own cultural landscapes and manage them accordingly (New Zealand Historic Places Trust Pouhere Taonga, 1998: 4).

The Review report summarised a range of concerns over cultural heritage and landscape protection that included inconsistencies found in interpretation of the RMA. Hypothetically speaking, if the existing Māori Heritage Council functioned within a designated Māori Heritage agency, then local councils would be obligated to transfer or delegate functions, powers and duties from their territorial authorities to iwi, hapū or Māori authorities. Provisions for transfer of functions, powers and duties to iwi authorities could then take place under Section 33 RMA.[5] But with an ongoing lack of interrelationship between relevant resource management and heritage laws, local authorities continue to neglect adequate Māori heritage protection mechanisms in their planning processes. Some remain reluctant to fully accept their duties and obligations under the Treaty of Waitangi. Even though iwi and hapū have a right to appeal resource consent decisions through the Environment Court, the threat of costs against litigants is often sufficient to impede them from proceeding further.[6] These disparities contribute to the general unwillingness of local authorities to devolve functions and powers to Māori, despite the opportunities to do so within Section 33 of the RMA.

In 1998, the Historic Heritage Management Review consultation hui inspired a series of potential solutions devised to address the poor treatment of Māori knowledge systems and lack of understanding by local authorities about Māori relationships with land, waterways, and their kaitiaki responsibilities. This coincided with elders and like-minded kaitiaki in Kuku moving towards rearticulating the local 'laws' that should govern tribal place, especially for natural and cultural significance. When they participated in the environmental case studies arranged for the region, interest grew in possible co-management models or opportunities. Other solutions that emerged from the hui included developing national policy statements and interim guidelines written by Māori, with an insertion of the Treaty of Waitangi as the founding principle of the RMA.

As the over-riding purpose of the RMA has been to promote the sustainable management of natural and physical resources, Part II of the act (Matters of National Importance) recognises and provides for Māori relationships with their ancestral lands, waters, sites, wāhi tapu and other taonga [section 6(e)]. Particular regard is also given for kaitiakitanga [section 7(a)] and the principles of the Treaty of Waitangi [section 8]. The RMA also aims to protect other historic heritage from inappropriate subdivision, use and development [section 6(f)]. While the HPA provides some heritage protection for particular sites defined as places of human activity before 1900, their investigations also provide important evidence of the history of New Zealand (O'Regan 1997: 33; Davidson 2003). In HPA [section 4], this clause recognises the traditional and cultural relationship Māori have with ancestral lands, water, sites and other taonga. It is important to reiterate that for archaeological areas, the HPA clearly states that it is unlawful for anyone to damage, modify or destroy a site or any part thereof [7] [section 10 (1)]. This applies when there is reasonable cause to even suspect that there is an archaeological site present. Despite this, the HPA site registration process does not automatically protect sites, or view them as areas of cultural significance hidden within landscape.

RMA Amendments introduced by the Labour-led government in 2004 (enacted in 2005), aimed to address problems with delays, costs, inconsistencies, uncertainty and national leadership regarding processes and decision-making. The amendments focussed on five key areas: decision-making; local policy and plan making; certainty for consultation; iwi resource planning; and natural resource allocation (Ministry for the Environment Manatū Mō Te Taiao 2007). For the purposes of the RMA, councils are required to keep and maintain a record of iwi authorities within their region or district and, if requested, groups representing hapū. The lack of statutory provision for joint management was addressed by providing a framework for public authorities, iwi authorities and groups (that represent hapū and recognised by iwi) to enter into joint management agreements over natural or physical resources. In consulting with tangata and mana whenua during the preparation of proposed policy statements or plans, councils are required to follow procedures that are aligned with the Local Government Act 2002.[8]

During the 2004 amendment process,[9] the terms 'cultural landscapes' and 'ancestral landscapes' were included in the definition of 'historic heritage' in the Resource Management Amendment Bill [No. 2].[10] The terms offered holistic definitions that reunited and revitalised core bio-cultural values[11] to protect and maintain connections between all entities within landscape. A later introduced Supplementary Order Paper deleted both terms and included an explanatory note to the effect that these terms were already covered by enhancement of amenity values and the maintenance and enhancement of the quality of the environment (Peart 2004: 17). In doing so, the maintenance of cultural and ancestral attributes was effectively minimised. Instead it was proposed to fortify Māori environmental perspectives within iwi management plans included in regional and district planning documents. Other possibilities included appointing more Māori as full members to Council Boards and Committees, with their approval sought for all resource and building consents, including non-notified applications. While it is difficult to achieve iwi management plans with added capability and capacity issues – insufficient qualified Māori able to fill positions on Boards and Committees[12] – councils are still statutorily obliged to work with iwi to affect better management.

Despite the RMA and HPA being two of the most important laws in Aotearoa that recognise culturally valued areas in landscape, they remain unconvincing when it comes to protecting wider or interrelated areas of Māori cultural and spiritual significance. This is due to a lack of coordination. Heritage landscape concepts may be present but interpretations are limited. There is no specific recognition of how whakapapa as a genealogical reference system relates people to lands, waterways, ecosystems and areas of spiritual importance. If a heritage landscape concept recognised and emphasised these intricacies, then laws might better reflect and respect the multiple narratives of iwi and hapū interaction with place, natural resources, and other influential events or experiences that remain embedded within landscape.

An overarching and supportive Māori Heritage Agency

It was during the course of the Historic Heritage Management Review (and picked up later by the Taonga Māori Review) that a Māori Heritage Agency within the Ministry for Culture and Heritage, was proposed. This agency was promoted as the entity to enable greater protection of Māori heritage values within cultural landscape. It aimed to advise the Minister for Culture and Heritage and the Minister of Māori Affairs on Māori heritage needs and issues. As a provider of national policy, the agency's standards of practice and procedural guidelines aimed to actively support iwi, hapū and whānau to protect and conserve their cultural landscape. If the agency or appropriate iwi authorities were affected parties in, for example, resource consent applications relating to Māori heritage, improved resource management responses would give clout to the issues facing iwi and hapū. The review aimed to encourage more effective and positive relationships between Māori, local and regional councils, developers and private landowners. Councils in particular, would then ensure that funds were available for Māori to participate more fully in local authority processes (New Zealand Historic Places Trust Pouhere Taonga 1998: 4). This would lead to more Māori being trained to tackle the resource consents process. The proposed agency would advise national agencies (ably assisted by local authorities) in *all* aspects of Māori cultural heritage management.

Importantly, if a Māori Heritage Agency had been established it would have assisted iwi, hapū and whānau in many ways, including the management of their own cultural landscape through a provision of funding, technical assistance, training and networking. The agency would have encouraged voluntary protection mechanisms; developed national public education programmes; compiled a comprehensive national database; and advised on heritage services as appropriate. A Māori heritage provider would have developed a national monitoring system to deliver clear protection strategies for land based heritage with conservation outcomes (Smith 2000: 285). The combination of activities would then have helped alleviate the collective concerns of iwi and hapū. But with Māori heritage consistently underfunded in comparison with non-Māori heritage, there were justifiable suspicions amongst iwi and hapū authorities over another Crown agency managing natural and cultural heritage as separate entities. Would the agency provide the protective mechanisms needed? Would the envisaged entity endorse effective partnerships or comanagement opportunities for Māori land and water based heritage?

Even though the major function of the agency was envisaged as a national channel for the Crown to address its Treaty obligations (Department of Conservation 1998: 23–25) for more effective Māori heritage management, the initiative did not eventuate. Despite being regarded as the agency with the potential to provide for Māori heritage leadership and policy, the government did not establish the Māori Heritage Agency. The recommendations were non-prioritised and the opportunity missed.

Taonga Māori Review 1999–2000

In 1999, Te Puni Kōkiri Ministry of Māori Development was instructed to undertake a review of government's role in Māori culture and heritage.[13] As reported to Cabinet, the review was called the Taonga Māori Review.[14] It had three main purposes. First, it tried to clarify the government's role in Māori culture and heritage. Second, it proposed organisational options for the development of more effective policies and delivery for the protection of Māori culture and heritage, which took into account the Treaty of Waitangi. Third, it aimed to develop options for the establishment of a Māori Heritage Agency, encompassing issues over functions, governance, funding, accountability, legislative implications, links with other agencies, and any other performance matters.

The scope of the review identified outputs delivered by public service departments that impacted on Māori culture and heritage. It aimed to ascertain the range of options and mechanisms that would develop and deliver more effective policies for government, and to devise objectives to improve outcomes for Māori culture and heritage. The review also attempted to analyse proposed government objectives and initiatives, and to assess their impact on Māori natural, environmental and cultural landscape values.

Issues that emerged during the course of the Historic Heritage Management Review were echoed in the Taonga Māori Review. There was a notable shortage of information about Māori culture and heritage, as well as limited policy development and strategic approaches that actively addressed issues. The review analysed the capacity of the culture and heritage sector to respond to key culture and heritage issues. It investigated opportunities for iwi and hapū involvement in management and decision-making.

When a draft policy statement summed up government's role in Māori culture and heritage, it clearly intended to provide and maintain an environment where Māori culture and heritage was respected, protected, and enhanced for future generations. It recognised that kaitiakitanga rested with whānau, hapū and iwi, and that the government needed to actively protect Māori culture and heritage by providing for and supporting participation in culture and heritage activities. The government had an interest in recognising that Māori culture and heritage was not static, that Māori contributed to an evolving national identity. It was also in the government's interest to support Māori culture and heritage as a unique part of New Zealand's identity to ensure that all New Zealanders benefited. The government agreed that in partnership with iwi and hapū they had duties derived from the Treaty of Waitangi to take reasonable action to protect cultural significance for Māori.[15]

The proposed heritage management system aimed to define the duties and functions of central and local government, to align decision-making as closely as possible with the affected communities of interest by maximising local community consultation and involvement within a national policy framework. Te Puni Kōkiri, therefore, developed the following policy statement, which set out the government's role in terms of Māori culture and heritage.

The role of Government is to foster an environment where Māori culture and heritage are respected, protected and enhanced for future generations.

Among the duties derived from the Treaty of Waitangi is the duty on Crown to actively protect Māori culture and heritage. In carrying out this obligation, Crown will take all reasonable and practicable steps to:

- *Recognise and support the rangatiratanga of whānau, hapū and iwi and Māori over their culture and heritage*
- *Uphold the principle of partnership; in developing and delivering policies that impact on Māori culture and heritage; in resolving differences with whānau, hapū and iwi over the impact of policies on their culture and heritage*

Government also has an interest in achieving culture and heritage outcomes for all New Zealanders, and therefore:

- Promotes Māori culture and heritage as a unique part of New Zealand's culture and heritage
- Recognises that a dynamic and vibrant Māori culture contributes positively to New Zealand's identity.

During the development of the review, it was understood that Māori knew best how to protect their own interests through the exercise of rangatiratanga and kaitiakitanga in their own areas. It was not the role of government to define the exact scope of the concept of Māori culture and heritage as the Treaty claims process had recognised that tino rangatiratanga maintained Māori peoples' ongoing distinctiveness as characteristic of their way of life.

The range of reports and reviews over the last fifteen years highlight government's lack of clear objectives for Māori culture and heritage in landscape. While the revised draft policy was intended as a government policy statement, it was not developed to be included in legislation.

Even though considerable time was invested in the Taonga Māori Review, it was not completed. The government's policy statement, which set out its role in terms of Māori culture and heritage, went into abeyance.

Heritage Think Tank 2003

On 7 April 2003 the New Zealand Historic Places Trust Pouhere Taonga chairperson Dame Anne Salmond, convened a Heritage Landscapes Think Tank. A large number of key personnel from across the culture and heritage sector, iwi and hapū leaders, academics, researchers, local and regional councils, and other Ministry representatives convened at Te Papa to discuss and investigate particular cultural landscapes issues with heritage significance.

The Think Tank identified the following issues and potentials. Heritage landscapes were defined as places where important historic events had occurred as part of New Zealand's emerging national identity. It was also identified that many of these heritage sites remain unacknowledged or ignored – heritage is well represented in archives, cenotaphs, libraries, and museums but rarely considered in the places where it occurred. With appropriate promotion and interpretation, such places could contribute significantly to local economic development through cultural tourism, as well as to national, regional and local pride (New Zealand Historic Places Trust Pouhere Taonga 2003: 2). Heritage landscapes are also not fixated on 'artefactual' or heritage buildings alone. They cover large geographic areas that may have multiple owners and represent a convergence of many experiences and interests. They reveal dynamic systems undergoing constant change and do not fit neatly into a single historical periods. They have composite layers of human interaction, with ongoing narratives of significance associated with each place (New Zealand Historic Places Trust Pouhere Taonga 2003: 4).

The Think Tank definition attempted to encompass iwi and hapū views and develop Māori cultural heritage significance by simultaneously capturing other historical relationships to land. Another concept known as braided cultural landscape was introduced to assist. This refers to the notion of place and peoples' place within it as informed by both Māori and non-Māori recollections of encounter and change within lands and peoples. The braided concept recognises other groups' intergenerational use of land. Such intertwining of stories and experiences offered ways of appreciating landscape from a bicultural or multicultural perspective as relevant in the present. The longevity of mana whenua relationships to lands, resources and waterways command respect, but a consideration for the way lands were alienated from collective tenure in the first place is also necessary. In contemporary times tensions have increased between private property rights, collective interests and the rights of iwi and hapū, and in order to realise more effective cultural landscape protection, intricacies and complex relationships to lands should be reconciled.

Ahi Kā Roa Cultural Landscape Assessment project[16]

In looking at the Kuku case study, the coastal, riverine and palustrine region under investigation for the Ahi Kaa Roa[17] Assessment research project has been the location of complex Māori history of warfare and conquest as a consequence of migrations from Kāwhia Harbour by Ngāti Toarangatira beginning in 1819 (Royal 1994: 7). More settled relationships to the Kuku coast began around 1822–23, with a later series of induced migrations south from the original homelands around Maungatautari, Waikato. Further lands in the Horowhenua region were allocated at the behest of leaders (see Oliver & Sparks 2006). When affiliates to Ngāti Tūkorehe established their customary mana whenua obligations over the coastal land and its resources, they enjoyed prosperous decades on the coastal plain that runs to the sea.

Iwi researchers understand how a braided cultural landscape concept can be applied. Particular landholders in the early twentieth century interacted closely with local tohunga or esoterically knowledgeable Māori. While it is true that some farmers may have disregarded and dismissed the understandings, others respected the request to safeguard cultural significance in land and waterways (Smith 2007). These farmers were privileged to learn about significant places with first-hand accounts of their importance. When areas were pointed out, they respected burial grounds, fresh water springs and shell middens. They clearly did not want to jeopardise resident Māori relationships to these regions and feared any possible transgression.

Today many hapū remain linked to these ancestral lands through continuous, shared resource use or repurchased land holdings. They represent ongoing connections with place, and undertake additional responsibilities to actively protect cultural landscape, enhance their identity in the present, and secure relationships for future generations. Despite the conclusions of the reviews and reports cited – that iwi and hapū cultural heritage is essential to the national identity of Aotearoa – the system still fails to advise and support Māori in the real work of protecting cultural landscape.

The Ahi Kā Roa Cultural Landscape Assessment through the Environment Sub-Committee of Te Iwi o Ngāti Tūkorehe Trust is a pilot project that seeks solutions to the ongoing lack of national and local direction for Māori cultural landscape. It uses GIS spatial modelling and GPS technology to comprehensively map significance within landscape. It draws together archaeological, ecological, natural and cultural attributes to explore all inter-relationships between physical evidence, cultural memory and identity. The Assessment is designed around people on the ground defining cultural landscape in their own terms and managing it accordingly. The project also samples the range of impacts on ecosystems and cultural values. It looks for ways Māori communities might reconnect with local coastal environments to exercise kaitiakitanga in modern times, promote sustainability, and strengthen tribal identity through a grounded relationship with Papatūānuku (earth mother), and ngā atua Māori (environmental entities).

The project attempts to understand the roles that spatial representation, effective communication of cultural or historic landscape values, and technology might play in creating outcomes that protect cultural landscapes. A larger action plan to encompass iwi and hapū knowledge, research and data; create visual Iwi Management Plans; collate Treaty Claims research; forge links to Māori Land Court databases; and compile information about coastal mātaitai and marine resources is also proposed. Iwi and hapū researchers have utilised existing information on the Historic Places Trust Register, the New Zealand Archaeological database, Landcare Research – Manaaki Whenua, and other agencies' databases.

It also aims to drive change towards practice, policy and ultimately, legislation. As well as accessing surveys and downloading relevant information, the team also adds high-definition aerial photos of the areas of interest. It is essential that the research team (on behalf of iwi and hapū) store all archaeological and heritage information so that control of and access to this knowledge remains with iwi and hapū. This is critical as archaeology consultancies and developers often overlook rūnanga, or local iwi and hapū requests to recognise their knowledge of place.

An interrelated landscape approach is preferable to the isolated-pockets-of-evidence model employed by most archaeologists. The cultural landscape model shifts notions of archaeological recording – where heritage areas or cultural values are defined as quantifiable areas of ground around which development can take place. This approach results in the damage or destruction of connecting factors between sites. Unfortunately, it is prevalent and contributes to significant loss of evidence about the way people lived and interacted with resources across landscape.

Another approach used by coastal land developers is to consult Māori individuals rather than groups mandated by consensus. This significantly impedes protection of ongoing ahi kā in coastal dune land systems. The Ahi Kā Roa approach avoids problems that arise when development turns up undiscovered evidence.[18] Furthermore the project has clearly signalled that regional iwi authorities need to re-examine their 'accidental find' scenarios of taonga or cultural material 'discovered' when subdivisions go ahead. Ill-considered sanction given to developers by individuals coupled with the lack of responsibility to resource management and heritage provisions in law, lead to paradoxical management mechanisms that allows cultural site destruction[19] to proceed unabated.

The pressure is on

The Kuku/Ōhau coastline of the western dune belt is a place of regular, sweeping coastal dune accretion and erosion. The range of papa kainga, pā and cultivations, and the areas of mahinga mātaitai and mahinga kai, represents layers of significance about particular hapū relationships to lands and waterways. To this day, many local Māori at Kuku (especially at the coast) retain ancestral lands as shareholders. Persistent, embedded cultural markers exist within the agriculturally modified landscape of the tribe's coastal dairy farm. The coast is still revered and respected because of the rights afforded by historic conquest, occupation and settlement, and the ongoing activities that define a people's long-term relationship with place.

There are other important drivers of ecosystem change that will increase in the 21st century. Climate change and excessive nutrient loadings will become more severe (Millennium Ecosystem Assessment Core Writing Team 2005). More localised extremes of climate change for the southwest coastal region of Kapiti to Horowhenua (including the Kuku/Ōhau coastline) are predicted as well as wide-ranging meteorological hazards – threats from frequent heavy rainfall and associated floods; sea level rises increasing the impact of high tides and storm adding to coastal erosion; aquifers near the coastline vulnerable to saltwater intrusion from flooding; and changes in temperature and rainfall causing problems for pest-eradication programmes (National Institute of Water and Atmospheric Research 2005). Climate change scenarios, the nitrification of water from intensified agricultural activities, and the possible increase in localised coastal subdivisions combine to create complex realities for kaitiaki. In the Kuku/Ōhau coastal region, public, local and regional government support is tantamount for preserving contiguous coastal dune wetland systems, and a dynamic coastline as significant cultural landscape.

The Ahi Kaa Roa Assessment project recognises the multiple pressures facing the region. In recent years, the actions of local councils and developers in the Horowhenua coastal region have alarmed kaitiaki. They have led iwi and hapū to create projects that collate, map, record and protect intricate and interrelated layers of bio-cultural diversity and cultural significance in landscape – as quickly as possible. If authorities respected iwi and hapū to lead in their regions (with mutually beneficial outcomes for the wider community) then agencies should devolve more environmental management functions to them. However, no local council has undertaken a transfer of powers to tangata or mana whenua, adding to a lack of progress in realising local Māori aspirations. If local councils question capacity and skills, or encounter difficulty in ranking responsibility for iwi and hapū, then practical arrangements are harder to realise. By developing partnerships any perceived deficiencies in capacity and responsibility can be readily overcome (Cooper & Brooking 2002: 197). However, local or regional authorities differ in standards and consistency of approach when addressing their statutory obligations over Māori landscape issues. Protection of significant sites is often non-prioritised[20] with destruction, loss and modification of cultural importance continuing at alarming rates.

Of interest to the Ahi Kā Roa Assessment project was a report entitled Processes of Coastal Change Manawatū-Horowhenua commissioned by the Manawatū Catchment Board and Regional Water Board in 1985. It recommended that serious thought be given to the physical forces of the coastal zone from Manawatū to Paekakariki. The report highlighted the effects of inappropriate foredune or land activities on physical processes that catalyse destructive shoreline responses. On the Kapiti Coast, developments on hazardous sites without due deliberation for the long-term stability and sustainability of the unique and dynamic dune coastline continue to occur.[21] As adjacent coastlines and inland uses are interconnected through wave action, wind, tides, currents and sediments, the best sustainable peri-urban development should respect foredunes as natural buffers against erosion, especially during periods of storm activity. A beach absorbs wave energy and to do this efficiently it adjusts its form and position. If wave action changes then the beach area compensates with a new pattern of surf energy. Sand is transported onshore by wave action, blown inland to form dunes, and is also transported offshore and alongside depending on wave conditions.[22]

Unfortunately, unsustainable peri-urban development proposed for sensitive fore dunes or dune systems increases drainage and runoff of fine sediments. This causes higher water tables in sandy beaches and the clogging of beach pore spaces with very fine particulate matter. These factors aggravate beach erosion further south (in the Kuku/Ōhau case) by creating impervious surfaces that increase the scouring effect of wave backwash (Holland & Holland 1985: 38). As the effects of different periods of urban development along the Manawatū, Horowhenua, and Kapiti coasts have worsened shoreline erosion (that stretches south to Paekakariki) such damage now requires considerable conservation, engineering, and expensive mitigating measures in the form of retaining walls erected against an encroaching sea. Peri-urban developments cannot be sanctioned when their effects stabilise[23] the unique coastal dune systems, which then impact on adjacent dune wetlands and lake systems. Stabilising sand impedes the system's intricate capacity to act as a natural buffer, absorb wave energy and therefore protect coastlines.

The Ahi Kā Roa Cultural Landscape Assessment project is a potential model for other entities to achieve beneficial outcomes for Māori cultural identity and community well being in healthy environments. National attempts at cultural landscape protection appear to cover complex needs but have failed to embed protective policies and laws with effective outcomes for iwi and hapū. Success in protecting landscape requires a generosity of spirit that acknowledges how different places will matter to different groups and that sometimes, the same place will have different significance (New Zealand Historic Places Trust Pouhere Taonga 2003: 19). The Kuku/Ōhau coastline has long been integral to iwi and hapū. The visual databases resulting from the project achieve goals of Māori cultural affirmation over complex but revered environments. They express tino rangatiratanga and kaitiakitanga determined by tikanga and guiding principles. Current generations are well aware of how ancestors came to occupy and utilise the Kuku/Ōhau coastline under a system of interlocking and overlapping usufructuary rights. Ahi Kā Roa remains the foundational tenet that reminds kaitiaki to keep the metaphoric home fires burning brightly on lands in the form of innovative projects that will benefit the environment as well as following generations.

Appendix I: Cabinet Minutes Relating to Māori Culture and Heritage.

Cabinet Agreements, *Historic Heritage Management,* CAB (97) M43/22.

TREATY OF WAITANGI CONSIDERATIONS

Noted that Article 2 of the Treaty of Waitangi guarantees Māori protection of their taonga, the Tribunal agree that wahi tapu are taonga, and that the Historic Places Act 1993 and the Resource Management Act 1991 provide statutory recognition of the importance of protecting taonga;

Agreed that the Crown, in partnership with Māori, has duties derived from the Treaty of Waitangi to take reasonable action to protect sites of significance to Māori;

Noted that objectives for the protection of sites of importance to Māori may, in some circumstances, be achieved though methods implemented by iwi/hapū authorities, local authorities and the private sector.

PROPOSED POLICY PRINCIPLES FOR THE REVIEW

Cabinet agreed that the following policy principles should inform preparation of the public discussion paper and subsequent processes in the Historic Heritage Management Review:

- The system should produce improved protection and management of Māori historic heritage
- The duties and functions of central and local government in historic heritage protection and management should be clearly defined
- There should be an increased emphasis on aligning decision-making processes as closely as possible to the communities of interest affected and maximising local community consultation and involvement, within a national policy framework ensuring clear national direction and consistency of standards and implementation;
- The system should provide for Māori to participate and be represented effectively in the protection and management of Māori historic heritage, consistent with the obligations of the Crown under the principles of the Treaty of Waitangi.

END NOTES

[1] Think Tank held at the Museum of New Zealand/Te Papa Tongarewa, Cable Street, 7 April 2003, Wellington.

[2] Since those times, kaitiaki representatives on the Te Iwi o Ngāti Tukorehe Trust Environmental Sub-Committee have been mapping land- and water-based areas of cultural significance using GIS technology. They are retaining the data and files for ongoing reference by iwi and hapū representatives.

[3] Since completing this PHD chapter in 2007, the author has been working with Horowhenua District Council, Rūnanga, iwi and hapū, developers, landscape architects and others within a wider group of stakeholders to improve matters covered under Section 6 of the RMA. As the Council are required to recognise and provide for these matters of national importance, they intend to rectify this under their District Plan Review, which will commence in late 2009.

[4] In January 1998, the Minister of Conservation, The Hon. Nick Smith, issued a discussion paper for public comment as the National and New Zealand First's coalition response to the PCE report.

[5] On 23 July 2006, Te Hākari Management Committee met with Horizons Regional Council on the One Plan, to outline the tangata whenua or kaitiaki perspective of leading and actualising positive environmental change in tribal regions. Hapū-led initiatives are now better supported by key staff at the Regional Council. However, it took over a decade to achieve better relationships with council representatives and for their understanding of iwi and hapū needs to develop.

[6] Under the RMA Part II Section 274, a person, parties, iwi or local authority can give notice to the Environment Court and to all parties after a notice of appeal has been lodged. In order to alleviate some of the financial constraints facing iwi and hapū organisations and the Environment Court, the Environmental Legal Assistance Fund (administered through the Ministry for the Environment) can help environmental, community, iwi and hapū groups to participate more effectively in the resource management process. The Fund helps with preparation, mediation and/or presenting resource management cases to the Environment Court and other courts. The Environment Legal Aid Fund also assists cases before the High Court or Court of Appeal in Aotearoa, particularly where the relevant Environment Court case was funded by the Environmental Legal Assistance Fund in the first instance, and where the group is defending a successful outcome from the Environment Court. The Fund is available to cover the time and expenses of legal representatives and/or expert witnesses used in preparing for, resolving and/or presenting cases before the court.

[7] The Historic Places Act 1993 regulates the modification of archaeological sites on all land. The Act makes it unlawful for any person to destroy, damage or modify the whole or any part of an archaeological site without the prior authority of the New Zealand Historic Places Trust Pouhere Taonga. This is the case regardless of whether:
- the site is registered or recorded
- the land on which the site is located is designated, or the activity is permitted under the District or Regional Plan
- a resource or building consent has been granted.

[8]The RMA amendments clarify that neither a resource consent applicant nor a local authority has a duty to consult any person about an application, although each must comply with a duty under any other enactment to consult any person about the application. Councils however, must still consider whether specific iwi or hapū are an affected party and contact the iwi or hapū to determine this.

[9]In 2009, the RMA is under review with the Resource Management (Simplifying and Streamlining) Amendment Bill. For iwi and hapū some of the key concerns include the possibility to remove non-complying activity status for resource consents and a presumption in favour of non-notification to the public. The latter means that instead of a council having to notify an application except in certain circumstances, a council will not now have to notify an application, except in certain circumstances. Notification is of fundamental importance for the public, for without it, they have no say on how the environment is used, developed or protected. The amendments will impact on public participation in resource management matters as Council decisions will then not reflect the true nature of the RMA, which is to balance all environmental components (social, cultural, economic and environmental). The public is very important in ensuring that all environmental components are explored and tested and that a decision represents sustainable management. (Sourced from www.eds.org.nz, the website for Environmental Defence Society.)

[10]Reported back to the House by the Local Government and Environment Select Committee in 2004.

[11]Spiritual, cultural, human and ecological values.

[12]One of the objectives of Te Reo a Taiao Raukawa Environmental Resource Centre (Taiao Raukawa) is to increase the capacity of Māori participation in resource and cultural landscape management processes for the wider region. Taiao Raukawa is a hapū driven entity for sustainable development, where hapū and participants can source expertise, resources and support for all environmental and cultural landscape matters. It is responsible for undertaking processes to achieve sustainable management of the natural and ancestral taonga within Ngāti Raukawa tribal area according to the tikanga of hapū and iwi of the region. It assists hapū in coordinating their approaches to resource and environmental management. The centre aims to lead on environmental matters for the community and build upon synergistic relationships with other Te Rūnanga o Raukawa projects and businesses.

The overall goals of Taiao Raukawa are to provide: strategic leadership in developing and implementing overarching environmental strategies for Ngāti Raukawa; to support hapū and iwi to develop respective environmental plans; build stakeholder relationships both internally with hapū and iwi, and externally with other authorities; lead and support RMA processes for active participants in natural resource management; encourage restoration and place-based education projects for natural ecosystems in wider tribal region, collate information and educational opportunities using databases and education programmes for hapū and wider communities and create and implement research and development opportunities.

[13]Cabinet Paper [CAB (99) M 17/18]

[14]The term 'taonga Māori' encompassed Māori culture and heritage. Taonga Māori was considered a very broad concept that includes both tangible and intangible aspects

incorporating land-based historic heritage, natural resources and wāhi tapu (sacred sites), and also matters such as cultural property, ngā toi Māori (arts) and te reo me nga tikanga (language and customs). Definitions of wāhi tapu, the cultural sector, cultural activity, historic heritage and the arts were informed by those used in the Culture and Heritage Sector Review and Historic Heritage Management Review.

[15]It was noted in Cabinet Agreements that the objectives for the protection of sites of importance to Māori may, in some circumstances, be achieved though methods implemented by iwi/hapū authorities, local authorities and the private sector. Cabinet Agreements, Historic Heritage Management, Reference CAB (97) M43/22.

[16]This research project is part of the Ngā Māramatanga-ā-papa (Ecosystem Services Benefits in Terrestrial Ecosystems for Iwi) supported by the Foundation for Research Science and Technology. It is a collaborative research project between Te Rūnanga o Raukawa, Te Wānanga o Raukawa, Te Iwi o Ngāti Tukorehe Trust, the New Zealand Centre for Environmental Economics, Landcare Research Manaaki Whenua both based at Massey University, and Massey University, Palmerston North.

[17]Ahi Kaa Roa is a metaphor for keeping the 'home fires long burning'. It refers to long-term occupation of iwi, hapū and whanau and their accumulated resource use rights, their experiences and relationships with lands and waterways that have accumulated over many generations.

[18]Sourced from the *Tirotirowhetu, Ōhau River* proposal 2007 for assessment by Susan Forbes of Kotuku Consultancy Ltd, Titahi Bay, near Wellington. She is a leading archaeologist who works with iwi and hapū to actively support ahi kā models of landscape assessment. Her practice well understands the complex human, ecological and cultural memory inter relationships that are present within coastal landscapes in Horowhenua that require urgent protection.

[19]Diane Lucas, June 2007. An Appeal Against the Decision of the North Shore City Council on Proposed Plan Change 6 and Variation 66 to the North Shore City District Plan under Clause 14(1) of the First Schedule of the RMA between Appellants, Respondent and Section 274 parties, ENV-2006-304-000-000404, Environment Court, Auckland Registry, Auckland.

[20]Cabinet Agreements, *Review of Protection Mechanism: Protection of Sites of Significance to Māori (Wahi Tapu),* Reference CAB (96) M 8/15.

[21]Cabinet Agreements, *Review of Protection Mechanism: Protection of Sites of Significance to Māori (Wahi Tapu),* II.

[22]Cabinet Agreements, *Review of Protection Mechanism: Protection of Sites of Significance to Māori (Wahi Tapu),* 42-44.

[23]There has been considerable impact on the dynamic Manawatū, Horowhenua and Kapiti west coast dune systems. It is important that dune systems move, however decades of agricultural, forestry and now peri-urban development threats, have limited the sand movement, with increased erosion in coastal regions and communities to the south.

Contributors

James Ataria

James Ataria, nō Rongomaiwahine, Ngāti Kahungunu, me Ngāti Tūwharetoa. Dr Ataria is an ecotoxicologist employed at Landcare Research, Manaaki Whenua specialising in the area of pest control and wildlife toxicology. He primarily works on environmental contamination issues affecting Māori communities but he is also carrying out research on emerging issues such as nanoparticles, building Māori research capability at Lincoln University and developing international linkages with other indigenous peoples who face similar environmental issues. His research interests include environmental risk assessment, ecotoxicology, chemical fate of pollutants, sewage sludge and ecotoxicological testing methods.

April Bennett

April Bennett is of Ngāti Tūwharetoa, Waikato, and Tūhoe descent. She currently works at Massey University as an independent contractor, teaching in resource management and doing social research with iwi and hapū in the environmental field. She has been passionate about the environment since she was a teenager. April has a Masters degree from Massey University.

Mason Durie

Mason Durie of Rangitane, Ngāti Kauwhata and Ngāti Raukawa is Professor of Māori Research and Development and Assistant Vice Chancellor (Māori) at Massey University, Palmerston North. Dr Durie is one of New Zealand's leading scholars and has been a major contributor to Māori development over the past thirty years.

Margaret Forster

Margaret Forster is from Rongomaiwahine and Ngāti Kahungunu. She is a lecturer at Te Pūtahi-a-Toi, School of Māori Studies, Massey University. Margaret is completing a doctoral study exploring the role of Māori communities, culture, and values in the environmental management of natural resources.

Angeline Greensill

Angeline Greensill is of Tainui, Ngati Porou, and Ngati Paniora descent, and currently resides in Kirikiriroa (Hamilton). She was raised at Te Kopua (Raglan), Whaingaroa on the turangawaewae of Tainui o Tainui ki Whaingaroa. Angeline is married to Alan Greensill and they have seven children and ten mokopuna. She was educated at Raglan Primary, Raglan District High School, Hamilton Technical College, Hamilton Teachers College and at Waikato University. She holds a Trained Teachers Certificate, LLB (Bachelor of Laws), Bachelor of Social Sciences with 1st class Honours and is currently completing a Masters of Social Science. She is a tenured lecturer in the Department of Geography, Tourism and Environmental Planning where she specialises in treaties, Māori Geography and Resource Management.

Jessica Hutchings

Jessica Hutchings is from Ngāi Tahu, Ngāti Huirapa and Gujurati, (India). Dr Hutchings is a mother, activist, educationalist, biodynamic gardener and is completing a Post-Doctoral Fellowship at Massey University. Jessica is a vocal opponent of genetic modification and other forms of biopiracy and has spoken both in Aotearoa and internationally on these issues. She is an active member of Te Waka Kai Ora, the Māori Organics Movement. Jessica and her whānau are currently developing a biodynamic permaculture property north of Wellington where they run Papawhakaritorito Organics offering organic educational courses to share and grow the skills of organic gardeners. Jessica continues to teach in Environmental Studies at Victoria University.

Lisa Kanawa

Lisa Kanawa, Ngāpuhi, Ngāti Raukawa and Ngāti Maniapoto, is passionate about Māori achieving their aspirations in regards to the environment and sustainable development. She has a background in Resource and Environmental Planning and Māori natural resource management. Lisa has a broad perspective having worked in private practice, with iwi and hāpu, in the public sector and research institutes. She enjoys the diversity of the communties she works with and the diversity of the aspirations. For Lisa, the oppportunity to do mahi that is challenging, innovative and for the benefit of Māori collectively is completely satisfying and provides her a path to contribute to the future of our tamariki.

Merata Kāwharu

Merata Kāwharu is Director of Research at the University of Auckland's James Henare Māori Research Centre. As a Rhodes Scholar, Dr Kāwharu read social anthropology at Oxford University, graduating with a DPhil in 1998. She graduated with a Post Graduate Diploma in Business Administration from the University of Auckland in 2004. She has published widely on Māori socio-environmental and development studies and has written reports for tribal groups, government and the Crown Forestry Rental Trust. She is a member of the New Zealand Historic Places Trust Board and the Māori Heritage Council.

Rangi Mataamua

Rangi Mataamua, from Tūhoe, spent his childhood in Levin attending local schools. He was also educated at Hato Paora College and after completing his final year moved to Wellington to attend Victoria University. Dr Mataamua was awarded a Bachelor of Arts degree in 1995, an Honours degree in 1996 and a Masters degree in 1998. In 2002 he moved to Massey University to manage research projects centred on Māori language revitalisation and broadcasting. In 2006 Dr Mataamua completed a PhD on Māori radio broadcasting and language revitalisation. In 2008 he relocated to Ruatāhuna in the heart of the Urewera, and now resides beside Mataatua marae. While still involved in a number of projects at both a local and national level, Dr Mataamua takes time to explore the native forest that surrounds his home.

Aroha Miller

Aroha is from Kai Tahu, Kāti Mamoe, Waitaha. She completed a PhD in Zoology, at Otago University in 2007, in which she investigated two invasive marine species in New Zealand. She has been working at Lincoln University since August 2007 as a Post-Doctoral Research Fellow in vertebrate pest management.

Pātaka J.G. Moore

Pātaka Moore, Ngāti Pareraukawa and Ngāti Raukawa, is a staff member at Te Wānanga-o-Raukawa in Ōtaki and whanau development co-ordinator for Ngati Pareraukawa. He has a background in Resource and Environmental Planning and Māori Resource development. His work has focused on the restoration of the Mangapouri Stream in Ōtaki and the Hōkio Stream west of Levin. He has collected oral history recordings from throughout Ngāti Raukawa about environmental injustice, tuna (eel) and aspects of culture and the environment that kaumātua are willing to share. He enjoys project management and the facilitation of positive Māori-led environmental initiatives. He enjoys playing rugby and listening to good home grown music from Aotearoa.

Malcolm Mulholland

Malcolm Mulholland, Ngati Kahungunu ki Wairarapa, is an editor at Te Putahi a Toi, Māori Studies, Massey University. He has been employed in a number of research positions involving Treaty of Waitangi claims. He is the author of "Beneath the Māori Moon: An Illustrated History of Māori Rugby" (Huia, 2009) and edited "State of the Māori Nation" (Reed, 2006).

Margaret Mutu

Margaret Mutu is of Ngāti Kahu, Te Rarawa, Ngāti Whātua and Scottish descent, and has three adult children and three grandchildren. Professor Mutu is the chairperson of the iwi authority, Te Rūnanga-ā-Iwi o Ngāti Kahu, the Professor of Māori Studies at the University of Auckland, the chairperson of both her home marae, Kāpehu, in the Northern Wairoa, and Karikari in the Far North and the chief negotiator for the settlement of

Ngāti Kahu's land claims. She has a BSc in mathematics, an MPhil with 1st class (Hons) in Māori studies and a PhD in Māori studies and linguistics. She also holds a Diploma in Teaching and a Certificate in Company Direction.

Marie Nixon-Benton

Marie Nixon-Benton is from Ngāti Mahuta, Tūrangawaewae marae, Tainui waka and has had a career in the global pharmaceutical industry as a pharmacologist and a pharmaceutical research director. Since returning to Aotearoa New Zealand Marie has used her extensive Western medical knowledge and combined this with traditional Māoritanga knowledge to address the current Type II diabetes epidemic. Dr Nixon-Benton completed a PhD about the long finned eel/tuna to prove her theory that the staple tuna diet prevented chronic non-communicable diseases from manifesting and validated that long finned tuna contained the essential fatty acid omega-3.

Shaun Ogilvie

Shaun Ogilvie is from Te Arawa (Ngāti Whakahemo) Ngāti Awa (Ngāti Pukeko). Dr Ogilvie has a PhD in Ecology from the University of Canterbury and is currently a Senior Lecturer in Wildlife Management at Lincoln University. Shaun is also the Tumuaki of the Kaupapa Māori Unit at Lincoln's Bio-Protection and Ecology Division. He was previously Principal Scientist - Māori Research at the National Institute of Water and Atmospheric Research in Christchurch and Scientist at Manaaki Whenua - Landcare Research. Shaun's research interests include the development of techniques for the management of animal pests. He has also been involved in projects investigating the fate of 1080 in the environment and has published a number of articles in this area. Shaun has a special interest in enhancing Māori research capability in the environmental arena.

Craig Pauling

Craig is a descendant of Ngāi Tahu tīpuna Te Ruahikihiki (nō Taumutu), Tūrakautahi (nō Kaiapoi) and Te Rakiwhakaputa (nō Rāpaki) and also has Kāti Mamoe, Waitaha, Ngāti Mutunga, English and Scottish ancestry. Craig is passionate about the protection, monitoring, and enhancement of native flora and fauna, particularly as it relates to Ngāi Tahu mahinga kai species and practices, and is also heavily involved in Ngāi Tahu based environmental education initiatives including Aoraki Bound and Te Tīra Horomaka. Craig shares his time looking after his three tamariki, Mihiroa, Meihana and Tainui and working part time as an Environmental Advisor for Toitū Te Whenua (the environmental management unit of Te Rūnanga o Ngāi Tahu) lecturing in Māori environmental management at Lincoln University and studying towards a Masters degree in Applied Science. Craig has worked for Te Rūnanga since 1999, after graduating from Lincoln University with a Bachelor of Resource Studies. He lives in Ōtautahi with his children and partner Janyne who is from Arahura on Te Tai o Poutini.

Rachael Selby

Rachael Selby, Ngāti Pareraukawa and Ngāti Raukawa is a writer, researcher and teacher. She resides in Ōtaki where she is a kaiāwhina at Te Wānanga-o-Raukawa and is a senior lecturer at Massey University. Rachael is an oral history researcher and has collected more than fifty interviews with Māori whose memories are recorded on audio-tape and deposited in library archives. She enjoys editorial work, mentoring young researchers and strengthening contacts with other indigenous researchers. Rachael chairs the Ngatokowaru Marae Committee, is a member of Te Runanga o Raukawa and the Raukawa Marae Trustees.

Cherryl Smith

Cherryl Smith is from Ngāti Apa, Ngāi Tumapuhiarangi and Te Aitanga a Hauiti. She is the Co-Director of Te Atawhai o te Ao: Independent Māori Research Institute for Environment and Health based in Whanganui. Dr Smith has a Ph.D in Education and has worked extensively on environmental and health issues. She is a grandmother of four mokopuna and raises her eldest mokopuna.

Huhana Smith

Huhana Smith is from Ngāti Tukorehe and Ngāti Raukawa. She is an artist, academic and Senior Curator Māori at the Museum of New Zealand, Te Papa Tongarewa. She is an iwi member on Te Iwi o Ngāti Tukorehe Trust's environmental committee and is an active researcher for a collaborative ecosystems services project. Dr Smith is currently working with key kaitiaki on the Ahi Kaa Roa mapping strategy for cultural landscape in the coastal Kūkū region. Since 1996 Huhana has supported the implementation of the Ōhau River 'loop' revitalisation programme for Tahamatā Incorporation (1997-); Te Hākari Dune Wetland (2000-) and Tikorangi Nursery (2005-) projects. These action projects encourage the protection of cultural landscape, sustainability of and enhancement of the dynamic coast, its waterways and indigenous biodiversity. Since 2006 Huhana and her partner Richard Anderson (Ngā Whenua Rāhui) have developed the Waikokopu stream rehabilitation project. Huhana also sits on the Environmental Legal Aid panel for the Ministry for the Environment, assisting parties with funding for Environment Court cases.

Veronica Tawhai

Veronica Tawhai is from Ngāti Porou, Uepōhatu. She is a lecturer in policy and politics at Te Pūtahi a Toi, School of Māori Studies at Massey University. After graduating from Massey with a Bachelor of Arts in Social Policy and Māori Studies and a Master of Education (Hons) her work and research interests have evolved around Māori political participation and political education. She is currently completing a PhD which focuses on citizenship education in bi-political states such as Aotearoa New Zealand.

Pou Temara

Pou Temara of Tūhoe is a professor at the University of Waikato and has written many publications and essays on issues currently affecting Māori. He is a recognized authority on Māori customary practice having taught at Victoria University and Te Whare Wānanga o Awanuiārangi as associate professor and head of the Faculty of Mātauranga Māori. He is also one of three directors of Te Panekiretanga o Te Reo, the Institute of Excellence in the Māori Language and a past member of the Māori Advisory Committee which produced essays for the Dictionary of New Zealand Biography. Professor Temara is a member of the Tūhoe Waikaremoana Māori Trust Board, a chairperson of Te Hui Ahurei a Tūhoe and chairperson of the Repatriation Advisory Panel to Te Papa. He was recently made a member of the Waitangi Tribunal.

Gail Tipa

Gail Tipa, Ngāi Tahu, is part of the Tipa whānau from Moeraki, North Otago. Dr Tipa has experience in health and environmental management. For the last 10 years she has been self employed which has enabled her to work on projects mainly for the benefit of iwi. A focus of her work has been freshwater issues within the South Island of New Zealand. She has been involved in acquiring and restoring wetlands. Jointly with Laurel Teirney they developed a Cultural Health Index for assessing stream health. In addition to a research interest in aquatic restoration, her recent research focuses on allocative decision making, specifically the development of new tools for Māori to use to help them determine appropriate stream flows. Gail has served on the Otago Conservation Board, Te Rūnanga o Ngāi Tahu, KTKO Ltd and the Otago DHB. She retains a range of environmental responsibilities for Te Rūnanga o Moeraki

Krystal Te Rina Warren

Krystal Te Rina Warren of Ngāti Whitikaupeka and Mōkai Patea with Ngāti Raukawa and Ngāti Rangitane whakapapa. She is actively involved with the development of iwi within Mōkai Patea where she is a delegate to Te Rūnanga o Ngāti Whitikaupeka and a representative on an environmental body named Ngā Pae o Rangitikei. Te Rina is passionate about iwi development. Te Rina has been involved in iwi research. She has also become involved in workforce development with a particular focus on the education sector, increasing Māori participation in higher education and Māori Immersion teaching.

Tracey Whare

Tracey Whare is from Ngāti Raukawa and Te Whānau a Apanui. She completed an LLB in 1996 at Victoria University of Wellington. Since that time she has practised in numerous areas of the law including Māori land, resource management, property and trusts. In 1998 she was awarded an indigenous fellowship with the United Nations Office of the High Commissioner for Human Rights in Geneva, Switzerland. She has continued to participate in United Nations meetings, in particular the working group on the Draft Declaration on the Rights of Indigenous Peoples, the previous working group on indigenous populations and the newly formed expert mechanism on the rights of indigenous peoples. Tracey is also a trustee of the Aotearoa Indigenous Rights Charitable Trust.

Bibliography

A

AC Neilson. 2001. *Review of the Local Government Act. Synopsis and Analysis of Submissions.* Wellington: Department of Internal Affairs.

Adkin, G.L. 1948. *Horowhenua: Its Māori Place-Names & Their Topographic & Historical Background.* Christchurch: Capper Press Ltd.

Agri*Quality* Laboratory Network, 131 Boundary Road, Lynfield, Auckland. [Unpublished raw data for assay test on long finned eel *anguilla dieffenbachii* to validate the fatty acid omega-3]. Reports 310956 & 209174 (2003).

Aitken, J. 2007. *Antibiotics.* Unpublished reference guide.

Alliston, L. and D. Cossar. 2006. *The Participation and Engagement of Māori in Decision-Making Processes and Other Government Initiatives.* Research New Zealand.

Anderson, A. 2002. 'A Fragile Plenty: Pre-European Māori and the New Zealand Environment', in E. Pawson & T. Brooking (ed.) *Environmental Histories of New Zealand* (pp. 19–34). Victoria, Australia: Oxford University Press.

Arthington, A., R. Tharme, S. Brizga, B. Pusey and M. Kennard. 2004. 'Environmental Flow Assessments with Emphasis on Holistic Methodologies' in R. Welcomme and T. Petr (eds) Proceedings of the Second International Symposium on the Management of Large Rivers for Fisheries, Volume II. RAP Publication 2004/17. Bangkok, Thailand: FAO Regional Office for Asia and the Pacific.

Atzert, S.P. 1971. A review of sodium monofluoroacetate (Compound 1080). Its properties, toxicology, and use in predator and rodent control. U.S. Bureau of Sport Fisheries and Wildlife, Special Scientific Report – Wildlife 146. 34 p.

Australian Government Fisheries Research and Development Corporation. 2004. *What's so Healthy about Seafood.* Canberra, Australia: Australian Federal Government.

B

Baker, S. 1993. 'The Principles and Practice of Ecofeminism', in *Journal of Gender Studies.* Vol. 2, no. 1, 4–26.

Ballara, A. 1990. 'Hine-i-paketia fl. 1850: 1870', in *Dictionary of New Zealand Biography, Vol. 1 (1769–1869)* (pp. 190–191). Wellington: Allen & Unwin/Dept of Internal Affairs.

Ballara, A. (1986). *Proud to be white? A survey of Pakeha prejudice in New Zealand.* Auckland: Heinemann.

Barnes, A. 2006. 'Citing Whaia te Mahere Taiao a Hauraki: Hauraki Iwi Environmental Plan (16/06/2006).'*Submission made by Alex Barnes: Resource Consent Number 102909 by Fonterra Cooperative Group Ltd for the Discharge to the Manawatu River of Milk Processing Wastewater and Condensate Cooling Water from their Longburn Factory.*

Bennett, A. 2007. 'Recognising and providing for Māori values in water allocation'. Unpublished Masters Thesis, Massey University, Palmerston North.

Bennetts, J. 2006, 2 August. 'Māori warn of battle over water'. *The Press.*

Benson-Pope, D. 2006. *Sustainable Water Programme of Action* New Zealand Government.

Best, E. 1972. *Tuhoe the Children of the Mist.* Wellington: A.H. & A.W. Reed Ltd.

Best, E. 1972. *The Astronomical Knowledge of the Māori.* Wellington: Government Printers.

Best, E. 'Waikaremoana The Sea of Rippling Waters: the lake, the land, the legends, with a tramp through Tuhoeland'. Unpublished typescript.

Beven, B.M., A. Harrison and P. Shaw. 1999. *Northern Te Urewera Ecosystem Restoration Project Te Urewera National Park.* Gisborne: Department of Conservation.

Best, E. 1935. *The Māori as He Was.* Wellington, New Zealand: Dominion Museum.

Best, E. 1942. *The Māori.* Wellington, New Zealand: The Polynesian Society.

Biggs, B.J., C. Kilroy and C.M. Mulcock. 2000. *New Zealand Stream Health Monitoring and Assessment Kit.* Christchurch: NIWA.

'Board has Big Plans for a Cleaner Manawatu.' *Evening Standard,* 17 April 1977.

Boast, R. (2004, Autumn Winter). Consitutional crisis over foreshore and seabed in Aotearoa. *Pacific Ecologist* .

Brookfield, F. M. (2003). Māori customary title to foreshore and seabed. *New Zealand Law Journal* , 295 - 297.

Buddle, T. 1860. *The Māori King Movement in New Zealand, with a Full Report of the Native Meetings held at Waikato, April and May 1860.* Christchurch: Kiwi Publishers.

Buick, T.L. 1903. *Old Manawatu.* Palmerston North: Buick & Young.

Burmil, S., T. Daniel and J.Hetherington. 1999. 'Human Values and Perception of Water in Arid Landscapes', in *Urban Planning.* Vol. 44, 99–109.

C

Cabinet Agreements. 1997 *Historic Heritage Management,* CAB (97) M43/22 Wellington: Parliament.

Cabinet Agreements. 1997. *Māori Language Policy: Options to Improve the Status and Vitality of the Language* [CAB (97) M 45/8C(4)] Cabinet Paper. Wellington: Parliament.

Cabinet Agreements. 1999. *Enhanced Ministry of Culture and Heritage* [CAB (99) M 17/18] Cabinet Paper. Wellington: Parliament.

Cabinet Agreements. 1999. *Review of Protection Mechanism: Protection of Sites of Significance to Māori (Wahi Tapu)*, CAB (96) M 8/15. Wellington: Parliament.

Cabinet Policy Committee [POL (01) 270]. (2001). *Review of the Local Government Act: Paper 7: Treaty of Waitangi and Local Government*. Available at: http://www.dia.govt.nz/Pubforms.nsf/wpg_CabinetPapers_LGAREV?OpenView

Cairns, D. 1941. 'Life History of the Two Species of New Zealand Fresh-water eel', in *New Zealand Journal of Science and Technology.* Vol. 24, 53B–72B.

Chapman, K. 2007. 'Dump Pollutes River.' *Manawatu Standard*, 5 October 2007), p. 1.

Chapman, K. 2007. 'Sewage Illegally Dumped into River.' *Manawatu Standard*, 10 October, 2007, p. 1.

Cheyne, C. M. 2006. *New Zealanders' Interactions with Local Government.* Palmerston North, New Zealand: School of Social Policy, Sociology and Social Work, Massey University.

Cheyne, C.M. and Tawhai, V.M.H. 2007. *He Wharemoa Te Rakau, Ka Mahue: Māori Engagement with Local Government. Knowledge, Experiences, and Recommendations.* Palmerston North: Massey University.

'City Objections to Fish Kill Blame Over-Ruled'. *Evening Standard*, 18 April 1984. p.4.

Clarkson, B.R., Sorrell, B.K., Reeves, P.N., Champion, P.D., Partridge, T.R. and Clarkson, B.D. 2003. *Handbook for Monitoring Wetland Condition.* Hamilton: Landcare Research.

Clarke, R. and G. Stankey. 1979. *The Recreation Opportunity Spectrum: A Framework for Planning, Management and Research.* USDA Forest Service, General Technical Report PNW-98.

Craig, D. 2005. *Indigenous Property Rights to Water: Environmental Flows, Cultural Values and Tradeable Property Rights.* www.law.mq.edu.au/MUCEL/craig/

Commission for the Environment. 1986. *New Zealand's Wetlands Management Policy.* Retrieved September 2006 from http://www.doc.govt.nz/Conservation/Wetlands/030-NZ-Management-policy/index.asp.

Coombes, B. 2007. 'Defending community? Indigeneity, Self-Determination and Institutional Ambivalence in the Restoration of Lake Whakaki' in *Geoforum.* Vol. 38 no. 1, 60–72.

Coombes, B. and S. Hill. 2005. *Fishing for the Land under Water: Catchment Management, Wetland Conservation and the Wairoa Coastal Lagoons.* Report prepared for the Crown Forestry Rental Trust. Auckland: School of Geography and Environmental Science, University of Auckland.

Cooper R. and R. Brooking. 2002. 'Ways through Complexities', in M. Kawharu (ed.) *Whenua: Managing Our Resources.* Auckland: Reed Publishing.

Crengle, H. 2002. 'The Legal Basis for a Consideration of Cultural Values' in G. Tipa, H. Crengle, K. Davis, B. Allingham and A. Symon (eds) *Cultural Impact Assessment – Project Aqua.* Christchurch: Meridian Energy Ltd.

Cummings, M. 2006. 'Troubled Waters.' *Manawatu Standard*, 8 August 2006, p. 1.

Cummings, M. 2006. 'Fonterra Dump Makes Only 'Minor' Difference.' *Manawatu Standard*, 10 August 2006, p. 1.

Cummings, M. 2006. 'Dumping Plan Could Change.' *Manawatu Standard*, 11 September 2006, p. 1.

Currie, K.J. 1977. *The Manawatu Catchment Board's Report on Water Quality Management in the Manawatu River below Palmerston North.* Palmerston North: Manawatu Catchment Board and Regional Water Board.

D

David, W.A.L. 1950. 'Sodium Fluoroacetate as a Systemic and Contact Insecticide, in *Nature*, Vol. 165, 493–494.

Davidson J. 2003. Wāhi Tapu and Portable Taonga of Ngāti Hinewaka: Desecration and Loss; Protection and Management. A report prepared for the Ngāti Hinewaka Claims Committee, February 2003.

Decision 1 (66) New Zealand Foreshore and Seabed Act 2004, CERD/C/66/NZL/Dec.1 (Committee on the elimination of all forms of racial discrimination March 2005).

Dell, P. 2004. *The Rotorua Lakes Protection and Restoration Programme: Outline of Project Structure and Timeline.* Whakatane: Environment Bay of Plenty.

Department of Conservation. 1994. *Possum Control in Native Forests.* Wellington: Department of Conservation.

Department of Conservation. 1998. Historic Heritage Management Review: Report to the Ministerial Advisory Committee. Wellington: Department of Conservation Te Papa Atawhai.

Department of Conservation. 2003. *Te Urewera National Park Management Plan.* Gisborne: Department of Conservation.

Department of Conservation & Ministry for the Environment. 2000. *The New Zealand Biodiversity Strategy.* Wellington: Department of Conservation & Ministry for the Environment.

Department of Internal Affairs. 2006. *Local Authority Election Statistics 2004.* Wellington: Department of Internal Affairs.

Dewes, W. and T. Walzl. 2007. *Issues Paper on the Impact of Rates on Māori Land: Prepared for the Local Government Rates Inquiry.* Wellington, New Zealand: Local Government Rates Inquiry.

Douglas E.M.K. (ed.). 1984. *Waiora, WaiMāori, Waikino, Waimate, Waitai: Māori Perceptions of Water and the Environment.* Hamilton: University of Waikato.

Dreaver, A. 2006. *Levin: The Making of a Town.* Levin: Horowhenua District Council.

Duckworth, J., B.M. Buddle and S. Scobie. 1998. "Fertility of Brushtail Possums (*Trichosurus vulpecula*) Immunised against Sperm', in *Journal of Reproductive Immunology,* Vol. 37, no. 2, 125–138.

Duckworth, J.A., K. Wilson, X. Cui, F.C. Molinia and P.E. Cowan. 2007. 'Immunogenicity and Contraceptive Potential of Three Infertility-Relevant Zona Pellucida 2 Epitopes', in *Reproduction,* Vol. 133, 177–186.

Durie, A.E. 1998. 'Me Tipu Ake Te Pono: Māori Research, Ethicality and Development', in T.P. Hauora (ed.) *Te Oru Rangahau Māori Research and Development Conference 7–9 July 1998: Proceedings.* Palmerston North, New Zealand: Te Putahi a Toi, School of Māori Studies, Massey University.

Durie, M. 1998. *Te Mana Te Kawanatanga: Politics of Māori Self-determination.* Auckland: Oxford University Press.

Durie, M. 1999. 'Marae and Implications for a Modern Māori Psychology: Elsdon Best Memorial Medal Address', in *Journal of the Polynesian Society,* Vol. 108, no. 4, 351–366.

Durie, M. 2004. 'A Māori Health Impact Framework' Power point presentation, *Health Impact Assessment Conference,* Wellington, 31 March 2004.

Dyberg, J. and H.O. Bang. 1979. 'Haemostatic Function and Platelet Polyunsaturated Fatty Acids in Eskimos', in *Lancet.* Vol. 2, 433–435.

E

Eason, C.T. 2002a. 'Sodium Monofluoroacetate (1080) Risk Assessment and Risk Communication', in *Toxicology,* Vols 181–182, 523–530.

Eason, C.T. 2002b. *Technical Review of Sodium Monofluoroacetate (1080) Toxicology.* Wellington: Animal Health Board. 25 p.

Ecological Society of America. 1998. 'Integrating Cultural, Economic and Environmental Requirements for Freshwater' in *Ecological Applications.* Vol. 8, no.3, p.xx

Ellison, B. 2007. *Wai Ki Uta – Wai Ki Tai: A Ngāi Tahu Leadership Initiative to Sustain the Freshwater Resources of Aotearoa/Te Waipounamu.* Christchurch: Te Rūnanga o Ngāi Tahu.

Environment Court New Zealand. 14 December 2004. Consent Order in the matter of Kenana Te Ranginui Marae Trust v Northland Regional Council, Far North District Council and Doubtless Bay Citizens and Ratepayers Association Incorporated (Environment Court, Auckland RMA0834/03).

Environment Waikato. 2008. *Regional Hazards and Emergency Management: Weather Hazards – Climate Change.* http://www.ew.govt.nz/Environmental-information/Regional-hazards-and-emergency-management/Weather-hazards/Climate-change/. Hamilton: Environment Waikato Regional Council.

Environment Waikato. 2008. 'Trends in water quality.' Retrieved March, 2008, from http://www.ew.govt.nz/enviroinfo/water/healthyrivers/waikato/facts6c.htm

F

Farming Futures. 2009. *Climate Change Series: Fact Sheet 3 – General adaptations for farmers and growers.* http://www.farmingfutures.org.uk.

Fisher, D. (2009, January 18). Māori deal with 'close access to public beaches'. *New Zealand Herald* .

Flanagan, C. and M. Laituri. 2004. 'Local Cultural Knowledge and Water Resource Management: The Wind River Indian Reservation,' in *Environmental Management.* Vol. 33, no. 2, 262–270.

G

Galindo, M.P.G. and J.A.C. Rodriguez. 2000. 'Environmental Aesthetics and Psychological Wellbeing: Relationships between Preference Judgments for Urban Landscapes and other relevant Responses,' in *Psychology in Spain.* Vol. 4, no. 1, 13–7.

Gibbs, M. and Bennett, A. 2007. 'Māori Claims to Ownership of Freshwater', in *Resource Management Journal* (August), 13–18.

Gold, J.R. 1980. *An Introduction to Behavioural Geography.* New York: Oxford University Press.

Goldie, W.H. 1999. *Māori medical lore.* Christchurch: Kiwi Publishers (originally documented and read to New Zealand Institute, Auckland, 7 September 1903).

Goldie, W. H. and E. Best. 1904. *Māori medical lore.* Auckland: The New Zealand Institute.

Good Earth Matters Consulting Limited. 2007. *New Zealand Pharmaceuticals Ltd – Liquid Waste Discharge Consents – Assessment of Environmental Effects: To Support Resource Consent Application 103907 Renewal of Process, Cooling & Stormwater Discharges. Revised AEE Incorporating Applicant's response to S92 Requests.*

Gordon, I.A. (ed.) 1978. *Mansfield, Katherine: The Urewera Notebook.* Christchurch: Oxford University Press.

Groenfeldt, D. 2004. *Water Development and Spiritual Values in Western and Indigenous Societies.* http://www.indigenouswater.org/IndigenousWaterManagement.html

Guijt, I. and A. Mosieev. 2001. *Resource kit for Sustainability Assessment.* Gland, Switzerland: IUCN.

H

Haggard, L. and D. Williams. 1992. 'Identity Affirmation through Leisure Activities – Leisure Symbols of Self', in *Journal of Leisure Research.* Vol. 24, 1–8.

Handford, P.A. & Associates Ltd. 2003. *Forest Monitoring Assessment Kit.* Wellington, NZ: MfE. www.formak.co.nz/default.aspx

Hannigan, J. 1982. 'Manawatu Catchment Board & Regional Water Board in Archives A175/66 Part 2: River Control' in *History of the Manawatu River and the Manawatu Catchment Board*. Palmerston North: Ian Matheson Archives.

Harawira, H. 2006. 'Government Confused and Confusing: Harawira.' Scoop, 13 September 2006.

Harding, J., P. Moseley, C. Pearson, and B. Sorrell. 2004. *Freshwaters of New Zealand*. Christchurch: Caxton Press for New Zealand Hydrological Society, New Zealand Limnological Society.

Harmsworth, G. 2002. *Coordinated Monitoring of New Zealand Wetlands, Phase 2, Goal 2: Māori Environmental Performance Indicators for Wetland Condition and Health*. Palmerston North: Landcare Research. www.landcareresearch.co.nz/research/social/Māoriindicators.asp

Harmsworth, G. 2005. *Good Practice Guidelines for Working with Tangata Whenua and Māori Organisations: Consolidating Our Learning*. Palmerston North: Landcare Research New Zealand.

High Court of New Zealand. 5 March 2001. Settlement Agreement between the Environmental Defence Society Inc., Te Rūnanga-ā-Iwi o Ngāti Kahu and the Far North District Council and Carrington Farms (High Court of New Zealand at Auckland M/404/45/01).

Holland M.K. and L.D. Holland. 1985. *Processes of Coastal Change Manawatu-Horowhenua*. Palmerston North: Manawatu Catchment Board and Regional Water Board Report.

Horizons Regional Council. 1994. *Decision of the Hearing Committee, Application by the Palmerston North City Council for Resource Consents relating to Awapuni Landfill*.

Horizons Regional Council. 2005. *State of the Environment Report of the Manawatu-Wanganui Region*. Horizons Regional Council Report 2004/EXT/608.

Horizons Regional Council. 2006. *Decision of the Hearing Committee: Application for Resource Consent No. 102909 by Fonterra Cooperative Group Ltd for the Discharge to the Manawatu River of Milk Processing Wastewater and Condensate Cooling Water from their Longburn Factory.*

Horizons Regional Council. 2006. *Managing Our Environment: A Real Look at the Water Quality in our Region*. Palmerston North: Horizons Regional Council.

Horizons Regional Council. 2007. *Proposed One Plan: The Consolidated Regional Policy Statement, Regional Plan and Regional Coastal Plan for the Manawatu-Wanganui Region*.

Horizons Regional Council. 11 July 2007. *Coal Tar Disposal – Awapuni Landfill*. Horizons Regional Council Report No: 07-08. File No: LR 00 00.

Horizons Regional Council. 2008. *Decision of the Hearing Committee: Application for Resource Consent No. 103907 by New Zealand Pharmaceuticals Limited for Discharge of Treated Wastewater from the Linton Plant to the Manawatu River.*

Howard, S. 2001. *Life, lineage and substance*. Nevada: Indigenous Peoples Council on Biocolonialism.

Hutchings, J. 1997. *A Māori Ecofeminist Model for Resource Management Consultation.* Unpublished Masters thesis. Victoria University, Wellington.

Hutchings, J. 2004. 'Tradition and Test Tubes, Māori and Science', in R. Hindmarsh and G. Lawrence (eds) *Recoding Nature: Critical Perspectives on Genetic Engineering.* Sydney: University of New South Wales Press. pp. 179–191.

I

Innes, J. and G. Barker. 1999. 'Ecological Consequences of Toxin Use for Mammalian Pest Control in New Zealand – An Overview' in *New Zealand Journal of Ecology,* Vol. 23, 111–127.

J

Jackson, S., M. Storrs and J. Morrison. 2005. 'Recognition of Aboriginal Rights, Interests and Values in River Research and Management: Perspectives from Northern Australia', in *Ecological Management and Restoration.* Vol. 6, no. 2, 105–110.

Jay, G. 2005. 'Whiteness Studies and the Multicultural Literature Classroom' in *MELUS,* Vol. 30, no. 2, 139–156.

Jellyman, D.J. 1992. *An Important fishery with an Uncertain Future: Freshwater Catch. Lake Ellesmere Catchment Intrinsic Values Report: Extract 6.* National conservation order application for Lake Ellesmere freshwater catch 32. Wellington: National Institute of Weather & Atmosphere.

Johnston, R., D. Gregory, G. Pratt, M. Watts. (eds) 2000. *The Dictionary of Human Geography.* Oxford: Blackwell.

Joy, M. 2006. *Open Letter: A Call for Action on Manawatu River Degradation.*

K

Kame'eleihiwa, L. 1992. *Native Land and Foreign Desires: Pehea Lā E Pono Aî?* Honolulu: Bishop Museum Press.

Kapiti Coast District Council. 1999. *A Guide to Growing Native Plants in Kapiti.* Paraparaumu: Natural Textures Information Graphics.

Kaplan, S. and R. Kaplan. 1977. 'The Experiences of the Environment', in *Man-Environment Systems.* Vol. 7, 300–305.

Kaplan, S. and R. Kaplan. 1982. *Cognition and the Environment: Functioning in an Uncertain World.* New York: Praeger Publishers.

Kaplan, R. and S. Kaplan. 1989. *The Experience of Nature: A Psychological Perspective* New York: Cambridge University Press.

Karetu, S.T. 1991. *Te Reo Rangatira.* Wellington: GP Print Limited.

Kawharu, I.H. 1977. *Māori Land Tenure: Studies of a Changing Institution.* Oxford: Oxford University Press.

Kawharu, I.H. 1975. *Orakei: A Ngati Whatua Community.* Wellington: New Zealand Council for Educational Research.

Kawharu, M. 1998. Dimensions of Kaitiakitanga: An Investigation of a Customary Māori Principle of Resource Management. D.Phil. thesis, University of Oxford.

Kawharu, M. 2000. 'Kaitiakitanga: A Māori Anthropological Perspective of the Māori Socio-Environmental Ethic of Resource Management', in *Journal of the Polynesian Society.* Vol. 110, no. 4, 349–70.

Kawharu, M. 2008. *Tāhuhu Kōrero: The Sayings of Taitokerau.* Auckland: Auckland University Press.

King, M. 2003. *The Penguin History of New Zealand.* Auckland: Penguin Books.

King, J., R. Tharme and C. Brown. 1999. *Definition and Implementation of In-stream Flows.* The World Commission on Dams (see http://www.dams.org)

Knack, M.C. and O.C. Stewart. 1984. *As Long as the River Shall Run: An Ethnohistory of Pyramid Lake Indian Reservation.* Reno & Las Vegas: University of Nevada Press.

L

Lambert, T. 1977. *The Story of Old Wairoa and the East Coast District, North Island, New Zealand.* Auckland: Reed Books (original published in 1925).

Lee, J.B.J. 2007. *Jade Taniwha: Māori-Chinese Identity and Schooling in Aotearoa.* Auckland: Rautaki.

Livingstone, P.G. 1994. 'The Use of 1080 in New Zealand', in A.A. Seawright and C.T. Eason (eds) Proceedings of the Science Workshop on 1080. *The Royal Society of New Zealand Miscellaneous Series 28.* 178 p.

Local Government New Zealand. 2004. *Local Authority Engagement with Māori: Survey of Current Council Practices.* Wellington: Local Government New Zealand.

Local Government New Zealand. 2007. *Co-Management: Case Studies Involving Local Authorities and Māori.* Wellington: Local Government New Zealand.

Loveridge, D.M. 1996. *Rangahaua Whanui National Theme k. Māori Land Councils and Māori Land Boards: A Historical Overview, 1900 to 1952.* Wellington: Waitangi Tribunal Rangahaua Whanui Series.

Long, R. 2007, 'Taniwha Terror? Lahar debacle'. *The Dominion Post*, 9 January 2007, p. 4.

'Longburn One Factor in Big Fish Kill.' *Manawatu Standard*, 22 February 1984. p.1.

M

MacDonald, C., Chamberlain, K., Long, N. 1997. 'Race, Combat, and PTSD in a Community Sample of New Zealand Vietnam War veterans', in *Journal of Traumatic Stress,* Vol. 10, no. 1, 117–124.

MacDonald, R.A. and O'Donnell, E. 1929. *Te Hekenga: Early Days in Horowhenua.* Palmerston North: G.H. Bennett & Co. Ltd.

Mahuta, R.T. 1990. *Tainui Lectures of Tawhiao's Vision.* Hamilton: University of Waikato.

Manawatu Regional Water Board. 1978. *Fish Kill Report – Manawatu River below Palmerston North.* Palmerston North: Manawatu Regional Water Board.

Marsden, M. 2003a. 'Kaitiakitanga: A Definitive Introduction to the Holistic Worldview of the Māori', in T.A.C. Royal (ed.) *The Woven Universe: Selected Writings of Rev. Māori Marsden* (pp. 54–72). Ōtaki: The Estate of Rev. Māori Marsden.

Marsden, M. 2003b. 'The Natural World and Natural Resources: Māori Value Systems and Perspectives', in T.A.C. Royal (ed.) *The Woven Universe: Selected Writings of Rev. Māori Marsden* (pp. 24–53). Ōtaki: The Estate of Rev. Māori Marsden.

Matiu, M., & Margaret M. (2003). *Te whānau moana – ngā kaupapa me ngā tikanga: customs and protocols.* Auckland: Reed Publishing.

Matunga, H. (2000). Decolonising planning: The Treaty of Waitangi, the environment and a dual planning tradition. In A. Memon, & H. Perkins (eds), *Environment, planning and management in New Zealand* (pp. 36–47). Palmerston North: Dunmore Press.

Mattingley, B. 2005. *Takiwā User Documentation.* Christchurch, NZ: ESR & Te Rūnanga o Ngāi Tahu.

Mattingley, B. 2007. *Takiwā 2.0 User Documentation.* Christchurch, NZ: ESR & Te Rūnanga o Ngāi Tahu.

McEwen, J.M. 1986. *Rangitane: A Tribal History.* Hong Kong: Reed Publishing.

McFadgen, B. 1997. *Archaeology of the Wellington Conservancy: Kapiti–Horowhenua. A Prehistoric and Palaeoenvironmental Study.* Wellington: Department of Conservation.

Mead, H.M. and N. Grove. 2001. *Nga Pepeha a nga Tipuna: The Sayings of the Ancestors.* Wellington: Victoria University Press.

Meyer, J.J.M. 1994. 'Fluoroacetate Metabolism of *Pseudomonas Cepacia*', in A.A Seawright and C.T. Eason (eds) Proceedings of the Science Workshop on 1080. *The Royal Society of New Zealand Miscellaneous Series 28*, pp. 54–58.

Milestad, R. 2003. *Building Farm Resilience: Prospects and Challenges for Organic Farming.* Uppsala, Sweden: Swedish University of Agricultural Sciences.

Millennium Ecosystem Assessment Core Writing Team. 2005. Millennium Ecosystem Assessment Synthesis Report. Washington, DC: United Nations Environment Programme, Millennium Ecosystem Assessment Secretariat, World Resources Institute.

Minhinnick, N. 1989. *Establishing Kaitiaki.* A report prepared for the Resource Management Law Reform. Auckland: Minhinnick, N.K.

Minhinnick N.K. 1984. In E. Douglas (ed.) 'Waiora, WaiMāori, Waikino, Waimate, Waitai: Māori Perceptions of Water and Environment', in Proceedings of a seminar sponsored jointly by the Commission for the Environment, Waikato University, Hamilton, New Zealand.

Ministry for the Environment. 1997 *Environmental Performance Indicators: Proposals for Air, Freshwater and Land.* Wellington: Ministry for the Environment.

Ministry for the Environment. 1997. *The State of the Environment.* Wellington: Ministry for the Environment, Manatū mō te Taiao.

Ministry for the Environment. 2003.*Dairying and Clean Stream Accord.* Retrieved 26 January, 2008, from www.mfe.govt.nz/publications/land/dairying-clean-steams-accord. html.

Ministry for the Environment. 2003b. *Microbiological Water Quality Guidelines for Marine and Freshwater Recreational Areas.* Wellington, NZ: Ministry for the Environment. www.mfe.govt.nz/publications/water/microbiological-quality-jun03/index.html

Ministry for the Environment. 2007a. *Environment New Zealand 2007.* Wellington: Ministry for the Environment.

Ministry for the Environment. 2007b. *Adapting to the Impacts of Climate Change.* http://www.mfe.govt.nz/issues/climate/adaptation/index.html. Wellington: Ministry for the Environment.

Ministry for the Environment Manatū Mö Te Taiao. 2007. *Resource Management Amendment Act 2005 – Summary.* Wellington: Ministry for the Environment.

Ministry for the Environment. (eds) 2008a. *Climate Change Effects and Impacts Assessment: A Guidance Manual for Local Government in New Zealand.* 2nd ed. Wellington: Ministry for the Environment. Xviii + 149 p.

Ministry for the Environment. 2008b. *How Might Climate Change Affect My Region?* http://www.mfe.govt.nz/issues/climate/about/climate-change-affect-regions/. Wellington: Ministry for the Environment.

Ministry of Agriculture and Forestry (MAF). 2008. *Climate Change and Land-Based Sectors – Preparing for the Future.* Wellington: Ministry of Agriculture and Forestry.

Ministry of Agriculture and Forestry (MAF). 2009. *Climate Change and Agriculture and Forestry – Issues and Responses.* http://www.maf.govt.nz/mafnet/rural-nz/sustainable-resource-use/climate/impact-on-industries//. Wellington: Ministry of Agriculture and Forestry.

Ministry of Economic Development. 2007. *Bioprospecting: Harnessing Benefits for New Zealand.* Wellington: Ministry of Economic Development.

Ministry of Health. 2000. *New Zealand Drinking Water Standards.* Wellington, NZ: MOH. www.moh.govt.nz/moh.nsf/0/70727db605b9f56a4c25696400802887?OpenDocument

Ministry of Social Development. 2006. *The Social Report.* Wellington: Ministry of Social Development.

Ministry of Works. 1957. *Pollution in the Lower Manawatu & Oroua Rivers.* Wellington: Ministry of Works with Health & Marine Depts & DSIR.

Mitsch, W. J. and J.G. Gosselink. 2000. *Wetlands.* 3rd ed. New York: John Wiley & Sons.

Moiseev, A., E. Dudley and D. Canti. 2002. *The Wellbeing of Forests: An E-Tool for Assessing Environmental Sustainability.* Gland, Switzerland and Cambridge, UK: IUCN.

Moon, P. 2003. *Tohunga Hohepa Kereopa.* Auckland: David Ling Publishing,

More T., S. Bulmer, L. Henzel and A. Mates. 2003. *Extending the ROS to Non Federal Lands in the North East: An Implementation Guide.* USDA Forest Service General Technical Report NE-309.

Moore, P. 2006. *Submission by Pataka Moore: Resource Consent Number 102909 by Fonterra Cooperative Group Ltd for the Discharge to the Manawatu River of Milk Processing Wastewater and Condensate Cooling Water from their Longburn Factory.*

Morrison, A. 2007. 'Short-term lahar solution may carry long-term risk'. *The Dominion Post*, 11 January 2007, B 5.

Moriarty, C. 1978. *Eels: A Natural and Unnatural History.* New York: Universe.

Mulholland (ed.), *State of the Māori Nation* (pp. 127–140). Auckland: Reed.

Mullan, B., D. Wratt, D. Dean, M. Hollis, S. Allan, T. Williams, G. Kenny and Ministry for the Environment (MfE). (eds) 2008. *Climate Change Effects and Impacts Assessment: A Guidance Manual for Local Government in New Zealand.* 2nd ed. Wellington: Ministry for the Environment. Xviii + 149p.

Mutu M. 2002. 'Barriers to Tangata Whenua Participation in Resource Management', in M. Kawharu (ed.) *Whenua: Managing Our Resources.* Auckland: Reed.

Mutu, M. 2006. 'Recovering and Developing Ngāti Kahu's Prosperity', in M.

Mutu, M. 2007. *Statement on behalf of Te Whānau Moana hapū and Karikari Marae in opposition to resource consent application RC 2060981 for Karikari 2J4 block.* Kaitāia: Te Rūnanga-ā-Iwi o Ngāti Kahu.

Mutu M. 2008. *Te Rūnanga-ā-Iwi o Ngāti Kahu.* Chairperson's Report October 2006 to March 2008. Kaitāia: Te Rūnanga-ā-Iwi o Ngāti Kahu.

N

Nara Document on Authenticity. 1994. Experts meeting, 1–6 November 1994, Nara, Japan.

Nash, T. 2002. 'Stop Poison Talk or We'll Sue: Council.' *Manawatu Evening Standard*, 20 May 2002, p. 1.

Nash, T. 2002. 'Resident Wants Coal Tar Removed from Landfill.' *Manawatu Evening Standard*, 20 May 2002, p. 5.

Nash, T. 2002. 'Landfill Neighbour Wants Tests.' *Manawatu Evening Standard*, 27 May 2002, p. 3.

National Institute of Water and Atmospheric Research (NIWA). 2008. *Māori Environmental Knowledge (MEK) of Weather and Climate.* http://www.niwa.co.nz//. Wellington: National Institute of Water and Atmospheric Research.

National Institute of Water and Atmospheric Research Ltd. 2005. *Executive Summary: Meteorological Hazards and the Potential Impacts for Climate Change in the Horizons Region.* Wellington: NIWA.

New Zealand Historic Places Trust Pouhere Taonga. 1998. *Historic Heritage Management Review Māori Consultation Round Key Points: Preliminary Report.* Wellington: NZHPT.

New Zealand Historic Places Trust Pouhere Taonga. 2003. *Heritage Landscapes Think Tank: Report on Proceedings.* Wellington: NZHPT.

New Zealand Law Reports, 1989. *The Environmental Defence Society Inc. and Taitokerau District Māori Council v Mangonui County Council* [1989]. NZLR 257.

New Zealand Māori Heritage Council. 2009. *Tapuwae. A Vision for Places of Māori Heritage.* Wellington: NZHPT.

Ngātokowaru Marae Committee Minute Book Number Five.

Ngati Kahungunu. 2007. *Crown Bioprospecting Consultation Hui Briefing Paper for*

Iwi. Wellington: Ngati Kahungunu.

Nikora, T.R. 2000. *Ko Wai a Tūhoe?* A report for the Waitangi Tribunal and the Office of Treaty Settlements.

NIWA. 2003. *Freshwater Fish Database.* Retrieved 18 July 2003 www.fbis.co.nz

NIWA. 2007. *Electric Fishing Machines.* Retrieved 28 June 2007 www.niwascience.co.nz/rc/instrumentsystems/efish

O

O'Gara, G. 2000. *What You See in Clear Water: Life on the Wind River Reservation.* New York: Knopf.

Ogilvie, S.C., L.H. Booth and C.T. Eason. 1998. 'Uptake and Persistence of Sodium Monofluoroacetate (1080) in Plants', in *Bulletin of Environmental Contamination and Toxicology*, Vol. 60, 745–749.

Ogilvie, S.C., J.M. Ataria, J. Waiwai, J.E. Doherty, M. Lambert, N. Lambert and D. King. 2006. 'Uptake and Persistence of the Vertebrate Pesticide, Sodium Monofluoroacetate (Compound 1080), in Plants of Cultural Importance', in *Ecotoxicology*, Vol. 15, 1–7.

Ogilvie, S. and B. Penter. 2001. *Stream Health Monitoring Assessment Kit for Māori.* Christchurch, NZ: NIWA http://www.smf.govt.nz/results/1027_finalreport.pdf

Orbell, M. 1985. *The Natural World of the Māori.* Auckland: Collins.

Office of Treaty Settlements. 2004. *Te Arawa and Arawa Māori Trust Board and Her Majesty the Queen in Right of New Zealand: Deed of Settlement of the Te Arawa Lakes Historical Claims and Remaining Annuity Issues.*

Office of Treaty Settlements. 2006. *Deed of Settlement between the Crown and Te Arawa for their Lakes and Annuity Claims: Summary of the Historical Background to the Lakes and Annuity Claims by Te Arawa.*

Office of Treaty Settlements. 2007a. *Draft Agreement in Principle between the Crown and Waikato-Tainui: For the Settlement of the Historical Claims of Waikato-Tainui in Relation to the Waikato River: Summary.*

Office of Treaty Settlements. 2007b. *Waikato-Tainui and Her Majesty the Queen in Right of New Zealand: Agreement in Principle for the Settlement of the Historical Claims of Waikato-Tainui in Relation to the Waikato River.*

Oliver W.H. and T. Sparks. 'Waitohi ? – 1839'. *Dictionary of New Zealand Biography*, updated 7 April 2006 Url: http://www.dnzb.govt.nz/

O'Regan G. 1997. *Bicultural Developments in Museums of Aotearoa: What is the Current Status? Ki te Whakamana i te Kaupapa Tikanga-a-rua ki roto i ngā Whare Taonga o te Motu: Kei Hea e Tū Ana?* Wellington: National Services Te Paerangi, Museum of Aotearoa New Zealand Te Papa Tongarewa.

Otaraua Hapū. 2003. *Kaimoana Monitoring Guidelines for Iwi and Hapū.* Wellington: MfE. www.mfe.govt.nz/publications/ser/kaimoana-oct03.html

Owens, J.M.R. 1972. *The Geography of the Manawatu. Miscellaneous Papers No.3: Early History of the Manawatu.* Palmerston North: Department of Geography, Massey University.

P

Palmerston North City Council. 2005. '71/3 Part 1', in *Sewage Treatment/Pollution of the Manawatu River 1967–1994.* Palmerston North: Ian Matheson Archives.

Panel, L.G.R.I. 2007. *Funding Local Government.* Wellington: Local Government Rates Inquiry.

Para, D. 1999. 'A Māori Perspective of Pest Control from within DOC', Manaaki Whenua Conference, Lincoln, 21 March1999. Pp. 1–7. www.landcareresearch.co.nz/news/conferences/manaakiwhenua/proceedings.asp

Park, G. 2001. *Effective Exclusion: An Exploratory Overview of Crown Actions and Māori Responses Concerning the Indigenous Flora and Fauna 1912–1983.* A report commissioned by the Waitangi Tribunal for the Wai 262 claim. Wellington: Waitangi Tribunal.

Park, G. 2002. '"Swamps which might Doubtless Easily be Drained": Swamp Drainage and its Impact on the Indigenous', in E. Pawson and T. Brooking (eds) *Environmental Histories of New Zealand* (pp. 151–165). Victoria, Australia: Oxford University Press.

Parliamentary Commissioner for the Environment. 1993a. *Investigation into the Management of Whakaki Lagoon.* Wellington: Parliamentary Commissioner for the Environment, Te Kaitiaki Taiao a Te Whare Paremata.

Parliamentary Commissioner for the Environment. 1993b. *Investigation into the Management of Whakaki Lagoon: Background Report.* Wellington: Parliamentary Commissioner for the Environment, Te Kaitiaki Taiao a Te Whare Paremata.

Parliamentary Commissioner for the Environment. 1996. Historic and Cultural Heritage Management in New Zealand. Wellington: Office of the Parliamentary Commissioner for the Environment.

Parliamentary Commissioner for the Environment. 2001. *Boggy Patch or Ecological Heritage? Valuing Wetlands in Tasman.* Wellington: Parliamentary Commissioner for the Environment, Te Kaitiaki Taiao a Te Whare Paremata.

Parliamentary Commissioner for the Environment. 2006. *Restoring the Rotorua Lakes: The Ultimate Endurance Challenge.* Wellington: Parliamentary Commissioner for the Environment.

Parliamentary Commissioner for the Environment 2008. *Levin Landfill Environmental Management Review.*

Pauling, C. 2003. *Ki Uta Ki Tai – Mountains to the Sea Natural Resource Management: A Scoping Document for Developing Mountains to the Sea Natural Resource Management Tools for Ngāi Tahu.* Christchurch: Te Rūnanga o Ngāi Tahu.

Pauling, C. 2004. *State of the Takiwā – Cultural Monitoring and Reporting on the Health of our Environment: A Scoping Document for Developing a Culturally Based Environmental Monitoring and Reporting System.* Christchurch: Te Rūnanga o Ngāi Tahu.

Pauling, C. 2007. *State of the Takiwā: Introducing a Culturally Based Environmental Monitoring and Reporting System for Ngāi Tahu.* Christchurch: Te Rūnanga o Ngāi Tahu.

Pauling, C., B. Mattingley and J. Aitken. 2005. *Te Ahuatanga o Te Waiau – Cultural Health Baseline Report 2005.* Christchurch and Wellington: Te Rūnanga o Ngāi Tahu/Ministry for the Environment.

Peart R. 2004. *A Place to Stand: The Protection of New Zealand's Natural and Cultural Landscape, Environmental Defence Society Incorporated Landscape Report, Executive Summary.* Auckland: Environmental Defence Society.

Petersen, G.C. 1973. *Palmerston North: A Centennial History.* Wellington: A.H. & A.W. Reed.

Plumwood, V. 1986. 'Ecofeminisn: An Overview and Discussion of Positions and Arguments', in *Australasian Journal of Philosophy.* Supplement to Vol. 64, 120–138.

Polkinghorne, I., D. Hamerli, P. Cowan and J. Duckworth. 2005. 'Plant-Based Immunocontraceptive Control of Wildlife – "Potentials, Limitations, and Possums"', in *Vaccine*, Vol. 23, 1847–1850.

Pond, W. 1997a. *The Land with All Woods and Water.* Rangahaua Whānui National Theme U. Wellington: Waitangi Tribunal.

Pond, W. 1997b. 'Loss of Harvest', in *The Land with All Woods and Water* (pp. 123–143). Rangahaua Whānui National Theme U. Wellington: Waitangi Tribunal.

Posey, D. 1999. *Cultural and Spiritual Values of Biodiversity.* London: Intermediate Technology Publications and UNEP.

Public Health Commission. 1991. *Our Health Our Future.* Wellington: Government Printers.

Pyke, D.A. 1999. *Preamble: The History of Diabetes.* London: John Wiley & Sons Limited.

R

Rammel, C.G. and P.A. Fleming. 1978. *Compound 1080: Properties and Use of Sodium Monofluoroacetate in New Zealand*. Wellington: New Zealand Ministry of Agriculture and Fisheries, Animal Health Division. 112 p.

Rangitīkei River Inter-tribal Working Party. 2004a. Ngā Pae o Rangitīkei discussion document. Unpublished document.

Rapport, D., C. Gaudet, J. Karr, J. Baron, C. Bohlen, W. Jackon, B. Jones, R Naiman, B. Norton and M. Pollock. 1998. 'Evaluating Landscape Health: Integrating Societal Goals and Biophysical Processes', in *Journal of Environmental Management*. Vol. 53, 1–5.

Report on the Crown's Foreshore and Seabed Policy, WAI 1071 (Waitangi Tribunal 2004).

Richardson, M. 2008. *Setting Community Boards in Context: A Report Prepared for the Royal Commission on Auckland Governance*. Auckland: Salt & Light IHS Limited.

Rikys, P. 2004. *Local Government Reform and Māori 1988 to 2002*. Waiheke: Te Ngutu o Te Ika.

Roberts, M., Norman, W., Minhinnick, N., Wihongi, D., and Kirkwood, C. 1995. 'Kaitiakitanga: Māori Perspectives on Conservation', in *Pacific Conservation Biology*. Vol. 2, 7–20.

Rout, E.A. 1926. *Māori Symbolism*. London: Kegan Paul, Trench, Trubner & Co.

Royal C.T.A. 1994. *Kāti au i konei: A Collection of Songs from Ngāti Toarangatira and Ngāti Raukawa*. Wellington: Huia Publishers.

Royal, T.A.C. 2002. *Indigenous Worldviews: A Comparative Study. A Report of Research in Progress*. Otaki: Te Wānanga o Raukawa.

Royal, Te A. C. 2003. *The Woven Universe: Selected Writings of Rev. Māori Marsden*. Otaki: The Estate of Rev. Māori Marsden.

Ruiter, A. (ed.). 1995. *Fish and Fishery Products*. Oxford: CAB International.

S

Salmond, A. 1978. 'Te Ao Tawhito: A Semantic Approach to the Traditional Māori Cosmos', in *Journal of the Polynesian Society*, Vol. 87, no. 1, 166–167.

Saunders, J. 1993. 'Group Attacking City over Sewage Discharge.' *Evening Standard*, 15 September, 1993, p.2.

Scarsbrook, M. 2006. *State and Trends in the National River Water Quality Network (1989–2005)*. Wellington: Ministry for the Environment.

Scott, R.R. 1984. *New Zealand Pest and Beneficial Insects*. Christchurch: Caxton Press.

'Sewerage Pollution under Council Microscope – Again'. *Evening Standard*, 23 September 1986. p.4.

Sheehan, J. 2001. 'Indigenous Property Rights and River Management', in *Water Science and Technology.* Vol. 43, no. 9, 235-42.

Shiva, V. 1998. *Biopiracy – The Plunder of Nature and Knowledge.* Cambridge: South End Press.

Shiva, V. 2000. *Tomorrow's Biodiversity.* London: Thames and Hudson.

Shreeve, C. 1992. *Fish Oil the Life Saver.* London: Thornsons.

Skutnabb-Kangas, T. 2000. *Linguistic Genocide in Education or Worldwide Diversity and Human Rights?* Mahwah, NJ: Lawrence Erlbaum Associates Inc.

Smith H. 2000. 'Taonga Tuku Iho, Taonga Māori: the Guardianship of Esteemed Treasures,' in Strelein, L & K. Muir (eds) *Native Title in Perspective: Selected Papers from the Native Title Research Unit, 1998–2000.* Canberra, Australia: Native Title Research Unit, Australian Institute of Aboriginal and Torres Strait Islander Studies.

Smith H. 2007. *Hei Whenua Ora: Hapū and iwi approaches for reinstating valued ecosystems within cultural landscape.* Unpublished Doctorate of Philosophy, School of Māori Studies Te Pūtahi-a-Toi, Massey University, Palmerston North.

Smith, L. T. 1999. *Decolonizing Methodologies: Research and Indigenous Peoples.* Dunedin: University of Otago Press.

Solomon, M., Nugent, D. (1995). *Commentary of the New Zealand Coastal Policy Statement 1994.* Wellington: Department of Conservation.

Statistics New Zealand. 2007a. *QuickStats about Māori: 2006 Census.* Retrieved 3 February 2009, from http://www.stats.govt.nz

Statistics New Zealand. 2007b. *QuickStats About Population Mobility.* Retrieved 2 February 2009, from http://www.stats.govt.nz

Stokes, E. 1985. 'Māori Research and Development', in R.U.f.M. Education (ed.), *The Issue of Research and Māori: Monograph No 9 (August 1992).* Auckland: University of Auckland.

Stauffer, C.E. 1996. *Fats and Oils.* St Paul, MN: Eagan Press.

Statement of Claim before the Waitangi Tribunal in the Matter of the Claim of Sharon Barcello-Gemmell, Harvey Ruru and Jane duFeu on Behalf of Te Atiawa. (3 December 2007).

Stavenhagen, R. (2006). *Report of the Special Rapporteur on the Situation of Human Rights and Fundamental Freedoms of Indigenous People. Mission to New Zealand.* E/CN.4/2006/78/Add.3. 13 March 2006. Geneva: United Nations Human Rights Commission.

Stewart, S. (1978). '70 km up the City's Sewer.' *Evening Standard*, 11 March 1978, p.3.

Stokes, E., J.W. Milroy and H. Melbourne. 1985. *Te Urewera, Ngā Iwi, Te Whenua, Te Ngāhere – People, Land and Forest of Te Urewera.* University of the Waikato (unpublished).

Stroombergen, A., A. Stojanovick, D. Wratt, B. Mulan, A. Tait, R. Woods, T. Baisden, D. Giltrap, K. Lock, J. Hendy and D. Kerr. 2008. *Ecoclimate Report 2008.* Wellington: Ministry of Agriculture and Forestry.

T

Tairawhiti Māori Land Court. 1893. *Wairoa Minute Book, No. 7.*

Tapsell, P. 1998. Taonga: A Tribal Response to Museums. D.Phil. thesis, University of Oxford.

Tau, T., A. Goodall, D. Palmer and R. Tau. 1990. *Te Whakatau Kaupapa: Ngāi Tahu Resource Management Strategy for the Canterbury Region.* Wellington: Aoraki Press.

Taupo District Council. 2009. *Taupo Iwi and Local Government Make History* [Press Release 9 January 2009]. Retrieved 6 February 2009, from http://www.infonews.co.nz/news. cfm?l=1&t=0&id=32263.

Taylor, R. 1997. *The State of New Zealand's Environment.* Wellington: Ministry for the Environment/Manatū mō te Taiao: GP Publications.

Taylor, R. and I. Smith. 1997. *The State of New Zealand's* Environment Report 1997. Wellington: Ministry for the Environment (MfE).

Teariki, C., P. Spoonley and N. Tomoana. 1992. *Te Whakapakari Te Mana Tangata. The Politics and Processes of Research for Māori.* Palmerston North: Department of Sociology, Massey University.

Te Puni Kokiri (TPK). 2009. *Te Kahui Mangai – Directory of Iwi and Māori Organisations.* http://www.tkm.govt.nz/map/. Wellington: Te Puni Kokiri.

Te Rūnanga o Ngāi Tahu. 2001. *Ngāi Tahu Vision 2025.* Christchurch: Te Rūnanga o Ngāi Tahu.

Terms of Agreement between Fonterra Co-Operative Group Ltd and Waitarere Environmental Care Association and Pataka Moore, Caleb Royal, The Manawatu Estuary Trust, Royal Forest and Bird Protection Society of NZ INC, Christina and George Paton and Foxton Waterfowl and Wetlands Club and Horizon Regional Council, (8/02/2007).

Te Rūnanga-ā-Iwi o Ngāti Kahu, February 2003. Minutes of the hui of Te Rūnanga-ā-Iwi o Ngāti Kahu held at Kenana marae, 18 January 2003. Kaitāia: Te Rūnanga-ā-Iwi o Ngāti Kahu.

Tesch, F.W. 1977. *The Eel: Biology and Management of Anquillia Eels.* London: Chapman and Hall.

Te Waka Kai Ora. 2006. *Evidence in Submission to Indigenous Flora and Fauna Inquiry Wai 262.* Rotorua: Rangitauira and Co.

Tharme, R.E. 1996. *Review of international methodologies for the quantification of the instream flow requirements of rivers: Water law review final report for policy development.* For Department of Water Affairs and Forestry, Pretoria. Capetown, South Africa: Freshwater Research Unit, University of Cape Town. 116 p.

Tipa G. and L. Tierney. 2003. *A Cultural Health Index for Steams and Waterways: Indicators for Recognising and Expressing Cultural Values.* Ministry for Environment Technical Paper 75. ME number 475. Wellington: Ministry for the Environment.

Tipa, G. and L. Tierney. 2006. *Using the Cultural Health Index: How to assess the health of streams and waterways.* Wellington: Ministry for the Environment.

Titchmarsh B.R and P.L. Blackwood. 1997. *Whakatane River Scheme Asset Management Plan.* Whakatane: Environment of Bay of Plenty

Toledo, V. 2008. *Indigenous Peoples and Biodiversity.* Accessed from: http://www.iea.ad/cbd/congres/cima99/toledo.pdf January 2008.

Tomlins-Jahnke, H. 1994. *Contemporary Perspectives of the Treaty of Waitangi: The Whakaki Lagoon – A Case Study.* A report prepared for the Whakaki Lake Trust. Palmerston North: Tomlins-Jahnke.

'Traditional Māori kai help in fight against cancer'. 2006. *New Zealand Herald,* 1 March 2006, p. A15.

Traditional Māori Oral History. 2000. *Taawhiao: King or Prophet.* Waikato: Turongo House.

Turner, A., M. Mutu, M. Solomon, D. Nugent et al. 1994. *The Report and Recommendations of the Board of Inquiry into the New Zealand Coastal Policy Statement.* Wellington: Department of Conservation.

U

United Nations Educational Cultural and Scientific Organisation. 1994. *Convention concerning the protection of the world cultural and natural heritage. World Heritage Committee, Phuket, Thailand, 12–17 December 1994.*

US Global Change Information Research Office (USGCIRO). 2009. *Global Warming and Climate Change – Part 1: What is Climate Change?* http://gcrio.org/gwcc/part1.html. Washington, DC: US Global Change Information Research Office.

US Climate Change Science Program (USCCSP). 2009. *Climate Literacy: The Essential Principles of Climate Science.* http://www.climatescience.gov. Washington, DC: US Climate Change Science Program.

W

Wairoa District Council. 2004. *Wairoa Coastal Strategy, Te Māhere Tātahi Ki Te Wairoa: A Community Partnership Initiative.* Wairoa: Wairoa Distrcit Council.

Waitangi Tribunal. 1984. *Kaituna Report.* Wellington: Brooker & Friend.

Waitangi Tribunal. 1988. *Muriwhenua Fishing Report: Wai 22.* Wellington: Brooker & Friend.

Waitangi Tribunal. 1991. *Ngai Tahu Report.* Wellington: Brooker & Friend.

Waitangi Tribunal. 1992. *Mohaka River Report* Wellington: Brooker & Friend.

Waitangi Tribunal. 1995. *Te Whanganui a Orotu Report.* Wellington: Brooker & Friend.

Waitangi Tribunal. 1998. *Te Ika Whenua River Report.* Wellington: Brooker & Friend.

Waldram, J.B., Herring, D.A., Young, T.K. 1995. *Aboriginal Health in Canada: Historical, Cultural, and Epidemiological Perspectives.* Toronto: University of Toronto Press.

Waldram, J.B., Herring, D.A., Young, T.K. 1995. *Aboriginal Health in Canada: Historical, Cultural, and Epidemiological Perspectives.* Toronto: University of Toronto Press.

Walker, R. 1990. *Ka Whawhai Tonu Matou: Struggle without End.* Auckland: Penguin Books.

Warren, K.T.F. 2004. Rūnanga: Mānuka Kawe Ake, Facilitating Māori aspirations. Unpublished Masters Thesis. Palmerston North: Massey University.

Warren, T. 2009. *Once Upon a Tikanga: A Literature Review of Early Māori Business Practice.* Palmerston North: Te Au Rangahau, Māori Business Management, Massey University. (Publication forthcoming)

Water & Care Environmental Association. 2008. *Notice of Appeal under Section 121 of the Resource Management Act.*

Water Programme of Action Interdepartmental Working Group. 2004. *Freshwater for the Future.* Wellington: Ministry for the Environment.

Watson, F. 1980. 'Quality of River will Improve'. *Evening Standard*, 27 February 1980, p.2.

Watson, F. 1980. 'Inaction over Pollution.' *Evening Standard*, 17 May 1980, p.3

'Well justified' *awards for top conservation efforts.* 1 February 2001. Media Statement from Hon. Marian Hobbs, Minister of the Environment and Hon. Sandra Lee, Minister of Conservation. Retrieved September 2006 from http://www.ramsar.org/wwd/1/wwd2001_rpt_newzealand3.htm.

Western D., R. Wright and S. Strum. 1994. *Natural Connections: Perspectives in Community-based Conservation.* Washington, DC: Island Press.

Whaanga, M. 2004. *A Carved Cloak for Tahu.* Auckland: Auckland University Press.

Whaley, K.J., B.D. Clarkson, D.K. Emmett, J.G. Innes, J.R. Leathwick, M.C. Smale et al. 2001. *Tiniroto, Waihua, Mahia and Matawai Ecological Districts: Survey Report for the Protected Natural Areas Programme.* Gisborne: Department of Conservation.

White, B. 1998a. *Inland Waterways: Lakes.* Rangahaua Whānui National Series. Theme Q. Wellington: Waitangi Tribunal.

White, B. 1998b. *Inland Waterways: Lakes.* Wellington: Waitangi Tribunal.

White, J. 2007. *An Uneasy Relationship: Palmerston North and the Manawatu River 1941–2006.* Masters thesis Massey University, Palmerston North.

Williams, H.W. 1985. *A Dictionary of the Māori Language.* Wellington: P.D. Hasselberg, Government Printer.

Wilson, N. 2007. 'No Evidence of River Contamination.' *Manawatu Standard*, 1 November 2007, p. 5.

Wilson, N. 2007. 'Tests Debunk Coal Tar Leak Scare.' *Manawatu Standard*, 17 November 2007, p .5.

Winiata, M.T. 2003. Interview for the Hōkio and Mangapouri Streams Oral History Project. Deposited in National Library and Te Wānanga-o-Raukawa library.

Working Party for Ngā Pae o Rangitīkei. 2005. *The Charter of Ngā Pae o Rangitīkei.* Rata: Te Maru o Ruahine Trust

Wright St Clair, R.E. 1986. 'Early Accounts of Māori Health and Diet', in *Historical Journal Auckland–Waikato.* Vol. 18, 20–23.

Y

Young, D. 2004. *Our Islands, Our Selves.* Dunedin: University of Otago Press.

Index